Identity Change and Foreign Policy

Identity has become an explicit focus of International Relations theory in the past two to three decades. Many early identity scholars were particularly attracted to and puzzled by the case of Japan. These constructivist typically ascribed Japan a 'pacifist' or 'antimilitarist' identity – an identity which they believed was constructed through the adherence to 'peaceful norms' and 'antimilitarist culture'. Due to the alleged resilience of such adherences, they predicted little change in Japan's identity and its international relations.

However, in recent years, Japan's foreign and security policies have begun to change, in spite of these seemingly stable norms and culture. This book seeks to address these changes through a pioneering engagement with recent developments in identity theory. In particular, most chapters theorize identity as a product of processes of differentiation. Through detailed case analysis, they argue that Japan's identity is produced and reproduced, but also transformed, through the drawing of boundaries between 'self' and 'other'. In particular, they stress the role of emotions and identity entrepreneurs as catalysts for identity change. With the current balance between resilience and change, contributors emphasize that more drastic foreign and security policy transformations might loom just beyond the horizon in Japan.

This book was originally published as a special issue of *The Pacific Review*.

Linus Hagström is East Asia Programme Director at the Swedish Institute of International Affairs and Professor of Political Science at the Swedish Defence University, Stockholm, Sweden. The author of *Japan's China Policy: A Relational Power Analysis* (Routledge, 2005), he recently published articles in the *European Journal of International Relations*, *Global Affairs* and *Review of International Studies*.

Identity Change and Foreign Policy

Japan and its 'others'

Edited by
Linus Hagström

LONDON AND NEW YORK

First published 2016
by Routledge
2 Park Square, Milton Park, Abingdon, Oxon, OX14 4RN, UK

and by Routledge
711 Third Avenue, New York, NY 10017, USA

Routledge is an imprint of the Taylor & Francis Group, an informa business

© 2016 Taylor & Francis

All rights reserved. No part of this book may be reprinted or reproduced or utilised in any form or by any electronic, mechanical, or other means, now known or hereafter invented, including photocopying and recording, or in any information storage or retrieval system, without permission in writing from the publishers.

Trademark notice: Product or corporate names may be trademarks or registered trademarks, and are used only for identification and explanation without intent to infringe.

British Library Cataloguing in Publication Data
A catalogue record for this book is available from the British Library

ISBN 13: 978-1-138-93160-2

Typeset in Times
by RefineCatch Limited, Bungay, Suffolk

Publisher's Note
The publisher accepts responsibility for any inconsistencies that may have arisen during the conversion of this book from journal articles to book chapters, namely the possible inclusion of journal terminology.

Disclaimer
Every effort has been made to contact copyright holders for their permission to reprint material in this book. The publishers would be grateful to hear from any copyright holder who is not here acknowledged and will undertake to rectify any errors or omissions in future editions of this book.

Contents

Citation Information vii
Notes on Contributors ix
Dedication xi

1. Japan and identity change: why it matters in International Relations 1
   Linus Hagström and Karl Gustafsson

2. The persistence of reified Asia as reality in Japanese foreign policy narratives 23
   Taku Tamaki

3. Shimane Prefecture, Tokyo and the territorial dispute over Dokdo/Takeshima: regional and national identities in Japan 47
   Alexander Bukh

4. The North Korean abduction issue: emotions, securitisation and the reconstruction of Japanese identity from 'aggressor' to 'victim' and from 'pacifist' to 'normal' 71
   Linus Hagström and Ulv Hanssen

5. The rise of the Chinese 'Other' in Japan's construction of identity: Is China a focal point of Japanese nationalism? 95
   Shogo Suzuki

6. Identity and recognition: remembering and forgetting the post-war in Sino-Japanese relations 117
   Karl Gustafsson

7. International and domestic challenges to Japan's postwar security identity: 'norm constructivism' and Japan's new 'proactive pacifism' 139
   Andrew L. Oros

Index 161

Citation Information

The chapters in this book were originally published in *The Pacific Review*, volume 28, issue 1 (March 2015). When citing this material, please use the original page numbering for each article, as follows:

Chapter 1
Japan and identity change: why it matters in International Relations
Linus Hagström and Karl Gustafsson
The Pacific Review, volume 28, issue 1 (March 2015) pp. 1–22

Chapter 2
The persistence of reified Asia as reality in Japanese foreign policy narratives
Taku Tamaki
The Pacific Review, volume 28, issue 1 (March 2015) pp. 23–45

Chapter 3
Shimane Prefecture, Tokyo and the territorial dispute over Dokdo/Takeshima: regional and national identities in Japan
Alexander Bukh
The Pacific Review, volume 28, issue 1 (March 2015) pp. 47–70

Chapter 4
The North Korean abduction issue: emotions, securitisation and the reconstruction of Japanese identity from 'aggressor' to 'victim' and from 'pacifist' to 'normal'
Linus Hagström and Ulv Hanssen
The Pacific Review, volume 28, issue 1 (March 2015) pp. 71–93

Chapter 5
The rise of the Chinese 'Other' in Japan's construction of identity: Is China a focal point of Japanese nationalism?
Shogo Suzuki
The Pacific Review, volume 28, issue 1 (March 2015) pp. 95–116

Chapter 6
Identity and recognition: remembering and forgetting the post-war in Sino-Japanese relations
Karl Gustafsson
The Pacific Review, volume 28, issue 1 (March 2015) pp. 117–138

Chapter 7
International and domestic challenges to Japan's postwar security identity: 'norm constructivism' and Japan's new 'proactive pacifism'
Andrew L. Oros
The Pacific Review, volume 28, issue 1 (March 2015) pp. 139–160

For any permission-related enquiries please visit:
http://www.tandfonline.com/page/help/permissions

Notes on Contributors

Alexander Bukh is Senior Lecturer in International Relations at Victoria University of Wellington, New Zealand. He has published academic articles and book chapters on Japan-Russia relations and Japan's national identity and foreign policy. His latest publications include articles in *Asian Perspective*, *International Relations of the Asia-Pacific*, and a chapter on early Soviet perceptions of Japan and China. He is the author of *Japan's Identity and Foreign Policy: Russia as Japan's Other* (Routledge, 2009).

Karl Gustafsson is a Research Fellow at the Swedish Institute of International Affairs, Stockholm, Sweden. His research interests include alternative approaches to security and issues related to identity and collective memory in international relations. Empirically, his primary research interest is Sino-Japanese relations. He recently published articles in *Asian Perspective*, *Asian Studies Review*, *Global Affairs* and *Cooperation and Conflict*.

Linus Hagström is East Asia Programme Director at the Swedish Institute of International Affairs and Professor of Political Science at the Swedish Defence University, Stockholm, Sweden. The author of *Japan's China Policy: A Relational Power Analysis* (Routledge, 2005), he recently published articles in the *European Journal of International Relations*, *Global Affairs* and *Review of International Studies*.

Ulv Hanssen has an MA in Japanese Studies from the University of Oslo, Norway, and is a PhD candidate in the Graduate School of East Asia Studies at the Freie Universität Berlin, Germany. He was previously a Research Associate at the Swedish Institute of International Affairs, Stockholm, Sweden. Hanssen recently published an article in *Review of International Studies*.

Andrew L. Oros is Associate Professor of Political Science and International Studies at Washington College, Chestertown, Maryland, USA, where he also serves as Director of International Studies. His publications include *Normalizing Japan: Politics, Identity and the Evolution of Security Practice* (Stanford University Press, 2008). He is currently working to complete a new book manuscript on Japan's evolving security policies "From Abe to Abe" with support from a Japan Foundation Abe fellowship.

Shogo Suzuki is a Senior Lecturer in the Department of Politics at the University of Manchester, UK. He is the author of *Civilization and Empire: China and Japan's Encounter with European International Society* (Routledge, 2009), as well as a number of articles that have appeared in *European Journal of International Relations*, *Third World Quarterly* and *Pacific Affairs*. Most recently, he has co-edited *International Orders in the Early Modern World: Before the Rise of the West* (Routledge, 2013).

Taku Tamaki is a Lecturer in International Relations in the School of Business and Economics at Loughborough University, UK. His work focuses on the intersection between International Relations theory and social theory, as well as the role of identity in Japanese foreign policy and the international politics of the Asia-Pacific region. He is the author of *Deconstructing Japan's Image of South Korea* (Palgrave, 2010), and has published in journals including *International Relations* and *International Relations of the Asia-Pacific*.

Dedication

To Marie Söderberg, with deep gratitude for her constant encouragement and advice

Japan and identity change: why it matters in International Relations

Linus Hagström and *Karl Gustafsson*

Abstract Two approaches to identity have been employed to explore issues in Japan's international relations. One views identity as constituted by domestic norms and culture, and as constitutive of interests, which in turn cause behaviour. Proponents view Japan's 'pacifist' and 'antimilitarist' identity as inherently stable and likely to change only as a result of material factors. In the other approach, 'Japan' emerges and changes through processes of differentiation vis-à-vis 'Others'. Neither 'domestic' nor 'material' factors can exist outside of such identity constructions. We argue that the second, relational, approach is more theoretically sound, but begs three questions. First, how can different identity constructions in relation to numerous Others be synthesised and understood comprehensively? Second, how can continuity and change be handled in the same relational framework? Third, what is the point of analysing identity in relational terms? This article addresses the first two questions by introducing an analytical framework consisting of three mutually interacting layers of identity construction. Based on the articles in this special issue, we argue that identity entrepreneurs and emotions are particularly likely to contribute to change within this model. We address the third question by stressing common ground with the first approach: identity enables and constrains behaviour. In the case of Japan, changes in identity construction highlighted by the articles in this special issue forebode a political agenda centred on strengthening Japan militarily.

Introduction

The literature on identity and Japan's international relations is dominated by two approaches. 'Norm constructivists' focus on explaining how a domestically constructed 'pacifist' or 'antimilitarist' identity influences foreign policy. The 'relational' approach, in contrast, concentrates on how 'Japan' is constructed vis-à-vis particular 'Others'. It treats identity as reminiscent of a dependent rather than an independent variable, paying less attention to the impact of identity on behaviour or policy. In addition, some scholars have emphasised the resilience of identity, whereas others have stressed its propensity for change. All contributions to this special issue deal with these matters. The main question addressed by all articles is whether and how Japanese identity is changing. Studying identity change is important because when identity constructions change they enable and constrain behaviour in ways that differ from what was previously the case. For example, this special issue highlights that changes in Japan's identity construction foreshadows a political agenda centred on strengthening Japan militarily. Most articles reach this conclusion by focusing on how Japanese identity is constructed in relation to a specific Other. The article written by Andrew Oros, in contrast, represents the norm constructivist position. It is included because it reflects on this position and the overall question of identity change in light of insights from the relational approach.

This introduction integrates the main contributions of the articles into a larger framework. Although we argue that the relational approach is theoretically sounder than norm constructivism, we develop a pragmatic analytical framework that nonetheless can incorporate most of Oros' findings. The article addresses three questions. First, how can different identity constructions in relation to numerous Others be synthesised and understood comprehensively? Second, how can continuity and change be handled in the same relational framework? Third, what is the point of analysing identity in relational terms?

The first section provides a background to research on identity in International Relations (IR) and more particularly Japan's international relations. The second one begins to examine how different findings in the special issue can be synthesised. Combined, the articles suggest that Japanese identity is constructed through the drawing of boundaries vis-à-vis *several* Others and in *multiple* contexts. We adopt a layered framework to examine how such identity constructions are maintained and how they transform (Wæver 2002). Based on the contributions to the special issue, section three suggests that two factors play particularly important roles in bringing about identity change: identity entrepreneurs and emotions. The fourth section addresses the question of why and how identities and identity change matter. We argue that the subject positions that emerge through processes of differentiation enable and constrain behaviour, and by extension foreign and security policy. The relational analysis of identity can thus be employed for a purpose strikingly similar to the one embraced by norm constructivists. A Japan constructed as 'abnormal' or 'pacifist' is thus believed to act differently from one understood as 'normalising' or 'normal'. Since the discussion draws on a number of case studies, we believe that it offers a firmer basis for making predictions about the future course of Japanese foreign and security policy than each article can do individually.

Japan and identity in its international relations

With the diffusion of constructivism and post-structuralism in the past few decades, identity has become an explicit and popular focus of IR research. Yet the concept is surrounded by contestation, complaints about its alleged 'vagueness' and 'slipperiness' (Chafetz, Spirtas, and Frankel 1998: vii; Kowert 1998: 4), and even allegations of 'definitional anarchy' (Abdelal, Herrera, Johnston, and McDermott 2006: 695). At the same time, identity shares the predicament of its definition being contested with 'power', 'culture', 'democracy', 'security' and many other concepts in the social sciences (Berenskoetter 2010). Although some scholars see contestation as a reason to discard the concept of identity altogether, in the end they rather tend to adopt different terminology, for instance by talking about 'identification', 'categorisation', 'self-understanding', 'social location', 'commonality', 'connectedness' and 'groupness' (Brubaker and Cooper 2000).

Moreover, assumptions about identity are not confined to recent decades of constructivist and post-structuralist research. For instance, realist scholars tend to view the anarchical international system as moulding security or power-maximising 'territorial states' (Rosecrance 1986). Although this 'status', or identity does not allow for much differentiation between states, the unequal distribution of capabilities still leads to some states being ascribed 'great power' or 'superpower' identities (Mearsheimer 2001; Waltz 1979) while others are known as 'middle powers' or 'small states'.

With its agglomeration of economic capabilities in the post-war period, Japan has commonly been ascribed the identity of an 'economic great power/superpower'. Observers more or less explicitly influenced by realism expected the country to develop commensurate political and military power, and to become a fully fledged 'great power'. However, when Japan failed to do so according to their estimations, the notion spread that the country was an 'anomaly' or 'abnormal' (Kennedy 1994; Layne 1993; Waltz 1993, 2000). The fact that scholars often ascribed Japan *other* identities than the 'normal' one prompted by realism – for instance, that of a 'trading state' (Rosecrance 1986), a 'civilian' power (Maull 1990/91; Funabashi 1991/92) or a 'reactive' and 'defensive' state (Calder 1988, 2003; Pharr 1993) – demonstrates exactly how central an essentialised and static 'territorial state'/'great power' identity is to realist theory. It also shows how deeply embedded that identity is in scholarly, media and policy discourses on Japan's foreign and security policy. Many observers – not all self-proclaimed realists – have continued to represent Japan as an economic 'giant' and a political and military 'pygmy' (Funabashi 1991/92; Inoguchi 1991).

The question of what kind of country Japan *is* has been pursued in earnest both inside and outside Japan, and not only in the literature on Japan's international relations (Befu 2001; Dale 1986; Littlewood 1996; Morris-Suzuki 1998: 173; Oe 1995: 53; Yoshino 1992). Identity first became the *explicit* focus of IR research related to Japan in the 1990s. Thomas U. Berger, and Peter J. Katzenstein and Nobuo Okawara tried to resolve the 'abnormality' which they saw at the heart of Japan's foreign and security policy by attributing to it a 'pacifist' or 'antimilitarist' identity. They did so through a focus on what they believed constituted that identity: 'peaceful cultural norms' (Katzenstein 1996a; Katzenstein and Okawara's 1993) and 'antimilitarist culture' (Berger 1993, 1996, 1998; cf. Oros 2008). The most important contribution of these constructivists was to illuminate the often tacit identity component of much IR research on Japan. Their work demonstrated that competing ideas about what Japan *is*, or is on the verge of *becoming*, fundamentally boil down to descriptions and predictions of identity. Article 9 of the post-war constitution was key to the identity analysis of these constructivists (Berger 1998; Katzenstein 1996a, 2008). It relinquished Japan's sovereign right to wage wars and to use force or the threat of force 'as means of settling international disputes', and established that 'land, sea, and air forces, as well as other war potential, will never be maintained' (Cabinet Office 1947). The influence of the early 'norm constructivists' on the analysis of Japan's international relations cannot be overestimated. A number of kindred studies have followed in their wake (Ashizawa 2008; Catalinac 2007; Oros 2008; Rozman 2012; Singh 2008).

These norm constructivists argue that identity matters primarily as a determinant of national interest, which they in turn believe to function as a source of foreign and security policy (Finnemore and Sikkink 1998; Hopf 2002; Katzenstein 1996b; Wendt 1999). National interest might seem like an unnecessary intervening variable here, stuck as it is between identity and behaviour. However, its place in the equation has to be understood from the perspective that IR theory has traditionally treated interests as the independent variable and behaviour as the dependent one. While in realism interests are predetermined and essentialised as physical security, liberals are open to the possibility that other interests – such as economic ones (Rosecrance 1986) – can emerge as a result of 'bottom-up' policy processes (Moravcsik 1997: 517). Norm constructivists, in turn, regard interests as socially constructed rather than given, and again consider norms, culture and identities as ideational 'stuff' involved in that social construction.

The debate between realists and these constructivists has often been framed as a struggle between essentially different independent variables –

structural/material factors for the former and ideational factors in case of the latter. Since even the norm constructivists also continue to attribute explanatory weight to structural/material factors, however, the distinction is not clearcut. Although they believe that norms and culture transform very slowly, and have thus predicted little change in Japan's foreign and security policy (e.g. Berger 1993: 140, 147; 1998: 208; Katzenstein and Okawara 1993: 104, 118), they argue that change will eventually have to come about as a result of changing structural or material conditions (Berger 1993: 120, 1998: 209; Oros 2008: 4, cf. ibid. 172: Friman, Katzenstein, Leheny, and Okawara 2006: 85–87).

By inferring that the international system might 'strike back' against Japanese identity independent of the meaning inter-subjectively ascribed to whatever events are labelled as 'shocks', and by confining the significance of identity to that of an intervening variable, norm constructivism could be criticised for accepting the rationalist terms of debate. It could also be faulted for viewing Japan's 'pacifist or antimilitarist identity' as an inherently and uniquely domestic product, thereby disregarding the notion that a 'domestic domain' is impossible other than in relation to an 'international' one.

Taken together, these points require a rather different concept of identity – a 'relational' understanding where demarcations between domestic and international, identity and difference, or Self and Other are exactly what *constitute* identity (Campbell 1994, 1998 [1992]; Connolly 1991; Neumann 1996; Rumelili 2004; Wodak, de Cillia, Reisigl, and Liebhart 2009 [1999]). The literature on Japan, which adheres to this concept, has identified a number of Others – both external ones, such as the West, Europe, the US, Asia, China, North Korea and South Korea, and internal ones, such as the outcast group at the bottom of Japan's social order – *burakumin*, the *ainu* people (often described as 'indigenous'), Okinawa and the Korean minority in Japan – and it has analysed how these Others have been juxtaposed with Japan to emphasise what Japan *is*, and hence to construct Japanese identity (Befu 2001; Bukh 2009, 2010; Guillaume 2011; Gustafsson 2011; Hagström 2014; Klien 2002; Morris-Suzuki 1998; Oguma 2002; Schulze 2013; Tamaki 2010; Tanaka 1993).

Analysing identity resilience and change: a layered model

Berger's and Katzenstein and Okawara's analyses predicted that Japan's identity would remain stable, and it is true that if identity were totally fluid, it would not carry enough meaning to function as an analytical device. Notwithstanding Emanuel Adler's contention that, 'if constructivism is about anything, it is about change' (Adler 2002: 102), much constructivist scholarship resembles research within other IR paradigms in that it focuses more on explaining resilience than change (Finnemore and Sikkink 1998: 888; Kowert and Legro 1996: 488). Instead of stipulating, for ontological reasons, that (Japanese) identity is fragile and provisional (Weldes, Laffey, Gusterson, and Duvall 1999: 16), or that it is fixed and stable (Chafetz, Spirtas, and Frankel 1998: x), the articles in this special issue depart from the ontology that identity's propensity for change is an empirical one (Abdelal, Herrera, Johnston, and McDermott 2006; Brubaker and Cooper 2000).

The question of continuity and change is closely related to the issue of agency vs. structure – a debate on which much ink has been spilled, not least in IR theory (for a revealing exchange see Doty 1997, 2000; Wight 1999, 2000). One way to analyse how change and continuity relate to agency and structure within the same analytical framework is to treat identity as layered, and simultaneously constituted on mutually interacting levels of inter-subjective meaning making. In such a framework, identity change in the less institutionalised layers interacts with and builds on layers that are more institutionalised – whether they too change or not. The latter layers are more 'fundamental' to the extent that they are 'more solidly sedimented and more difficult [for actors] to politicise and change' (Wæver 2002: 31; cf. Laclau and Mouffe 1985: viii). In other words, more sedimented layers of identity construction can enable different identity constructs in less sedimented layers and even sharp turns in identity construction, but changes in the latter can also affect the former (Wæver 2002: 33–42).

We suggest that the most sedimented layer of Japanese identity construction is an understanding of Japan's position in hierarchical terms, where Japan is constructed through its differentiation from Others, who are alternately understood as superior or inferior to Japan (cf. Hagström 2014). As Tamaki's article in this special issue demonstrates, Japanese narratives have tended to portray Asia as inferior to Japan (cf. Tamaki 2010). A critical realist, Tamaki assumes that identity becomes resilient through reification, and he has argued elsewhere that the notion of *kokutai* ('national polity') embodies a resilient Japanese identity, namely, a 'hierarchic worldview' and an 'associated sense of Japanese "uniqueness"', which 'can be identified within the postwar *heiwa/shonin kokka* [peace/trading state] narratives' (Tamaki 2010: 62). Xavier Guillaume, who subscribes to a relational ontology, agrees that *kokutai* has been a 'key narrative matrix' in Japanese identity construction (Guillaume 2011: 63–99). Hence, there is agreement that since the second half of the 19th century Japanese identity narratives have positioned Japan between an 'inferior Asia' and a 'superior West'. They have thus reflected desires to catch up with and to be recognised by the West (Suzuki 2005, 2009). As Tamaki's contribution clarifies, these narratives also continue to emphasise Asia's externality to Japan, sometimes as an opportunity that needs to be taken advantage of, but more often in the form of a threat that needs to be handled.

The middle layer is where the more exact distinctions and demarcations between Self and Other are negotiated. At this level, we find *multiple* identities that describe the Others and consequently also the Self. Some identities are more important in certain contexts and in relation to particular Others (Lupovici 2012; Murray 2010: 665). These identities involve concrete self-descriptions, such as 'rational' or 'democratic', as well as corresponding Other-representations such as 'emotional' and 'undemocratic' – the specific traits that are given priority within the hierarchical matrix.

'Othering' is often associated with a negative and dichotomised imagination of difference (Lebow 2008) but this is not necessarily the case (Rumelili 2004). There are various ways of relating to difference, including comparison and integration (Abizadeh 2005; Guillaume 2011). An example is Tamaki's observation that 'Asia' tends to be reified in Japanese narratives as either an opportunity or a threat. In addition, not all of a state's identities need to be constructed in relation to *external* Others. As Gustafsson's article in this special issue suggests, post-war Japan's 'peaceful' identity has to a large extent been constructed in relation to its own wartime 'aggressive' Self (cf. Abizadeh 2005: 58). At the same time, it is possible that Japan's identity as 'peaceful' might be retained through differentiation from 'less peaceful' external Others (Hagström and Hanssen 2013). Another possibility is the construction of a collective identity *with* other states (Wæver 2002; cf. Wendt 1999: 336–343). If, for example, the middle layer stresses Japan's identity as a democratic state, this involves emphasis on both the difference from 'undemocratic' states and the similarity with other 'democratic' ones.

The least institutionalised layer is where policies and specific political issues are discussed and where agents operate. The way in which bilateral problems are discussed and understood in this layer is constrained by and has consequences for identity constructions in the other layers, particularly identity constructions in relation to specific others in the middle layer. If the behaviour of several Others is similarly interpreted in relation to a number of issues, it may affect multiple middle-layer identities. For example, if Japan's Others are depicted as behaving as 'bullies', it is likely that the Self's identity as a victim will be strengthened in the middle layer, as is illustrated in several contributions to this special issue and discussed in greater detail below.

Factors contributing to identity change

As is noted above, based on the contributions to this special issue, two factors have been identified that arguably play important roles in effectuating identity change within the layered model: identity entrepreneurs and emotions.

Identity entrepreneurs and identity change

The notion that research should trace the process whereby identity is constructed means that it should account for the *contestation* involved, or the *politics* of identity (Neumann 1996: 165; Abdelal, Herrera, Johnston, and McDermott 2006: 696; Guillaume 2011). Actors seem to *realise* that much is at stake in identity politics. As Oros discusses in his article in this special issue, conservative Japanese political actors have attempted to change Japan's security identity throughout the post-war period. Bukh also emphasises the role of contestation as he shows that regional actors from Shimane prefecture, in defiance of central national elites, have played an important role in promoting the Takeshima issue and in contributing to identity change. Other research shows that conservative Japanese actively try to influence not only Japanese but also Chinese identity (Gustafsson 2014).

Like 'norm entrepreneurs', identity entrepreneurs call attention to, or even create, issues 'by using language that names, interprets, and dramatizes them', thereby promoting the identities that they themselves espouse (Finnemore and Sikkink 1998: 897; see also Keck and Sikkink 1998). In other words, as Bukh, Gustafsson, Hagström and Hanssen, and Suzuki all show, identity entrepreneurs are political actors who promote their desired versions of Japanese identity through the discursive representation of issues and actors. These entrepreneurs operate most obviously at the least sedimented layer where agency is less constrained by structure. Their representations are likely to influence identity constructions in relation to Others in the middle layer. In addition, identity entrepreneurs do not merely reproduce but also seek to alter identities. Oros is also concerned with the agency exercised by actors, who at the same time promote different identity conceptions and security policies, but his focus is on 'domestic institutions and electoral politics'.

While some observers argue that identities can be manipulated (Kowert and Legro 1996: 493), others question the extent to which it is possible for actors to be autonomous of identity narratives (Campbell 1998 [1992]: 218; Suzuki 2007: 27). The latter view implies that there is a limit to how far identity discourses can be 'actorised', and that identity entrepreneurs are not cynical, rational actors who tamper with identities in an instrumentalist and strategic way in order to achieve their purposes without themselves being under the influence of identities (cf. Wodak, de Cillia, Reisigl, and Liebhart 2009 [1999]: 31–32).

This point could be rephrased by saying that two kinds of power are at work in the construction of identities. Discursive, narrative or productive power works to produce and maintain identity constructions, or to transform them when discourses are pitted against each other (Barnett and Duvall 2005; Digeser 1992). At the same time, a relational understanding of power suggests that actors at times play a privileged role in the formation, maintenance and transformation of identities (on 'relational power' see Baldwin 2013 [2002]; Hagström 2005).

The issues discussed in the articles are all closely linked to particular Others: South Korea for Bukh, North Korea for Hagström and Hanssen, and China for Gustafsson and Suzuki. The concrete issues analysed all emerged with force in the mid-2000s, in some cases after having been long dormant, and this might lead to more substantial changes in Japanese identity construction in the middle layer. These issues have provided a window of opportunity for identity entrepreneurs to discredit Japan's 'pacifist' or 'peaceful' post-war identity as 'mistaken', 'abnormal' and 'weak'. They seem to regard it as *excessively* or *naively* peaceful, because it enables other states to 'bully' Japan. The negative adjectives associated with Japan's Others, in contrast, include 'arrogant', 'aggressive', 'undemocratic', 'immoral', 'irrational', 'unreasonable', 'nationalistic', 'disrespectful of international law' and 'emotional', suggesting that unlike them Japan could remain peaceful, albeit not excessively so (cf. Hagström 2012).

Hagström and Hanssen, as well as Suzuki, suggest that the tables have recently been turned in Japanese discourses on Japan-North Korea relations and Sino-Japanese relations. The previously dominant discourses on North Korea and China as 'victims' of Japanese aggression during the war have largely been replaced by discourses in which North Korea and China are constructed as 'aggressors' or 'bullies' that make 'unreasonable demands', and Japan is portrayed as the 'victim'. Similarly, in discussions of Chinese 'anti-Japanism' outlined in Gustafsson's article, the customary understanding of what the 'history problem' in Sino-Japanese relations consists of is increasingly challenged as China is seen to be denying Japan's peaceful identity. This identity change from 'aggressor' to 'victim' exemplifies how the work of identity entrepreneurs at the least sedimented layer has consequences for identity construction in the middle layer.

Emotions and identity change

Even though often discussed in classical texts, IR theory during the Cold War largely ignored the role of emotions. It did so because it viewed states as rational actors making decisions based on given national interests within boundaries set by material structures. In realism, only one emotion is regarded as legitimate and rational: fear (Crawford 2000; Hall 2006; Weber 2010: 14–36). Moreover, rational fear was equated with physical threats and the pursuit of physical security (Saurette 2006: 495–496). With the exception of research on misperceptions in foreign policy decision-making, emotions remained largely neglected in IR until the late 1990s. However, fear linked to issues traditionally not associated with 'hard' threats to physical security, along with other emotions such as shame, anxiety, sympathy, anger and feelings of insult, could play an important role in identity change in all three layers of our model.

Mainstream approaches have thus tended to portray emotions as irrational. However, it has been convincingly argued that the distinction between rationality and emotion is untenable. Rational action requires emotion since actors have to empathise to make rational decisions (Mercer 2010). Moreover, as Bleiker and Hutchison (2008: 123) argue, '[e]motions help us make sense of ourselves, and situate us in relation to others and the world that surrounds us'. Identity is thus constructed through the forging of an emotional allegiance that makes us feel like we belong. As Jan Assmann observes, '[c]ollective identity is a matter of identification on the part of the participating individuals. It does not exist "in itself", but only ever to the extent that specific individuals subscribe to it. It is as strong – or as weak – as it is alive in the thoughts and actions of the group members, and able to motivate their thoughts and actions' (Assmann cited in Heer and Wodak 2008: 7). When one identifies with a particular notion, one *feels* part of a certain collective. It follows that without emotional attachment, identities are difficult to construct. In such a situation, identity entrepreneurs appear more seldom and are much less likely to succeed.

The link between emotion and identity is particularly clear in discussions of nationalism and patriotism (cf. Mercer 2010). Some scholars argue that nationalism involves 'malign' feelings of superiority, which may lead to *hatred* of the Other, whereas patriotism is 'benign' or 'healthy' and associated with *love* for one's own nation (Gries, Zhang, Crowson, and Cai 2011; Kosterman and Feshbach 1989). Others argue that a strong love for and pride in one's country is not necessarily benign as it is a more basic motivation for self-sacrifice than hatred of the Other, and therefore a more fundamental reason for people's willingness to go to war (cf. Anderson 1983: 7; Billig 1995: 55–59). In addition, love or pride in one's own country implies comparison, and it therefore often involves feelings of disdain in relation to the Other. Either way, it is clear that emotions form the basis of both patriotic and nationalistic identities. This is especially clear in the Japanese language, where a literal translation of the word for patriotism is love-country-feeling (*aikokushin*).

At the same time, the Self is often represented as rational and unemotional, whereas the Other is depicted as excessively emotional in its expression of national identity (Billig 1995: 43–46, 55–59; Mercer 2010: 21). For example, as the articles in this special issue highlight, Japanese discourses portray both China and South Korea as emotional in contrast to Japan. Yet emotions paradoxically play a key role in the strategies of Japanese identity entrepreneurs. For example, Hagström and Hanssen shed light on how emotional traumas related to the North Korean abduction issue are involved in attempts to effectuate identity change. They do not understand trauma as an external 'shock', but as the specific emotional interpretation of an event. Hagström and Hanssen emphasise that the diffusion of emotions of sympathy and anger within Japan contributed to the collectivisation and politicisation of the abduction issue in a way that makes Japanese identity change possible.

Gustafsson's analysis suggests that the perceived Chinese denial of recognition of Japan's peaceful identity produces feelings of shame and insult, also contributing to identity change. Some approaches to ontological security argue that actors feel shame when there is dissonance between their actions and their self-identity (Steele 2008). When faced with denials of recognition, moreover, actors can either accept how they are described and experience shame, or refuse to accept the description and instead feel insulted, much like the Japanese actors in Gustafsson's account (cf. Ringmar 1996, 2012). Both shame and feelings of insult are emotions closely linked to an agent's sense of Self, and as such they function as drivers of identity change.

Japanese discussions of Japan as 'weak' and 'inferior', in Suzuki's analysis, could also be interpreted in terms of shame. In an international society that values 'great powerness' or 'superpowerness', weakness is typically understood as embarrassing or even shameful. As Suzuki points out, Japanese politicians are criticised for 'making Japan look weak' vis-à-vis China. Since their behaviour is understood as embarrassing or shameful, they are urged to act more decisively.

Bukh's analysis also suggests that identity change can be generated by ontological insecurity or anxiety about one's sense of Self. In a similar way to Tamaki's treatment of Japanese discourses on Asia, Bukh argues that Japanese identity has consistently been constructed in relation to a notion of South Korea as inferior. Until recently, Japan's ontological security at the most sedimented layer of the model was confirmed by the inferior economic status of South Korea. However, South Korea's economic development has arguably made the country increasingly like Japan. This has made it difficult to maintain a Japanese sense of uniqueness or superiority in relation to South Korea in this dimension. This is not a threat to Japan's physical security or survival, but a threat to its ontological security. A similar argument might be made in relation to China, which surpassed Japan as the world's second largest economy in 2010 (Schulze 2013).

Bukh argues that this anxiety has been handled by emphasising that South Korea is 'emotional', 'nationalistic' and 'lacking respect for international law' in its behaviour towards the Takeshima/Dokdo dispute and related issues such as education. In this way, the fundamental hierarchical matrix has been stabilised through an adjustment in the middle layer of the framework. Hence, Japan is still depicted as superior, albeit not in the area of economics but in its 'disposition' or 'national character'. In contrast to South Korea, Japan is described as more 'mature', 'rational' and 'law-abiding'.

Suzuki's and Gustafsson's analyses similarly highlight how Japan is differentiated from China. Now that Japan is no longer economically superior to China in terms of GDP, it is depicted as superior in other spheres. Chinese denial of Japan's 'peaceful' identity, and its 'arrogant', 'bullying' and 'overbearing' behaviour in bilateral disputes, is therefore stressed, and China is portrayed as 'undemocratic', 'irrational', 'unreasonable', 'immoral', 'anti-Japanese' and 'lacking respect for international law'. This suggests that Japan, in contrast, is 'democratic', 'reasonable', 'moral' and 'law-abiding'.

On the basis of this discussion, norm constructivists, such as Oros in this special issue, might conclude that material factors cause identity change. After all, it might be argued that the economic development of China and South Korea threatens Japan's ontological security. We suggest, however, that this is a spurious conclusion. First, agents may attempt to substantiate their socially constructed identities in material practices and capabilities, thereby making them *appear* as brute facts (Murray 2010: 663–667). In addition, it is only because Japan's identity (or one of its identities) was that of an 'economic power', and hence constructed on the basis of material factors, that China and South Korea's economic development has produced anxiety in Japan. Japan's other identities, for example that of a 'peaceful state', were not threatened by the economic development of South Korea and China. We do not contest the existence of structural and material factors, or of a reality external to thought, but we do contest the possibility that these factors can have any precise or clear meaning independent of the discourses in which they are constituted as objects (cf. Laclau and Mouffe 1985: 108). For example, a forest can be viewed as an obstacle to the construction of a highway, a source of material when building wooden houses or a scenic area in need of protection from the former. Similarly, the 'rise of China' can be interpreted as an opportunity, as a threat, or in other ways.

Why and how identity (change) matters in International Relations

As is discussed above, post-war Japan was ascribed the identities of an 'economic great power/superpower/giant' and a 'military dwarf', and those of a 'passive', 'reactive' and overall 'abnormal' state because its foreign and security policy was interpreted as deviating from the inter-subjectively defined international standard. Hence, there is a tacit connection between the identities that are more or less habitually ascribed to states, such as Japan, and their policies or behaviour. When norm constructivists, such as Katzenstein and Berger, introduced the concept of identity into the literature on Japan's international relations in the 1990s, they did so explicitly to explain policies or behaviour. These constructivists held that identities constitute national interests, which in turn shape or regulate behaviour (Finnemore and Sikkink 1998; Hopf 2002; Katzenstein 1996b; Wendt 1999).

When constructivism and post-structuralism adopted a relational view on identity, by contrast, there was a tendency to analyse identity more for its own sake, to make sense of the formation, maintenance and transformation of collective identities such as 'state' and 'nation', and by extension to understand the production and reproduction of the 'interstate' and the 'international' (Williams 1998). Hence, such research treated identity as reminiscent of a dependent variable, and the social construction of identity was analysed mostly through variations of discourse analysis (cf. Phillips and Hardy 2002: 2).

Described as such, relational identity analysis appears incommensurable with the norm constructivist analysis of identity presented above. However, although few relational analyses of identity elaborate in detail on the analytical role of identity – beyond stipulating the intrinsic value of elucidating and problematising the construction of 'imagined communities' – some works do argue that there is a connection between discursively constructed social identities, 'interpretative dispositions' and propensities for action (Doty 1993: 298).

The question is thus not only how identities emerge as a product of narratives and discourses but also how emergent subjects 'live out their identities and act' (Howarth and Stavrakakis 2000: 12). The question could be rephrased by interrogating what behaviour or policy discursively produced identities enable or constrain, by either promoting or excluding certain possibilities (Phillips and Hardy 2002: 21) – that is, by delineating the 'range of imaginable conduct' (Doty 1993: 299). Hutchison argues that traumas play an important role in destabilising identities and making possible their reconfiguration in ways that facilitate hawkish security policies (Hutchison 2010: 66–68, 81–83).

The recognition or denial of recognition that Others bestow on the Self's construction of identity also influences its propensities for action (Ringmar 2012). Erik Ringmar puts it succinctly: 'It is only *as some-one* that we can want *some-thing*, and it is only once we know who we *are* that we can know what we *want*' (Ringmar 1996: 13, italics in original). Identity, then, is fundamentally about agency. If we do not know who we are we will not know what to do. Since the 'range of imaginable conduct' is defined, inter alia, through the production and reproduction of discursively emergent norms and institutions, there is again notable common ground with norm constructivism.

While Michel Foucault sought to analyse how discourses on 'madness' and 'punishment' affected medical, psychiatric and legal practices and institutions, and Edward Said aimed to demonstrate how statements about 'the Orient' provided the 'means for the appropriation of the Orient by successive waves of European colonialization and imperialism' (Howarth 2000: 68), several articles in this special issue address the question of how discourses on Asia, China and the two Koreas affect the practices and institutions of Japanese foreign and security policy, and produce the range of possible Japanese conduct vis-à-vis its neighbouring countries.

Hence, even if one acknowledges that states are constructions of the imagination that come into being through the collective meaning-making of human beings, for example, through 'foreign and security policy', on another level it seems perfectly reasonable to ask what consequences such identity constructions might have for foreign and security policy. Although we define identity differently from norm constructivists, we agree that action can be understood from the viewpoint of identity. However, while the mapping of a certain discourse 'does not explain *specific* decision-making processes' (Neumann 2003: 48 emphasis added) or provide unambiguous 'templates for action' (Jackson 2004: 286), it can illuminate the overall past policy direction. Most importantly, perhaps, it can be used to make negative predictions (Wæver 2002: 32) – to suggest policies that are unlikely to be implemented in the foreseeable future. A sufficient number of negative predictions, moreover, implies a set of possibilities or positive predictions.

The discourse/identity literature rarely theorises the connection between discursively constructed identity and propensities for action further than this. Jack Holland, however, has criticised some of this literature for conflating 'imaginability', 'conceivability' and 'thinkability', on the one hand, and 'possibility', on the other. He argues that a course of action becomes possible not only by being conceivable, but that 'communicability' and 'coerciveness' are also necessary. He thus advises analysts of political possibility to address 'how thinkable', 'how resonant' and 'how dominant' a particular action is (Holland 2013: 52). We agree that communicability and coerciveness are crucial, but believe they are already inherent in the notion of conceivability – or at least that they should be. Something only becomes *collectively* conceivable if it is at the same time communicable and coercive. Perhaps Holland conflates conceivability with 'utterance', as when he states that '[p]olitical possibility is not achieved in the utterance alone (ibid. p. 53). However, crucially, *collective* inconceivability does not mean that something is *individually* inconceivable. It merely means that it will not be supported or accepted by the collective. Oros' article illuminates this issue as he shows how the Japanese identity entrepreneurs attempting to refashion Japan's security identity have long found themselves constrained by the strength of domestic antimilitarism.

With the exception of Bukh, all articles included in this special issue endeavour to make analytical connections between identity and propensity for action – both policy developments in the past and present, and possible future directions. Suzuki argues that the increasingly similar construction of a 'bullying Chinese Other' on the political right and left could have the consequence that 'Japanese politicians come under increased criticism for following this relatively moderate "established" policy towards China' and that 'Tokyo will be less afraid of "straining" Sino-Japanese relations further'. He warns that 'if China continues to be "Othered" as a high-handed, arrogant neighbour, we could be set to witness many more diplomatic standoffs between these two great powers of East Asia for some years to come'.

Tamaki, moreover, argues not only that a resilient notion of Asian Otherness continues to define the range of conceivable conduct in Japan, but also that widespread narratives of Asia in terms of 'threat' or 'danger' currently set much narrower confines than previously. These dangers, which are associated with North Korea, China and Russia, have for example made it possible or even seem necessary to strengthen Japan's military capabilities, reorganise command structures and increase the Japanese defence budget. As Tamaki notes, it is also within this context that debates over collective self-defence – a reinterpretation or a possible revision of Article 9 of the constitution – have been 'revisited'.

The developments and possible future trajectories that Tamaki highlights are often known as Japan's 'normalisation' or 'remilitarisation'. Gustafsson, and Hagström and Hanssen present different arguments as to why this might indeed be the direction in which Japanese foreign and security policy is headed. Gustafsson argues that China's non-recognition of Japan's allegedly 'peaceful' identity in the post-war period presents an opportunity for Japanese conservatives to argue that the 'peaceful' identity should be exchanged for the identity of a 'normal' state, which in turn enables a revision of Article 9 and the strengthening of the Japanese military. Hagström and Hanssen, furthermore, contend that the abduction issue can be understood as a 'vehicle for renegotiating Japanese identity'. Through the diffusion of emotions – particularly through the discursive construction of Japan as 'victim' and North Korea as 'aggressor' – the issue has been securitised and collectivised so that 'normalisation'/'remilitarisation' has become politically possible.

As Oros describes in his article, throughout the post-war period conservative lawmakers in the Liberal Democratic Party (LDP) have pursued a political agenda centred on Japan's 'normalisation' as a nation state and revision of the constitution. Indeed, the aims of amending Article 9 and remilitarising Japan were allegedly a driving factor behind the LDP's establishment in 1955 (Hagström 2010: 513). Some observers interpreted this agenda as a step towards Japan's remilitarisation already in the 1980s (Hook 1988, 1996), but it is arguably more accurate to characterise the post-war era as a constant tug of war between concomitant forces working towards remilitarisation and demilitarisation. Hence, the pacifist policies of the Japan Socialist Party (JSP) were distinct from the policies of the LDP in that they opposed both the security treaty with the United States and the establishment of Japan's Self-Defense Forces. The JSP, moreover, was strong enough to provide a viable political alternative to the LDP. This has even been taken as evidence that two opposing identities were at work in post-war Japan – one 'pacifist' (*heiwa shugi*) and one 'traditional statist' (*dentōteki kokka shugi*) (Soeya 2005). The fact that the political left has become politically weak might also suggest that the 'pacifist' identity has weakened. Most of the current opposition parties support variations of the agenda to alter Article 9.

Having previously been collectively inconceivable, we therefore argue that revision of Article 9 and remilitarisation have come to appear politically possible in large part because this agenda has become more resonant and ubiquitous. As Hagström and Hanssen show, its dominance has been achieved through verbal and physical sanctions – in their case against dissenters in the abduction issue debate. Oros, moreover, points out that it has become less costly in terms of political capital to adopt policies contrary to the hitherto dominant security identity, which he sees as one of anti-militarism. Nonetheless, to argue that revision of Article 9 and remilitarisation have entered the realm of the politically possible is not the same as stating with any degree of certainty how likely it is that such policy changes will take place – or when they might happen. As Oros writes, although the current Prime Minister, Abe Shinzō, and many other conservative politicians do not subscribe to the 'core tenets of anti-militarism', they remain highly constrained by them.

Conclusions

This article argues that a relational concept of identity is theoretically more sound than the identity concept espoused by the norm constructivists, who nonetheless have to be lauded for their instrumental role in explicitly introducing identity into the study of Japan's international relations. Fundamentally, we argue that the notion of 'domestically produced identities' is problematic, because it reifies the very boundaries between inside and outside that investigations into identity should seek to understand and problematise. Moreover, although the norm constructivists predicted little change in Japan's foreign and security policy, they believed that change would eventually have to occur as a result of an outside shock defined in material terms. While we agree that material factors may play some role, we argue that this role is indeterminate and that the meaning ascribed to material conditions does not necessarily follow from 'brute facts'. One example is the notion that post-war Japan was a 'military dwarf', which has been reproduced in many contexts despite the fact that Japan at the same time had one of the largest defence budgets in the world, and also one of the world's most technologically advanced defence forces (Hagström 2005). Hence, we argue that the meaning of these 'material factors' is discursively constructed.

In line with their different ontologies, some relational accounts of identity emphasise the possibility of identity being resilient, while others are more inclined to stress fragility and fluidity. In this article, in contrast, we adopt an ontology on the basis of which both are possible and where the question can only be illuminated through empirical enquiry. More specifically, an analytical model consisting of three mutually interacting layers, in which identities are institutionalised to different degrees, allows us to account for both continuity and change. Equipped with this model, we are able to synthesise the findings of this special issue in a more comprehensive assessment. Based on the contributions, we argue that identity entrepreneurs and emotions play important roles in effectuating identity change within the layered model. Entrepreneurs have some agency but are also constrained by more institutionalised layers. Emotions, moreover, are produced and reproduced in all three layers, and thus comprise aspects of both agency and structure. Finally, we argue that identity understood in relational terms shares one important analytical application with the identity concept developed by norm constructivists in that it is seen to enable and constrain behaviour or policy.

Based on the individual contributions, we conclude that at the most sedimented layer, Japan remains constructed as 'superior'. It is mainly at the middle layer that a more general Japanese identity shift is taking place from that of an 'economic giant' to that of a mature, moral and law-abiding country, which is threatened and even victimised by morally inferior neighbours. Moreover, all the contributions, in one way or another, relate to Japan's 'pacifist' or 'antimilitarist' identity. Suzuki suggests that some identity entrepreneurs regard this identity as a reason for Japanese weakness, which makes it possible for China to 'bully' Japan. Similarly, Tamaki proposes that 'Asia' is increasingly understood as a threat, which necessitates Japan's 'normalisation' as a nation state. Gustafsson, furthermore, argues that the 'peaceful' identity becomes easier to change in such a direction due to the Chinese denials of it. Hagström and Hanssen's analysis reveals how North Korean abductions are interpreted as a trauma that could have been avoided had Japan not been excessively and 'abnormally' 'peaceful'. Japan's 'pacifist' identity in the post-war period is thus depicted as a threat to Japan's 'true' identity and physical survival. Hence, this identity is now more easily portrayed as mistaken and 'abnormal', and it might therefore have to be abandoned or at least altered to make it possible for Japan to deal with its difficult Others. Oros agrees that Japan's post-war identity is 'under siege', but also persuasively demonstrates how a security identity of domestic antimilitarism continues to constrain the sometimes ambitious political agendas of political actors, such as that of Prime Minister Abe Shinzō. Nonetheless, despite the continuing constraining power of this identity, it has probably never been more thoroughly challenged than it currently is.

Acknowledgements

For insightful comments on earlier drafts of this article we would like to thank Stefan Borg, Alexander Bukh, Björn Jerdén, Andrew Oros and one anonymous reviewer.

References

Abdelal, R., Herrera, Y. M., Johnston, A. I. and McDermott R. (2006) 'Identity as a variable', *Perspectives on Politics* 4(4): 695–711.
Abizadeh, A. (2005) 'Does collective identity presuppose an other? On the alleged incoherence of global solidarity', *American Political Science Review* 99(1): 45–60.

Adler, E. (2002) 'Constructivism and international relations', in W. Carlsnaes, T. Risse and B. Simmons (eds) *Handbook of International Relations*, New Delhi: SAGE, pp. 95–118.

Anderson, B. (1983) *Imagined Communities: Reflections on the Origin and Spread of Nationalism*, London: Verso.

Ashizawa, K. (2008) 'When identity matters: state identity, regional institution-building, and Japanese foreign policy', *International Studies Review* 10(3): 571–98.

Baldwin, D. A. (2013) [2002] 'Power and international relations', in W. Carlsnaes, T. Risse and B. Simmons (eds) *Handbook of International Relations*, New Delhi: SAGE, pp. 273–97.

Barnett, M. and Duvall, R. (2005) 'Power in international politics', *International Organization* 59(1): 39–75.

Befu, H. (2001) *Hegemony of Homogeneity: An Anthropological Analysis of Nihonjinron*, Melbourne: Trans Pacific Press.

Berenskoetter, F. (2010) 'Identity in international relations', in R. Denemark (ed) *The International Studies Encyclopaedia*, Oxford: Wiley-Blackwell.

Berger, T. U. (1993) 'From sword to chrysanthemum: Japan's culture of anti-militarism', *International Security* 17(4): 119–50.

Berger, T. U. (1996) 'Norms, identity, and national security in Germany and Japan', in P.J. Katzenstein (ed) *The Culture of National Security: Norms and Identities in World Politics*, New York: Columbia University Press, pp. 317–56.

Berger, T. U. (1998) *Cultures of Antimilitarism: National Security in Germany and Japan*, Baltimore: Johns Hopkins University Press.

Billig, M. (1995) *Banal Nationalism*, London: SAGE.

Bleiker, R. and Hutchison, E. (2008) 'Fear no more: emotions and world politics', *Review of International Studies* 34(1): 115–35.

Brubaker, R. and Cooper, F. (2000) 'Beyond "identity"', *Theory and Society* 29(1): 1–47.

Bukh, A. (2009) 'Identity, foreign policy and the "Other": Japan's "Russia"', *European Journal of International Relations* 15(2): 319–45.

Bukh, A. (2010) *Japan's National Identity and Foreign Policy: Russia as Japan's 'Other'*, London: Routledge.

Cabinet Office (1947) *The Constitution of Japan*, accessed at http://www.kantei.go.jp/foreign/constitution_and_government/frame_01.html, 30 October 2014.

Calder, K. (1988) 'Japanese foreign economic policy formation: explaining the reactive state', *World Politics* 40(4): 517–41.

Calder, K. (2003) 'Japan as a post-reactive state?', *Orbis* 47(4): 605–16.

Campbell, D. (1994) 'Policy and identity: Japanese Other/American Self', in N. Inayatullah, S. J. Rosow and M. Rupert (eds) *The Global Economy as Political Space: A Crucial Reader in International Political Economy*, Boulder: Lynne Rienner, pp. 147–69.

Campbell, D. (1998) [1992] *Writing Security: United States Foreign Policy and the Politics of Identity*, Manchester: Manchester University Press.

Catalinac, A. L. (2007) 'Identity theory and foreign policy: explaining Japan's responses to the 1991 Gulf War and the 2003 US War in Iraq', *Politics & Policy* 35(1): 58–100.

Chafetz, G., Spirtas, M. and Frankel, B. (1998) 'Introduction: tracing the influence of identity on foreign policy', *Security Studies* 8(2–3): 7–22.

Connolly, W. E. (1991) *Identity/Difference: Democratic Negotiations of Political Paradox*, Minneapolis: University of Minnesota Press.

Crawford, N. C. (2000) 'The passion of world politics: propositions on emotion and emotional relationships', *International Security* 24(4): 116–56.

Dale, P. N. (1986) *The Myth of Japanese Uniqueness*, London: Routledge.
Digeser, P. (1992) 'Fourth face of power', *Journal of Politics* 54(4): 977–1007.
Doty, R. L. (1993) 'Foreign policy as social construction: a post-positivist analysis of US counterinsurgency in the Philippines', *International Studies Quarterly* 37 (3): 297–320.
Doty, R. L. (1997) 'Aporia: a critical exploration of the agent-structure problematique in International Relations theory', *European Journal of International Relations* 3(3): 365–92.
Doty, R. L. (2000) 'A reply to Colin Wight', *European Journal of International Relations* 5(3): 387–90.
Finnemore, M. and Sikkink, K. (1998) 'International norm dynamics and political change', *International Organization* 52(4): 887–917.
Friman, R. H., Katzenstein, P. J., Leheny, D. and Okawara, N. (2006) 'Immovable object? Japan's security policy in East Asia', in P. J. Katzenstein and T. Shiraishi (eds) *Beyond Japan: The Dynamics of East Asian Regionalism*, Ithaca: Cornell University Press, pp. 85–107.
Funabashi, Y. (1991/92) 'Japan and the new world order', *Foreign Affairs* 70(5): 58–74.
Gries, P. H., Zhang, Q, Crowson, H. M. and Cai, H. (2011) 'Patriotism, nationalism and China's US policy: structures and consequences of Chinese national identity', *The China Quarterly* 205: 1–17.
Guillaume, X. (2011) *International Relations and Identity: A Dialogical Approach*, London: Routledge.
Gustafsson, K. (2011) *Narratives and Bilateral Relations: Rethinking the History Issue in Sino-Japanese Relations*, Ph.D. dissertation (Stockholm Studies in Politics 139), Stockholm: Stockholm University.
Gustafsson, K. (2014) 'Memory politics and ontological security in Sino-Japanese relations', *Asian Studies Review* 38(1): 71–86.
Hagström, L. (2005) 'Relational power for foreign policy analysis: issues in Japan's China Policy', *European Journal of International Relations* 11(3): 395–430.
Hagström, L. (2010) 'The democratic party of Japan's security policy and Japanese politics of constitutional revision: a cloud over Article 9? *Australian Journal of International Affairs* 64(5): 510–25.
Hagström, L. (2012) '"Power shift" in East Asia? A critical reappraisal of narratives on the Diaoyu/Senkaku Islands incident in 2010', *The Chinese Journal of International Politics* 5(3): 267–97.
Hagström, L. and Hanssen, U. (2013) 'What "peace" enables: from 'normalisation' of Sino-Japanese relations to the 'normalisation' of Japanese foreign and security policy?', *Paper Presented at the Workshop 'The Rise and Demise of Asian World Supremacy: Power, Effects and Identities'*, Swedish Institute of International Affairs, Stockholm; 28–29 August.
Hagström, L. (2014) 'The "abnormal" state: identity, norm/exception and Japan', *European Journal of International Relations*. doi:10.1177/1354066113518356.
Hall, M. (2006) 'The fantasy of realism, or mythology as methodology', in D. H. Nexon and I. B. Neumann (eds) *Harry Potter and International Relations*, Lanham, MD: Rowman & Littlefield, pp. 177–93.
Heer, H. and Wodak, R. (2008) 'Introduction: collective memory, national narratives and the politics of the past, the discursive construction of history', in H. Heer, W. Manoschek, A. Pollak and R. Wodak (eds) *The Discursive Construction of History: Remembering the Wehrmacht's War of Annihilation*, Basingstoke: Palgrave Macmillan, pp. 1–16.
Holland, J. (2013) 'Foreign policy and political possibility', *European Journal of International Relations* 19(1): 49–68.

Hook, G. D. (1988) 'The erosion of anti-militaristic principles in contemporary Japan', *Journal of Peace Research* 25(4): 381–94.

Hook, G. D. (1996) *Militarization and Demilitarization in Contemporary Japan*, London: Routledge.

Hopf, T. (2002) *Social Construction of International Politics: Identities & Foreign Policies, Moscow, 1955 & 1999*, Ithaca: Cornell University Press.

Howarth, D. (2000) *Discourse*. Buckingham and Philadelphia: Open University Press.

Howarth, D. and Stavrakakis, Y. (2000) 'Introducing discourse theory and political analysis', in D. Howarth, A. J. Norval and Y. Stavrakakis (eds) *Discourse Theory and Political Analysis: Identities, Hegemonies and Social Change*, Manchester: Manchester University Press, pp. 1–23.

Hutchison, E. (2010) 'Trauma and the politics of emotions: constituting identity, security and community after the Bali bombing', *International Relations* 24(1): 65–86.

Inoguchi, T. (1991) *Japan's International Relations*, Oxford and San Francisco: Westview Press.

Jackson, P. T. (2004) 'Hegel's House, or "People are states too"', *Review of International Studies* 30(2): 281–7.

Katzenstein, P. J. (1996a) *Cultural Norms and National Security: Police and Military in Postwar Japan*, Ithaca: Cornell University Press.

Katzenstein, P. J. (1996b) 'Introduction: Alternative perspectives on national security', in P. J. Katzenstein (ed) *The Culture of National Security: Norms and Identities in World Politics*, New York: Columbia University Press, pp. 1–32.

Katzenstein, P. J. (2008) *Rethinking Japanese Security: Internal and External Dimensions*, London: Routledge.

Katzenstein, P. J. and Okawara, N. (1993) 'Japan's national security: structures, norms, and policies', *International Security* 17(4): 84–118.

Keck, M. E. and Sikkink, K. (1998) *Activists Beyond Borders: Advocacy Networks in International Politics*, Ithaca: Cornell University Press.

Kennedy, P. (1994) 'Japan: A twenty-first-century power?', in C. C. Garby and M. Brown Bullock (eds) *Japan: A New Kind of Superpower?*, Baltimore: John Hopkins University Press, pp. 193–9.

Klien, S. (2002) *Rethinking Japan's Identity and International Role: An Intercultural Perspective*, London: Routledge.

Kosterman, R. and Feshbach, S. (1989) 'Toward a measure of patriotic and nationalistic attitudes', *Political Psychology* 10(2): 257–74.

Kowert, P. A. (1998) 'National identity: inside and out', *Security Studies* 8(2–3): 1–34.

Kowert, P. and Legro, J. (1996) 'Norms, identity, and their limits: a theoretical reprise', in P. J. Katzenstein (ed.) *The Culture of National Security: Norms and Identity in World Politics*, New York: Columbia University Press, pp. 451–97.

Laclau, E. and Mouffe, C. (1985) *Hegemony and Socialist Strategy: Towards a Radical Democratic Politics*, London: Verso.

Layne, C. (1993) 'The unipolar illusion: why new great powers will rise', *International Security* 17(4): 5–51.

Lebow, R. N. (2008) 'Identity and international relations', *International Relations* 22(4): 473–92.

Littlewood, I. (1996) *The Idea of Japan: Western Images, Western Myths*, Chicago: Ivan R. Dee.

Lupovici, A. (2012) 'Ontological dissonance, clashing identities, and Israel's unilateral steps towards the Palestinians', *Review of International Studies* 38(4): 809–33.
Maull, H. W. (1990/91) 'Germany and Japan: the new civilian powers', *Foreign Affairs* 69(5): 91–106.
Mearsheimer, J. J. (2001) *The Tragedy of Great Power Politics*, New York: W. W. Norton.
Mercer, J. (2010) 'Emotional beliefs', *International Organization* 64(1): 1–31.
Moravcsik, A. (1997) 'Taking preferences seriously: a liberal theory of international politics', *International Organization* 51(4): 513–53.
Morris-Suzuki, T. (1998) *Re-inventing Japan: Time, Space, Nation*, Armonk: M.E. Sharpe.
Murray, M. (2010) 'Identity, insecurity, and great power politics: the tragedy of German naval ambition before the First World War', *Security Studies* 19(4): 656–88.
Neumann, I. B. (1996) 'Self and other in international relations', *European Journal of International Relations* 2(2): 139–74.
Neumann, I. B. (2003) *Mening Materialitet Makt* [Meaning, Materiality, Power], Lund: Studentlitteratur.
Oe, K. (1995) *Japan, the Ambiguous, and Myself: The Nobel Prize Speech and Other Lectures*, Tokyo: Kodansha.
Oguma, E. (2002) *A Genealogy of 'Japanese' Self-Images*, Melbourne: Trans Pacific Press.
Oros, A. L. (2008) *Normalizing Japan: Politics, Identity and the Evolution of Security Practice*, Stanford: Stanford University Press.
Pharr, S. J. (1993) 'Japan's defensive foreign policy and the politics of burden-sharing', in G.L. Curtis (ed) *Japan's Foreign Policy After the Cold War: Coping with Change*, Armonk: M. E. Sharpe, pp. 235–62.
Phillips, N. and Hardy, C. (2002) *Discourse Analysis: Investigating Processes of Social Construction*. New Delhi: SAGE.
Ringmar, E. (1996) *Identity, Interest and Action: A Cultural Explanation of Sweden's Intervention in the Thirty Years War*, Cambridge: Cambridge University Press.
Ringmar, E. (2012) 'Introduction: the international politics of recognition', in T. Lindemann and E. Ringmar (eds) *The International Politics of Recognition*, Boulder: Paradigm, pp. 3–23.
Rosecrance, R. (1986) *The Rise of the Trading State: Commerce and Conquest in the Modern World*, New York: Basic Books.
Rozman, G. (2012) 'Introduction', in G. Rozman (ed) *East Asian National Identities: Common Roots and Chinese Exceptionalism*, Stanford: Stanford University Press, pp. 1–16.
Rumelili, B. (2004) 'Constructing identity and relating to difference: understanding the EU's mode of differentiation', *Review of International Studies* 30(1): 27–47.
Saurette, P. (2006) 'You dissin me? Humiliation and post 9/11 global politics', *Review of International Studies* 32(3): 495–522.
Schulze, K. (2013) 'Facing the 'rise of China': changes in Japan's foreign policy identity', unpublished Ph.D. Thesis, Department for Social Sciences/Institute of East Asian Studies, Duisburg: Duisburg-Essen University.
Singh, B. (2008) 'Japan's security policy: from a peace state to an international state', *The Pacific Review* 21(3): 303–25.
Soeya, Y (2005) *Nihon no 'midoru pawā' gaikō* [Japan's Middle Power Diplomacy], Tokyo: Chikuma Shobō.

Steele, B. J. (2008) *Ontological Security in International Relations: Self-Identity and the IR State*, London: Routledge.

Suzuki, S. (2005) 'Japan's socialization into Janus-faced European international society', *European Journal of International Relations* 11(1): 137–64.

Suzuki, S. (2007) 'The importance of "othering" in China's national identity: Sino-Japanese relations as a stage of identity conflicts', *The Pacific Review* 20(1): 23–47.

Suzuki, S. (2009) *Civilization and Empire: China and Japan's Encounter with European International Society*, London: Routledge.

Tamaki, T. (2010) *Deconstructing Japan's Image of South Korea: Identity in Foreign Policy*, Basingstoke: Palgrave Macmillan.

Tanaka, S. (1993) *Japan's Orient: Rendering Pasts into History*, Berkeley, Los Angeles and London: University of California Press.

Wæver, O. (2002) 'Identity, communities and foreign policy: discourse analysis as foreign policy theory', in L. Hansen and O. Wæver (eds) *European Integration and National Identity: The Challenge of the Nordic States*, London: Routledge, pp. 20–49.

Waltz, K. N. (1979) *Theory of International Politics*, New York: McGraw-Hill.

Waltz, K. N. (1993) 'The emerging structure of international politics', *International Security* 18(2): 44–79.

Waltz, K. N. (2000) 'Structural realism after the cold war'. *International Security* 25(1): 5–41.

Weber, C. (2010) *International Relations Theory: A Critical Introduction*, London: Routledge.

Weldes, J., Laffey, M., Gusterson, H. and Duvall, R. (1999) 'Introduction: constructing insecurity', in J. Weldes, M. Laffey, H. Gusterson and R. Duvall (eds) *Cultures of Insecurity: States, Communities, and the Production of Danger*, Minneapolis: University of Minnesota Press, pp. 1–33.

Wendt, A. (1999) *Social Theory of International Politics*, Cambridge: Cambridge University Press.

Wight, C. (1999) 'They shoot dead horses don't they? Locating agency in the agent-structure problematique', *European Journal of International Relations* 5(1): 109–42.

Wight, C. (2000) 'Interpretation all the way down: a reply to Roxanne Lynn Doty', *European Journal of International Relations* 6(3): 423–30.

Williams, M. C. (1998) 'Identity and the politics of security', *European Journal of International Relations* 4(2): 204–25.

Wodak, R., de Cillia, R., Reisigl, M. and Liebhart, K. (2009) [1999] *The Discursive Construction of National Identity*, 2nd edn, Edinburgh: Edinburgh University Press.

Yoshino, K. (1992) *Cultural Nationalism in Contemporary Japan*, London: Routledge.

The persistence of reified Asia as reality in Japanese foreign policy narratives

Taku Tamaki

Abstract Asia is narrated in Japanese foreign policy pronouncements as an opportunity as well as a threat. Despite the purported transformation from militarism to pacifism since August 1945, the reified images of Asia as an 'entity out there' remain resilient. The image of a dangerous Asia prompted Japan to engage in its programme of colonialism before the War and compels policy makers to address territorial disputes with Asian neighbours today. Simultaneously, Asia persistently symbolises an opportunity for Tokyo to exploit. Hence, despite the psychological rupture of August 1945, reified Asia remains a reality in Japanese foreign policy.

Introduction

Despite the end of the Second World War, which saw pre-war militarism superseded by post-war pacifism, Japan's outlook on Asia remains largely unchanged. Official Japanese narratives still display a sense of awkwardness about its Asian existence. The Japanese government's reaction to the resurgence of territorial disputes with its neighbours since the summer of 2012 reinforced the image of Asia as a potential threat – an idea reminiscent of the pre-war interpretation of the international environment that prompted Japan to engage in its own programme of colonisation at the turn of the last century (Iriye 1991: 13–15). Simultaneously, Tokyo is keen to leverage the economic dynamism of Asia as a potential solution to its 'lost decades', providing another parallel to Japan's pre-war Asia imaginary: that Asia is a source of opportunity indispensable to Japan's wellbeing. Hence, Asia remains a socially constructed entity that poses opportunities for Japanese leadership to exercise its self-proclaimed leadership role, on one hand; but the legacies of the past and the concomitant absence of regional institutional structure means that Asia is understood as a dangerous place, on the other. In short, Asia remains a reified entity with multiple meanings for the Japanese leadership.

This poses a puzzle. Despite the purported changes in August 1945, there is a lingering image of Asian Otherness as an awkward 'thing out there'. What might explain the persistence of reified Asia in Japanese foreign policy narratives? And what implications does this have for Japan's foreign policy preference?[1] The purported psychological rupture of August 1945 has not fundamentally changed Japanese leadership's outlook on Asia. On the contrary, Asia is reified into a dichotomous entity posing both a threat and opportunity within Japanese foreign policy narratives. Perhaps this is due to the international environment, such as the pre-war *Realpolitik*, the Cold War environment in which Communist China became an important player, and the lingering animosities between Japan and its most immediate neighbours. It seems as if the change in Japanese identity has not moved in tandem with transformations in political economic challenges facing Japan. In short, 'opportunity' and 'threat' had become a default set of signifiers within Japanese foreign policy circles to 'talk about' international challenges facing Japan.

This article investigates how the Japanese constructions of Asian Otherness have reified Asia into a 'thing out there' to be identified as an opportunity as well as a threat in foreign policy narratives through the decades, and explores the implications for Japanese foreign policy today. The first section provides a brief overview of the main issues surrounding Japan's relations with Asia. The second section takes reification seriously, focusing on the possibility of reification as a social phenomenon with implications for policy outcomes. Reification matters, since it allows policy makers and theorists alike to talk about complex entities as tangible things to be studied and analysed. I argue that Asia has generally been reified into a notional entity with multiple meanings across the decades. However, it is also the case that the particular Japanese constructions of Asian Otherness have reified Asia into symbols that signify both an opportunity and a threat – a signifier that provides a frame of reference for contemporary Japanese foreign policy narratives. The third section explores the enmeshing of threat and opportunity in pre-war Japanese foreign policy narratives, while the fourth section looks at the constructions of Asia during the Cold War. The fifth section investigates contemporary foreign policy narratives that reproduce the image of Asia as both an opportunity and a threat. The sixth section explores the implications for Japanese foreign policy. Japanese policy makers reify Asia the way they do because they need to be able to 'talk about' the challenges posed by the inherently complex region. This is why reification needs to be taken seriously.

Japan and Asia

Japan's geographical proximity to the Asian continent implies that Asia remains firmly within Japanese policy makers' gaze. Yoon (1997: 176–77) notes that Asia constitutes a signifier that exemplifies Japan's position as a 'non-Western' nation, while the perceived backwardness of Asia reinforced Japan's perceived uniqueness. Japanese elites in the nineteenth century shared the view that a weak Asia was being devoured by the West, ultimately symbolising Asia's purported 'backwardness'. This translated into the notion that Japan, which embarked on rapid modernisation following the Meiji Restoration of 1868, was superior to backward Asia (Yoon 1997: 79). As Takeuchi (1993: 294) notes, such hierarchicalised worldview also translated into a sense of camaraderie (*rentai*) between Japan and Asia.

In a similar vein, Iriye (1966: 42–43) observes that 'prewar Japanese leaders thought Japan and China should co-operate to establish peace and prosperity in Asia, but witnessing China's weakness, Japanese leaders also felt that Japan needed to establish itself as a leader (*meishu*) of Asia'. Japan's pre-war militarism underpinned by such an egotistical liberator identity compelled Japanese leadership to force change upon Asia (Iriye 1966: Chapter 6). Iriye (1991: 13–18) further notes that the pre-war elites felt that the West and Japan were fundamentally irreconcilable, lending credence to the egotistical notion that Japan should lead the rest of Asia in its resistance against the West. Such views also encouraged intellectuals to justify the War as a war of liberation (Takeuchi 1979).

The pre-war liberationist narrative was superseded by its post-war counterpart, in which a pacifist Japan was determined to pursue peaceful interdependence. Superficially, the pre-war Japanese Self of egotistical liberator seems to have been superseded by a peaceful Japanese Self after the War. Yet, the indications are that Asia remains reified as symbolising Japan's precarious position. Bert Edström (1999: 51) observes that 'Japan saw its role in Asia as a promoter of peace, as well as a bridge between the East and West'. Reflecting on Prime Minister Satō Eisaku's February 1970 speech, Edström (1999: 63) argues that,

> The oldish view of Japan as excelling over Asia is seen in one statement Japan should build a base for a spiritually as well as materially rich national life in 'advance of all other countries in the world' as a country that was to excel over other Asian countries in the quest for welfare and prosperity. It was 'significant from the point of view of the history of the world civilization that such things should be realized by Japan, which is a member of Asia'.

Edström (1999: 146) notes that such a view continued into the post-Cold War period, with Prime Minister Kaifu Toshiki suggesting that Japan needed to be a spokesman for Asia, *vis-à-vis*, the 'West'. Hence, Asia remains a recurring theme in Japanese foreign policy narratives.

As Wakamiya (2006: 121) states, 'Japan never felt it lost Asia. While the Western "enemies" evolved into "allies", the sense of superiority towards Asia remained intact'. Hook *et al.* (2012: 162) also suggest that '[the legacies of colonialism have] served as a structural barrier to distance Japan from closer political, economic and security ties with the region in the post-war era'. For them (2012: 163), 'the aftermath of the implosion of Japanese imperialism and the political space that it produced helped to create a geographical landscape conducive to the application of bipolarity and the emergence of a new Cold War order in the region'. Hence, within the Japanese policy elites' gaze, Asia remains an opportunity as well as a source of threat. According to Hook *et al.* (2012: 232), Japan's defeat 'raised once again the international structural barrier of the legacy of colonialism to security interaction between Japan and the newly independent states of the region', and that,

> Japanese policy makers themselves also remain reluctant to exercise leadership from the front; to exploit the opportunities of Asianism and internationalism to the full; and to endorse frameworks which could form an exclusive regional body centred upon Japan, and which would generate tensions with China, the US and other states in the region. (Hook *et al.* 2012: 252)

Therefore, Asia remains a notional entity for generations of Japanese policy makers to 'talk about' and reification is employed to expedite foreign policy making. The meanings attached to Asia might be ethnocentric and egotistical with a tinge of condescension. In any event, reified Asia is a product of Japan's exposure to the challenges posed by events in and around Asia.

Reification as social reality

The term reification is usually a curse in International Relations (IR) theorising, employed mainly to criticise fellow theorists for their failure to consider the complexities of social reality. The accusations and counter-accusations of reification have become more familiar in IR theory debates following the emergence of Constructivism and the subsequent turn to Metatheory and the Philosophy of Social Science (see Kessler 2012; Michel 2012, 2009; Schiff 2008). Yet, there is an important facet to reification: reification of social constructs enables social actors to talk about complex intangible entities as if they are identifiable things. While reification as part of an ontological commitment in theory-building might be controversial (Jackson 2011), there is nothing inherently wrong with applying this term to the psychological landscapes shared by practitioners, just as IR theorists share epistemological landscapes when they tell stories about the complexities of the international environment. In short, practitioners and theorists alike employ reification to render complex reality into workable models.

Humans employ reification as a way to navigate the complex social world (Searle 1995). As Colin Wight (2004: 270) puts it,

> [reification of complex social reality] is so common place that it seems churlish to challenge it. After all, if social actors treat the state in this manner, what right have social scientists to question it?

A similar sentiment is shared by Anderson (1991: 59) who argues that symbols and ideas are reified into obdurate social facts that persist unless manipulated by significant external forces. In other words, however much the ideas of Asian Otherness may be a figment of collective imagination, such images do translate into policy making and implementation. In short, reification plays a vital role.

Examples of reified Asia in Japanese foreign policy narratives include Prime Minister Kishi Nobusuke stating in 1957 that, 'while Asia is not one, I did not think that Asia was divided into two groups [the Communists and the Free World]' (Kwon 2000: 177), as well as the Ministry of Foreign Affairs (MOFA) stating in 1970 that the 'situation in Asia is an admixture of stability and instability' (MOFA 1970: 74). In both cases, it was a way for the Japanese government to 'talk about' the complex region. To paraphrase Patrick Jackson (2011: xii; xiii), reification allows us to 'hook up to the world'. We need to bear in mind that policy makers actively reproduce reifications and they act on them. Hence, reification is not just a theoretical relic. As Brubaker and Cooper (2000: 5) argue, 'reification is a social process, not only an intellectual practice'. As such, reification is necessary if policy makers are to analyse macro-level social phenomena, including the international environment. The main function of reification is to make this process more bearable. Such reification should be taken seriously, since policy elites in Japan and elsewhere can only grasp the vast complexities by reifying Asia into a notional entity that means various things under various circumstances. In short, reification is part and parcel of international life, and it needs to be scrutinised if we are to appreciate the 'reality' encountered by policy elites.

Reified Asia in pre-war Japan

Asia as a diverse region provided a fertile platform upon which reification was employed to rationalise its inherent complexities. As a notional entity, as well as a geographical reality, pre-war Japanese foreign policy narratives constructed Asia into a symbol denoting Japan's perceived vulnerability, as well as opportunities that needed exploiting. Asia has been imagined as a potential conduit for Western colonisers who were already 'devouring' China, as well as an object of desire in Japan's self-proclaimed identity as a 'liberator' and as a valuable source of resources. The variations in Japanese images of Asian Otherness derived from the various ways in which pre-war policy elites in Tokyo attached meanings determined by the perceived diplomatic imperatives and national interests of the time.

Threat and opportunity enmeshed

Maruyama (1961: 9) argues that the 'opening' (*kaikoku*) in the mid-1850s was tantamount to an exposure to the *Realpolitik* of Great Power rivalry. The decision to send troops to Taiwan in 1874, followed by an expedition to Korea in 1875, needs to be interpreted as an effort at addressing Japan's purported security concerns. As Seki (1999: 3) notes, while the political debate of 1873–75 revolved around whether or not to invade Korea, ultimately the issue was about the timing of Japan's Asia expedition, reinforcing the sense that Asia was a 'thing' to be desired and subjugated for the sake of Japan's own security. The purported 'punishment' of Taiwan and Korea in the 1870s, and the 'taming' of China following the Sino-Japanese War of 1894–95, represented Japan's increasing sense of vulnerability as a result of Asia's perceived weaknesses. Put differently, the policy elites felt that Asia required disciplining to prevent further exploitation by the West. Field Marshall Yamagata Aritomo, in his March 1890 memo to the government, argued for the delineation of a 'sovereignty line' (*shuken sen*) and the 'national interest line' (*rieki sen*), defining the 'national interest line' as 'where our "sovereignty line" borders our neighbours'; and that the 'focal point of our *rieki sen* lies in none other than Korea' (Hirono 1999: 51). This highlighted the Japanese leadership's perception of Asia as a source of existential threat for Japan. The cabinet decision in 1903 reiterated such sentiment, arguing that 'our focus on the East Asian continent should be to maintain security of our Empire by encouraging Korean independence in the north and to bring the south of China, starting from Fujian, into our sphere of interest' (Iriye 1966: 39). Foreign Minister Komura Jutarō repeated this assessment in 1904 when he suggested that China was too weak to maintain its own autonomy (Iriye 1966: 39). Gotō Shimpei, the president of South Manchurian Railway, stated in July 1907 that it was important to 'encourage the powerful people in China (*Shina no yūryokusha*) to gain international awareness, and to convince them of the idea of Asia for the Asians as a way for them to understand the essence of Asianism' (Yamamuro 2001: 621). Thus, Asia was simultaneously a source of threat as it was an opportunity.

Similarly, Ugaki Kazushige, a former War Minister and Foreign Minister in the 1920s and the 1930s, considered China as a potential bulwark against further Western incursion. In his diary (December 1941), he argued that Japan should have 'tamed' (tenazukeru) China, and co-operated with it to push Soviet Union away from East Asia. Had Japan and China co-operated — and enhanced China's capabilities — then this should have been possible. However, he also suggested that if this proved to be impossible, then force should have been employed (Matsuura 2010: 201–2). Ugaki also recognised that, so long as 'China's unification movement encompassed anti-Japanese sentiments, then the survival of both Japan and China was at stake' (Tobe 1999: 249). For Ugaki, China was an opportunity intertwined with threat.

Matsui Ukon of the Imperial Army General Staff Office likened the Sino-Japanese conflict to a sibling rivalry within the Asian household (Ajia no ikka): it was a way for the elder brother (Japan) to instil repentance on the younger brother (China) purely out of brotherly love (Matsuura 2010: 512). Similarly, Foreign Minister Ishii Kikujirō wrote in July 1931 that 'it is imperative that we use our holy interests as a shield with which to refuse pleasure to backward peoples' (Yamamuro 2001: 575), reiterating Japan's self-professed mission to civilise Asia. Even the liberal foreign minister, Shidehara Kijūrō, stated in August 1931 that 'our interests in Manchuria are inextricably linked to the activities of our nation, and however much we might be generous towards the Chinese government, we have no intention of forfeiting our rights and interests' (Iriye 1966: 96). The August 1936 meeting of the prime minister, foreign- and finance ministers, as well as the army- and naval ministers stated that,

> Our continental policy centres on the healthy development of Manchukuo, along with the strengthening of Japan-Manchukuo security alliance. We will realise our economic development through strengthening the Japan-Manchukuo-China tripartite alliance, and by ridding the threat from northern Soviet Union, as well as preparing against the Americans and the British. (Iriye 1966: 110)

It was this ethnocentricity which justified the War as brought about by the greed of the USA and Britain, as stated in the Declaration of the Greater East Asian Conference in November 1943 (Harada 1975: 264). Hence, Asia was seen as a dangerous neighbourhood that made Japan vulnerable. Simultaneously, Japanese policy elites' confidence in considering Japan to be the most modern nation in Asia implied that Asia became synonymous with opportunity — an opportunity to realise Japan's leadership potential.

While the focus on Northeast Asia, and China in particular, elicited a sense of vulnerability and danger, Southeast Asia was merely seen as an opportunity. Colonel Watanabe Wataru of the Malayan Military Administration stated in May 1941 that,

> The indigenous peoples who had submitted themselves to the British rule for such a long time must be made aware of their need to reflect on their conduct and must be taught to endure hardship as citizens of Greater Asia for its prosperity. They can no longer be allowed to indulge themselves in a hedonistic and wasteful way of life that is eating up their mind and spirit.... The fundamental principle of my nationality policy is to require them to account for their past mistakes and to make them ready to give up their lives and property. Only when they repent their wrongdoing, will I allow them to live, and I will return their property once they repent. (Akashi 2008: 39)

However much condescending such a view might have been, there was a fleeting sense of opportunity as well – an opportunity to turn purportedly backward people into acceptable subjects of the empire. In a similar vein, Marquis Tokugawa Yoshichika stated in June 1942 that 'Malays [should] be indoctrinated in the Japanese spirit to be the emperor's subjects, and pay a visit to Syonan [Singapore] Jinja enshrined with the ancestral god of their imperial family' (Akashi 2008: 43). To be sure, these sound as if they were intended to camouflage the true intent of the Japanese government to exploit natural resources. General Okada Kikujirō asserted in November 1941 that 'what is most valuable for us in [Southeast Asia] is the oil' (Gotō 1995: 27). This was repeated in MOFA's Guidelines for Greater East Asia Strategy of May 1943 which explicitly stated that 'Southeast Asia provides crucial resources for the empire' (MOFA 2010b: 1486). Southeast Asia was an opportunity for the Japanese to turn its people into faithful subjects in the imperial project, and as a way to exploit resources. Effectively, Southeast Asia represented a hedge against the existential threat posed by Asia in general. Hence, Asia in pre-war Japanese foreign policy narratives enmeshed threat and opportunity: because of the perceived threat emanating from Asia, it also became an opportunity for Japanese government to exploit it in the name of Japan's imperial project.

Japan's gaze on Asia during the Cold War

The May 1950 MOFA document on economic relations called for pragmatism, stating that 'now that China was lost, it is Japan's destiny (*unmei*) to expand trade with Southeast Asia' (Hatano and Satō 2007: 5–6). Superficially, Communist China may have been a threat during the Cold War, but the sense of danger was rather nuanced. As Prime Minister Yoshida Shigeru wrote to John Foster Dulles in December 1951,

The Japanese Government ultimately wants to establish trade and political relations with our neighbour China; and while it is in our best and realistic (*genjitsu-teki de saizen*) interest, we can guarantee that we have no intention of establishing bilateral relations with the People's Republic of China. (Wakamiya 2006: 128)

Other policy makers shared similar optimism. Prime Minister Kishi Nobusuke stated in January 1958 that,

Concerning Japan-China relations, the government has so far acted on the course of promoting trade and cultural exchange and of aiming at the solution of fishery and other problems to the maximum extent possible, given the present position of our country, and it wants to go on with this course. I hope and expect that both sides will come to understand each other's position where they have to conduct trade and cultural exchange in the present situation when national relations are not formally restored. (Edström 1999: 43)

Hence, the threat of Communist China needs to be understood within the context of this latent pragmatism within Japanese foreign policy circles.

Communist China as threat and opportunity

The focus of Japanese foreign policy on Southeast Asia in the first two decades following the end of the War represented perceived threat, rather than opportunities, from China (MOFA 1957: 13). As early as 1953, Nakasone Yasuhiro warned that 'it is dangerous to hope for trade with China' given its close ties with the Soviet Union (Kanda 2013: 58). It is noteworthy that Yoshida himself mentioned similar intentions in November 1954, stating that 'Japan would strengthen its relations with Southeast Asian countries with the ultimate goal of strengthening the bulwark against "the Communist offensive"' (Edström 1999: 20). Kishi reiterated this position after visiting Southeast Asia in 1957, commenting on his willingness to 'talk to [the US] about what they are doing in Southeast Asia, and to discuss what Japan needs to do, given that the turmoil in Southeast Asia could precipitate a Communist invasion which would be detrimental to the world' (Wakamiya 2006: 135).

The MOFA had been forthright about the dangers of Communist China. Its 1960 *Diplomatic Bluebook*[2] stated that, 'needless to say, we need to refute misunderstandings by the Chinese Communists. Yet, it is important for Communist China not to be arrogant' (MOFA 1960: 6). In the 1962 edition, MOFA stated that the Chinese membership of the United Nations 'poses potential danger (*kiken*) for the future, and therefore needs to be treated seriously' (MOFA 1962: 19). Furthermore, the same issue noted that, 'depending on the way the [membership] issue is dealt with, it can seriously affect world peace, and thus is an extremely complex issue' (MOFA 1962: 20). Prime Minister Ikeda Hayato reiterated such sentiment in December 1962, stating that Communist China – and the march of Communism in Asia in general – made pursuit of relations with the 'free countries' of Asia important; and that Japan needed to become 'a pillar of the "free camp" along with North America and Western Europe' (Edström 1999: 53).

Eventually, the normalisation of Sino-American relations elicited a more positive outlook. MOFA's *Diplomatic Bluebook* for 1974 (MOFA 1974: 126) stated that the normalisation of relations with China 'brings about an end to the 23 years of unnatural and abnormal relationship since the end of the War'. In the following year, MOFA (1975: 39) saw Indochina as representing the persistence of Communist threat in Asia, but the 'events in Asia have changed from confrontation to communication (*taiketsu kara taiwa*)', in a clear reference to Sino-Japanese *rapprochement*. There was an enhanced sense of optimism in the 1978 *Diplomatic Bluebook*, when MOFA (1978: 20) argued that 'good neighbourly relations between Japan and China hold significance for the peaceful international environment in Asia'. The change from threat to opportunity was defined primarily by international events. Nevertheless, it reveals that China still signified the duality of Asia as representing threat and opportunity for Japanese policy elites.

Southeast Asia as an opportunity

To the extent Communist China represented a threat, Southeast Asia presented opportunities. As the MOFA *Diplomatic Bluebook* pointed out in 1959, while the relations with China remained sensitive (1959: 72–73), Southeast Asia was identified as the focal point of Japan's Asia diplomacy (MOFA 1959: 56). Not dissimilar to pre-war Japanese interests in the region, MOFA stated in 1957 (1957: 23) that,

> With their foodstuffs and raw materials necessary for sustaining our industries, Southeast Asian states remain important as sources of our imports. Furthermore, as important markets for our industrial products, their importance for the stability and prosperity of our postwar economy means that they are becoming increasingly indispensable.

A similar sentiment was repeated in 1958, when Southeast Asia was identified as an important region for the economic prosperity, as well as political stability, for Japan (MOFA 1958: 35) – an outlook that continued into the 1960s.

To a certain extent, the focus on Southeast Asia was borne of necessity. For Yoshida, Southeast Asia was effectively a 'substitute for the loss of Chinese market' (Edström 1999: 23–24). At the same time, the region was seen as a source of stability during the Cold War. Prime Minister Hatoyama Ichirō stated in January 1956 that the 'expansion of Japan's economic relations with Southeast Asia [through] economic diplomacy (*keizai gaikō*) [was to become] the focal point of Japan's Asia policy' (Edström 1999: 33). The creation of Association of Southeast Asian Nations (ASEAN) in August 1967 enhanced the image of Southeast Asia as an oasis of stability. Speaking in December 1972, Foreign Minister Ōhira Masayoshi stated that '[o]ur intention is to join co-operative efforts with Southeast Asian states intent on forging stability and prosperity as a peace-loving member of Asia' (Tamaki 2013: 272). In the 1973 *Diplomatic Bluebook* for the same year, MOFA identified ASEAN as 'seeking to avoid unwanted external interference while strengthening autonomy', thereby contributing to the stability of Asia as a whole (Hatano and Satō 2007: 161).

Thus, Asia as a whole continued to be narrated as an entity that posed challenges to Japan's interests, whether be it in the guise of national security or as a test of Japan's post-war international legitimacy. Likewise, Southeast Asia provided a stark contrast to Northeast Asia yet again, depicting a region of relative stability and an important lifeline for Japan. In other words, the challenges of Cold War international politics resulted in the reproduction of a familiar dichotomy in Japan's images of Asia.

Narrating the reified Asia today

Contemporary Japanese foreign policy narratives continue to reproduce the dichotomous images of Asia as both an opportunity and a threat, though the stress is predominantly on the dangers posed by China since Summer 2012 as representative of the challenges Asia poses to the Japanese government. The 2014 *Defence Whitepaper* published by the Ministry of Defence (MOD) explicitly identified China as 'seeking to unilaterally change the *status quo*, potentially inciting crisis through escalation' (*Nihon keizai shimbun* 2014). For the Tokyo government, the reification of Asia into a set of challenges remains a default worldview through which the international environment is understood.

Asia as still a threat

Already back in 1969, a report by MOFA considered China to represent an 'eventual threat' symbolising dangerous Asia (Tanaka 1997: 220). This image was revisited in the mid- to late-2000s, when the MOD made explicit mentions of China's power projection capabilities. The National Institute for Defence Studies (NIDS) (2011: iii) published its *China Security Report* in 2011, stating that, while the *Report* did not reflect official views of the Japanese Government, the authors argued that they were compelled to analyse China's opaque military build-up. The 2009 *East Asian Strategic Review*, also published by the NIDS (2009: i), suggested that the 'maintenance of peace and stability in East Asia entails an objective understanding of the region's security environment', and such objectivity translated into identifying China as a main concern.

The territorial dispute over Senkaku/Diaoyu Islands that resurfaced in September 2010 reinforced that message. The 2011 edition of MOFA's *Diplomatic Bluebook* (2011: 17) stated that, 'there exist not only non-traditional threats, but also traditional threats in the East Asian region surrounding Japan. The year 2010 made it evident that the security of East Asia is still severe; and that situations remain indeterminate and unstable'. Considering the March 2010 sinking of a South Korean corvette, *Cheonan*, along with the North Korean shelling of Yongbyon Island in November that year, such pessimism was understandable. The *Bluebook* added that, 'while a rapidly developing China insists on a peaceful rise, their opaque military spending and maritime activities pose regional- as well as international concerns' (MOFA 2011: 17). These events reinforced the worldview shared among foreign policy elites that China and the Korean Peninsula still symbolised risks to Japan's security — very similar to the threat perception at the turn of the last century (Iriye 1966: 30–32). In short, it was understood as the persistent reality of Japan's Asian predicament.

Not surprisingly, the MOD was more pessimistic. Just as in other official publications, it recognised in its 2010 edition of the *Defence White Paper* that Asia was a rapidly expanding region, and as such, the region provided Japan with opportunities. However, it also suggested that, 'despite the end of the Cold War, conflicts and disputes remain; and while a dramatic shift in the security environment was experienced in Europe, there remain territorial, as well as unification, problems [in East Asia]' (MOD 2010b: 3). The MOD (2010b: 3–4) went on to list perceived threats emanating from the familiar triad of Japan's security concerns — the Korean Peninsula, China, and Russia. It identified general concerns with respect to North Korea, as well as the opacity of Chinese military spending (MOD 2010b: 4), along with Russia's military modernisation (MOD 2010b: 4), arguing that, 'as such, the region still retains vague and indeterminate factors' (MOD 2010b: 4). Foreign Minister Asō Tarō reiterated this, stating that 'the problem remains China's military spending that is increasing annually at double-digit figures (*nenkan futaketa no wariai*). And there is absolutely no sense that it is transparent.... It is natural for neighbours to be alarmed by it. It would be unnatural if we kept quiet about it' (Chūō kōron 2006: 47). Similarly, Noda Yoshihiko (2011: 100), on the verge of taking over as the prime minister, admitted that, while Japan was heavily dependent on Chinese economy, he was also apprehensive about 'China's opaque military spending, along with its strategic thinking, [they] are both concerns not just for Japan, but also to other countries in the region. Recent, aggressive, Chinese foreign policy stance (*taigai shisei*) through military activities in the South China Sea potentially upsets the regional international order'.

Thus, China's military spending and modernisation defined Asia as a dangerous neighbourhood for Japanese foreign policy circles. The result was the further reproduction of the familiar reification of Asia into signifying threat for Japan. The then-leader of LDP, Tanigaki Sadakazu, suggested in 2010 that:

> China is an important neighbour, and closer relations would bring benefits to our economy as well. Yet, China has a different face (*betsu no kao*) militarily. Its maritime and airborne operations pose concern for Japan and the surrounding countries. To pretend that we can maintain good relations with China and not worry about it can potentially endanger the security not just of Japan, but also of the Asia-Pacific region. (Chūō kōron 2010: 137–38)

This sentiment was reiterated by Abe Shinzō on his second stint as the prime minister. In a forthright interview with The Washington Post (2013) in February 2013, Abe argued that:

> In the process of [patriotic education], in order to gain natural resources for their economy, China is taking action by coercion of intimidation, both in the South China Sea and the East China Sea. This is also resulting in strong support from the people of China, who have been brought up through this educational system that attaches emphasis on patriotism. This, however, is also a dilemma faced by China. That is to say, the mood and atmosphere created by the education in China attaching importance to patriotism – which is in effect focusing on anti-Japanese sentiment – is in turn undermining their friendly relationship with Japan and having an adverse effect on its economic growth. And the Chinese government is well aware of this.

While this did not constitute a conflation, *per se*, it represented Abe's view that Asia remained dangerous because of China's rise.

Hence, the psychological landscape shared by Japanese policy makers focused primarily on China as a source of threat for Japan's security. It was China which seems to have represented Asia as a dangerous place. On one hand, Asia still remained a threat because China made it so. As such, the security – and the larger international – environment has changed since the Cold War, let alone the turn of the last century. Yet, on the other hand, even if today's Japanese policy makers face issues that are different from the previous era, it seems that the reified image of Asia as symbolising threat has been recycled. In short, reified Asia remains relevant for policy makers in 'talking about' the changing international environment.

Asia remains an opportunity

Given Japan's reliance on Asian and Chinese economies, it is not surprising that Asia is seen as the next growth centre holding the key to Japan's own economic recovery. The MOFA (2010a: 20) stated in the 2010 edition of the *Diplomatic Bluebook* that the 'realisation of a prosperous, stable, and an open Asia-Pacific region is indispensable to Japan's peace, stability, and prosperity', and that the construction of the 'East Asian Community is a vital element' in this process, hoping that an increased 'intra-Asian demand' (*Ajia naiju*) would help pull Japan out of its lost decade (MOFA 2010a: 20). In the 2011 edition, MOFA (2011: 25) reaffirmed the importance of Asian economy, stating that the 'Asia-Pacific region is increasingly becoming crucial for Japan – both politically and economically', and 'it is for this reason that Japan is determined to contribute to the prosperity of Asia; and to use Asia's vitality and demand (*katsuryoku, juyō*) as a stimulus for Japanese economy as well'. In a similarly optimistic language, the *White Paper on International Economy and Trade* published by the Ministry of Economy, Trade, and Industry (METI) focused on the opportunities posed by Asia. In its 2009 edition, METI (2009: 270) identified Asia as a '21st Century growth-centre', in the hope of leveraging Asian 'wealth, trade, and investment for the benefit of Japanese employment and innovation', while the 2010 edition invoked the narrative of Asia again as a 'growth centre', suggesting that Japan needed to 'contribute towards Asia's growth as a way of leveraging our own economy' (METI 2010: 156).

Foreign policy elites reconstruct the reified image of Asia as an opportunity. Asō stated in 2006 with a hint of condescension reminiscent of the pre-war era that, 'until about 30 years ago, Asia was almost synonymous with poverty.... Now, I am quite optimistic about the Asian region in the medium- to longer term' (Chūō kōron 2006: 47). In a characteristic reification that leaves Asia under-defined, a former foreign minister, Okada Katsuya of the Democratic Party of Japan (DPJ), admitted in 2009 that the USA–Japan alliance was important, but suggested that 'Asia is another area where we will need to focus our attention... We are fortunate to be located in Asia, where the economy is expanding' (Sekai 2009: 141). Reiterating the *Trade White Paper*, Okada argued that, 'we need to realise Japan's stability and prosperity within the East Asian Community (EAC). Enhancing the economic linkages can only be achieved within interdependence, so it is our policy to construct (*kumitateru*) our Asian diplomacy'

(Sekai 2009: 141). Here again, we witness the identification of dynamic Asia as a 'tool' to help stimulate Japanese economy.

Gemba Kōichirō, another former DPJ foreign minister, argued that 'a democratic, prosperous, and stable Asia is indispensable for Japan's national interest' (Gaikō 2012: 15), adding: 'we need to improve our domestic public sentiments (*kokumin kanjō*) in order to forge more mature Sino-Japanese relations, so that we can enhance our strategic partnership in establishing rules for the Asia-Pacific region' (Gaikō 2012: 17). For Gemba, the Sino-Japanese relationship epitomised Japan's relations with Asia. In a similar vein, Noda (2011: 100) stated that the 'world around us is changing. Our economic and political position in the Asia-Pacific is also changing. China is the engine for growth; and if China's development is harmonious with the international community, then that provides opportunities for Japan as well'. Here again, even the changing economic environment of the twenty-first century elicited familiar recycling of reified Asia as an opportunity, once again highlighting the inherent dichotomy in the Japanese constructions of Asia as an entity 'out there'.

Southeast Asia as a beacon of stability

Southeast Asia is still perceived as an oasis of stability in the region, and the closer relations with ASEAN is seen as a counter-balance to the perceived instability of Northeast Asia. Prime Minister Obuchi Keizō, commemorating the 30th anniversary of ASEAN in 1997, used the occasion to hold what was to become the ASEAN+3 meetings (Wakamiya 2006: 238), representing how Southeast Asia provided diplomatic opportunity for Japan. The sense of opportunity was also highlighted in January 2002 by Prime Minister Koizumi Junichirō, who argued that 'in the 21st century, Japan and ASEAN under the principle of "acting together and advancing together" should enhance co-operation and construct a community' (Sadakata 2011: 208).

The importance of stability in Southeast Asia has been a recurring theme in Japanese foreign policy narratives. The 2004 *Diplomatic Bluebook* suggested that 'it is important for Japan to co-operate with ASEAN for it to become a force for political and economic stability. Japan intends to enhance co-operation with ASEAN in an effort at contributing to the political and economic stability of Southeast Asia, as well as the wider East Asia' (MOFA 2004: 56). For that purpose, MOFA claimed that ASEAN was an important partner (MOFA 2004: 59), while also noting that ASEAN was the largest destination for Japanese foreign direct investment (MOFA 2004: 59). Similar sentiments were reiterated in subsequent publications, with the 2006 edition highlighting the 30 years of 'ASEAN-Japan friendship' (MOFA 2006: 47), arguing that the relationship is evolving into a 'strategic partnership' (MOFA 2006: 49). The 2007 *Diplomatic Bluebook* reaffirmed 'Japan to proactively support the stability of ASEAN' (MOFA 2007: 37), while the 2008 edition identified 'ASEAN as the most important investment partner' (MOFA 2008: 37). The 2009 *Diplomatic Bluebook* quoted Foreign Minister Kōmura Masahiko proclaiming that 'the development of Mekong is to the benefit of ASEAN; and the growth in ASEAN is beneficial to Japan' (MOFA 2009: 41).

Hence, Southeast Asia is consistently represented as an opportunity for Japan. As Hook *et al.* (2012: 211) suggest,

> Japan at the start of the twenty-first century has worked hard to cement good relations with ASEAN and to realize many of the goals of the Fukuda Doctrine from the 1970s. However, it is important to note that Japan's proactivity towards ASEAN has been driven in large part by concerns that Japan's 'special relationship' with Southeast Asia is now increasingly threatened by the rise of China as a competitor for regional leadership.

This is not dissimilar to the focus on Southeast Asia in the decades following the War. Southeast Asia remained an opportunity, precisely because Asia, and China in particular, remained a dangerous neighbourhood.

The implications of reified Asia

The recent territorial conflicts since 2010 prompted the Japanese government to adopt a sterner language. Before the landslide victory by the LDP in both the December 2012 and July 2013 elections, the preceding DPJ government revised the *National Defence Programme Guidelines* (*Bōei taikō*) and the *Midterm Defence Programme* (*Chūkibō*) in December 2010, over concerns that the security environment was deteriorating. The Chief Cabinet Secretary, Sengoku Yoshito, referred to the need for enhancing defence capabilities, given the heightened tensions (MOD 2012c), while the Defence Minister, Kitazawa Toshimi, stated that:

> With the existence of military power with nuclear capabilities, along with many states modernising their military power, the time has come for us to move from passive deterrence (*seiteki yokushi*) in which we rely solely on existing defence capability, to a more dynamic deterrence (*dōteki yokushi*) in which we show national determination (*kokka no ishi*) and a high level of defence capability (*takai bōei nōryoku*) on a continuous basis. (MOD 2012b)

The *Bōei taikō* itself stated that the balance of power had shifted, and that many states are modernising their military, before explicitly naming

North Korea, China, and Russia as involved in such activities (MOD 2010a: II-2). The *Chūkibō* augmented this by arguing for the necessity of strengthening response capabilities, particularly in the Southwest islands, including the deployment of radars and reconnaissance aircraft, along with transport helicopters (MOD 2012a: III-1(2)). Furthermore, the MOD (2012a: III-4(1)) stated that it was crucial to reorganise the command structure so that 'multiple events' (*fukugō jitai*) can be addressed swiftly through the implementation of joint command.

Following the change of government in December 2012, the new LDP administration initiated a review of the defence budget. Citing new developments, the Abe cabinet decided in January 2013 to abandon the 2010 *Chūkibō*, explicitly referring to repeated territorial infringement by the Chinese, while reiterating the necessity of enhancing defensive capacity in the Southwest islands (MOD 2013b). As Abe noted in the February 2013 Washington Post (2013) interview,

> Accordingly, for the first time in 11 years, I have increased our defense budget, as well as the budget for the Japan coast guard. It is important for us to have them [China] recognize that it is impossible to try to get their way by coercion or intimidation.

It is noteworthy that the reified notion of Asia as a dangerous neighbourhood is represented yet again within the *Defence Posture Review Interim Report*, which identified North Korea, China, and Russia as main concerns – again similar to the pre-war sense of vulnerability (MOD 2013a).

It is within this context that the debate over collective self-defence had been revisited. The sense of Asia as a dangerous neighbourhood was repeated in an interview given by Kitaoka Shin'ichi, chairman of the committee tasked with assessing the legal framework for collective self-defence. In the interview, Kitaoka suggested that 'there is a country with nuclear arms that infringe our territorial waters. Unless Japan invests in its own nuclear weapons programme, there is no way Japan can fend for itself', adding that 'the times have changed; and the weapons technology is constantly evolving. With the rise of China and North Korea, can we work within the [old] rules [as prescribed by Article 9 of the Constitution]?' (Asahi shimbun 2013). Defence Minister Onodera Itsunori denied that collective self-defence is about sending troops abroad, but as if to prepare for an armed conflict with China over the Senkakus/Diaoyus, he pointed out instead that there was the need to debate what Japan should do if US warships trying to defend Japan came under attack in high seas – ostensibly helping to protect Japanese territory from Chinese invasion (Nihon keizai shimbun 2013). Another manifestation of this sense of danger is the launch of the new helicopter destroyer *Izumo*. Inoue (2013) interprets this as a natural response to Chinese naval activities around the East China Sea, commenting that possessing a helicopter carrier would be useful in enhancing the control of the airspace. This assessment is similar to an analysis by Kyle Mizokami (2013), suggesting that 'the Izumo and the rest of Japan's amphibious and helicopter escort ships could theoretically provide air and sea lift to transport Japan's nascent marine infantry, the Western Army Infantry Regiment based in Southern Japan' – something that is reflected in the *Bōei taikō* and the now-abandoned *Chūkibō*.

The government in Tokyo is not yet actively preparing for war. However, the rhetoric seems to suggest that the officials are compelled to pronounce Japan's readiness to do so. Indeed, Abe told *The Wall Street Journal* (Baker and Nishiyama 2013) in October 2013 that, 'I've realised that Japan is expected to exert leadership not just on the economic front, but also in the field of security in the Asia-Pacific', warning that if China 'opts to [change the status quo by force], then it won't be able to emerge peacefully'. Such words precipitate a vicious circle of invectives that might instantiate an actual conflict. As Linus Hagström (2012: 297) argues, the narrative emphasising 'Chinese aggressiveness' has agency precisely 'because the more dominant it becomes the more inevitable it is that other states will take recourse to potentially dangerous balancing behaviour *vis-à-vis* China'. In a similar vein, we can argue that Japan's reification of Asia into a dangerous neighbourhood embodies a potential for self-fulfilling prophecy. Japan's contemporary foreign policy narratives view Asia, and China in particular, with a significant amount of scepticism, interpreting China's rise as 'detrimental to the security of the seas around China (*Chūgoku wo torimaku kaiyō no anzen-hoshō kankyō ni hitei-teki na eikyō*), and the areas around East Asia are no exception' (NIDS 2011: 44). These images of Asia and China conspire to complete the vicious circle in which the reified Asian Otherness representing threat trumps symbols of opportunity, thereby reinforcing the sense of Japan under siege.

Conclusions

Tokyo is constantly reminded of the fact that its existence is inextricably intertwined with events in Asia. For Japan situated in the eastern-most edge of Asia, Asia ceases to be a mere geographical designation: it constitutes a reality. Yet, there are multiple realities in that Asia poses both an opportunity as well as a potential threat. From a simple geographical perspective, it is not surprising. Japan cannot wish away neither the nuclear weapons of North Korea, nor territorial disputes with China and South Korea. Simultaneously, Asia provides opportunities, if not a lifeline, for Japan that is lacking in natural resources, as well as a possible solution to its economic problems. Hence, Asia remains a reified social construct that signify both an opportunity and a threat. Such narratives are becoming more salient following the flare-up in territorial disputes between Tokyo and its neighbours.

The answer to the puzzle of resilient reification seems to lie with the international environment. The consistent reification of Asia into a set of signifiers by generations of Japanese policy elites points to its resilience in providing a continuous psychological landscape for understanding the constraints encountered by the Japanese government. To be sure, reified Asia might be a figment of imagination within the minds of policy makers. Yet, it is precisely due to the policy implications of such social constructs that reified Asian Otherness has remained potent throughout the decades. Put differently, even if Japanese identity had transformed since August 1945, the basic constraints of the international environment seems to have persisted in the minds of Japanese policy makers. The Korean peninsula remains unstable as a by-product of the Cold War; China still represents both a threat and opportunity for Japan; and Southeast Asia represents a friendly sphere for Japan in stark contrast to the dangerous Northeast Asia. In order to address these challenges, Asia has been reified into a familiar dichotomy of threat and opportunity. In short, Japanese foreign policy elites recycled the images of Asia to be able to 'talk about' and 'deal with' the complexities of international life in East Asia. Reification enabled Japanese policy makers to formulate and execute policies including recasting military capabilities to address mounting tensions with China, while identifying Asia as a source of economic salvation. These reified images prompted policy makers to take action, and this is the reason why reifications must be said to possess policy implications. To that effect, we need a better handle on reification. Without such an insight, Japanese debates on constitutional amendment, as well as the new thinking on the future defence of the Southwest islands, cannot be fully appreciated. After all, Japan's actions to counter China's rise are 'rational' insofar as they are contextualised within the narratives of reified Asia. The debates on collective self-defence and the launch of the helicopter destroyer are facets of the Japanese Self responding to the meanings attached to the narratives of Asian Otherness.

Hence, reifications are important. Japanese policy makers act on these perceptions. It means that Asia remains an awkward entity for Japan, and despite the narratives such as 'Japan in Asia', the two can never be synonymous, providing a particular template for the formulation of a particular policy preference. As such, Asia remains a 'thing out there' within Japanese policy narratives. Throughout the centuries of Japan's socialisation process in and around Asia, the foreign policy narratives suggest that Tokyo never identified itself fully with Asia, consistently utilising Asia as a signifier for Japan to proclaim itself as neither Western nor Asian. Hence, Asia remains a 'thing' that is potentially dangerous, but also a 'thing' that is beneficial for Japan. It is to be hoped that the events since the summer of 2012 do not portend a resurgence of Japanese narratives that marked the decades leading up to the 1930s and the 1940s.

Acknowledgements

I am extremely grateful to Linus Hagström for his piercing and insightful comments throughout the drafting of this article. I also thank the reviewers and the participants at Focus Asia: Collective Memory, Identity and International Relations in East Asia, Lund University, 6–7 November 2012, for their helpful comments on the earlier versions of this article.

Notes

1. I thank Linus Hagström for pointing out the 'puzzle'.
2. While the name *Diplomatic Bluebook* (*Gaikō seisho*) did not appear until the 1980s, I will refer to the series of publications as *Diplomatic Bluebook*.

References

Akashi Y. (2008) 'Colonel Watanabe Wataru: The architect of the Malayan military administration, December 1941–March 1943', in Y. Akashi and M. Yoshimura (eds) *New Perspectives on the Japanese Occupation of Malaya and Singapore, 1941–1945*, Singapore: NUS Press, chapter 2.

Anderson, B. (1991) *Imagined Communities*, London: Verso.

Asahi shimbun. (2013) 'Senshu-bōei towa "kōgeki zero" denai: Kitaoka zachō-dairi ichimon-itto' [An exclusively self-defence policy is no "zero offensive": Q&A with Vice Chairman Kitaoka], 10 August; accessed at http://digital.asahi.com/articles/TKY201308090428.html?ref=comkiji_txt_end_kjid_TKY201308090428, 9 August 2013.

Baker G. and Nishiyama, G. (2013) 'Abe says Japan ready to counter China's power: premier urges China to refrain from using force', *The Wall Street Journal*, 26 October; accessed at http://online.wsj.com/news/articles/SB10001424052702304799404579157210861675436>, 31 October 2013.

Brubaker, R. and Cooper, F. (2000) 'Beyond "identity"', *Theory and Society* 29(1): 1–47.

Chūō kōron (2006) 'Kore ga gaikō no hinkaku da' [This is the dignity of diplomacy], July, pp. 36–47.

Chūō kōron (2010) 'Ajia no "kōkyō-zai" Nichibei-dōmei wo kijuku ni hoshu-seiji wo saisei suru' [Reviving conservative politics based on US-Japan alliance as Asia's 'public good'], March, pp. 136–45.

Edström, B. (1999) *Japan's Evolving Foreign Policy Doctrine: From Yoshida to Miyazawa*, London: Macmillan.

Gaikō (2012) 'Nichi-bei-chū taiwa no toki' [The time for Japan-US-China trilogue], Vol. 11, January, pp. 12–21.

Gotō K. (1995) *Kindai Nippon to Tōnan-ajia: Nanshin no 'shōgeki' to 'isan'* [*Modern Japan and Southeast Asia: The 'Shock' and 'Legacies' of Southern Policy*], Tokyo: Iwanami shoten.

Hagström, L. (2012) '"Power shift" in East Asia? A critical reappraisal of narratives on the Diaoyu/Senkaku Islands incident in 2010', *The Chinese Journal of International Politics* 5: 267–97.

Harada K. (1975) *Dokyumento Shōwa-shi 4: Taiheiyō-sensō* [*Document History of Showa 4: The Pacific War*], Tokyo: Heibonsha.

Hatano S. and Satō S. (2007) *Gendai Nippon no Tōnan-Ajia seisaku (1950-2006)* [*Modern Japan's Southeast Asian Policy (1950-2006)*], Tokyo: Waseda daigaku shuppanbu.

Hirono Y. (1999) 'Yamagata Aritomo: "Yamagata Aritomo Ikensho"' ['Yamagata Aritomo: "The Opinion of Yamagata Aritomo"'], in Seki S. (ed), *Kindai Nippon gaikōshisō-shi nyūmon* [*Introduction to Modern Japanese Diplomatic Thought*], Kyoto: Minerva, chapter 3.

Hook, G. D., Gilson, J., Hughes, C. W. and Dobson, H. (2012) *Japan's International Relations: Politics, Economics and Society* (3rd ed.), London: Routledge.

Inoue H. (2013) 'Hiroshima genbaku no hi, kūbo-gata goeikan "Izumo" no meimei shinsuishiki ni omouno wa "heiwa-boke" Nippon' [Pondering Japan's peace-numbness on the day of destroyer Izumo's launch], *Gendai bijinesu* [*Contemporary Business*], 8 August 2013; accessed at gendai.ismedia.jp/articles/print/36653, 9 August 2013.

Iriye A. (1966) *Nippon no gaikō* [*Japan's Diplomacy*], Tokyo: Chūkō shinsho.

Iriye A. (1991) *Shin Nippon no gaikō* [*New Japan's Diplomacy*], Tokyo: Chūkō shinsho.

Jackson, P. T. (2011) *The Conduct of Inquiry in International Relations*, London: Routledge.

Kanda Y. (2013) '1980-nendai no reisen to Nippon gaikō ni okeru futatsu no chitsujo-kan: Nakasone-seiken no tai-Chū gaikō wo juku toshite' ['Two Conceptions of Order During the Cold War of the 1980s and Japanese Diplomacy: Focusing on Nakasone Cabinet's China Diplomacy'], *Ajia-taiheiyō tōkyū* [*Asia-Pacific Research*] 19: 53–69.

Kessler, O. (2012) 'On logic, intersubjectivity, and meaning: is reality an assumption we just don't need?' *Review of International Studies* 38(1): 253–65.

Kwon Yongseok (2000) 'Kishi no Tōnan-ajia rekihō to "tai-bei jishu" gaikō' [Kishi's Southeast Asia tour and "autonomous diplomacy" against the US], *Hitotsubashi ronsō* [*Hitotsubashi Papers*] 123(1): 170–89.

Maruyama M. (1961) *Nippon no shisō* [*Japanese Thought*], Tokyo: Iwanami shinsho.

Matsuura M. (2010) *'Dai-tōa sensō' wa naze okita noka: Han-ajia-shugi no seiji keizai-shi* [*Why the 'Great Far Eastern War' Happened: The Political Economic History of Pan-Asianism*], Nagoya: Nagoya daigaku shuppankai.

Michel, T. (2009) 'Pigs can't fly, or can they? Ontology, scientific realism and the metaphysics of presence in international relations', *Review of International Studies* 35(2): 397–419.

Michel, T. (2012) 'In Heidegger's shadow: a phenomenological critique of critical Realism', *Review of International Studies* 38(1): 209–22.

Ministry of Economy, Trade, and Industry (METI) (2009) *Tsūshō hakusho 2009*, Tokyo: METI.

METI (2010) *Tsūshō hakusho 2010* [*The Trade White Paper*], Tokyo: METI.

Mizokami, K. (2013) 'Japanese "helicopter destroyer" stirs regional tensions', *USNI News*, 12 August; accessed at news.usni.org/2013/08/12/japanese-helicopter-destroyer-stir-regional-tensions?utm_source=feedly, 15 August 2013.

Ministry of Defence (MOD) (2010a) *Heisei 23-nendo ni kakawaru bōei keikaku no taikō* [*Mid-term Defence Guidelines for FY 2011*], 17 December 2010, Section II-2, Tokyo: MOD.

MOD (2010b) *Nippon no bōei 2010*, Tokyo: MOD.

MOD (2012a) *Chūki bōeiryoku seibi keikaku (Heisei 23-nendo kara Heisei 27-nendo) ni tsuite* [*Mid-term Defence Planning for FY2011-FY2015*], 17 December 2012, Section III-1 (2), Tokyo: MOD.

MOD (2012b) 'Heisei 23-nendo ikō ni kakawaru bōei keikaku no taikō' oyobi 'Chūki bōeiryoku seibi keikaku (Heisei 23-nendo kara Heisei 27-nendo)' no kettei ni tsuite [Decisions on the Defence Programme Guidelines for FY2011 and Beyond; and the Mid-term Defence Guidelines for FY2011-FY2015], 17 December 2012, Tokyo: MOD.
MOD (2012c) Naikaku kanbō chōkan danwa [Statement by the Chief Cabinet Secretary], 17 December 2012, Tokyo: MOD.
MOD (2013a) Bōeiryoku no arikata kentō ni kansuru chūkan hōkoku [Interim Report on the Defence Capability], 26 July 2013, Tokyo: MOD.
MOD (2013b) Heisei-25nendo no bōeiryoku seibi tō ni tsuite [Upgrading Defence Capabilities for FY 2013], 25 January 2013, Tokyo: MOD.
Ministry of Foreign Affairs (MOFA) (1957) Waga gaikō no kinkyō September 1957, Tokyo: MOFA.
MOFA (1958) Waga gaikō no kinkyō March 1958, Tokyo: MOFA.
MOFA (1959) Waga gaikō no kinkyō March 1959, Tokyo: MOFA.
MOFA (1960) Waga gaikō no kinkyō June 1960, Tokyo: MOFA.
MOFA (1962) Waga gaikō no kinkyō June 1962, Tokyo: MOFA.
MOFA (1970) Waga gaikō no kinkyō FY1969, Tokyo: MOFA.
MOFA (1974) Waga gaikō no kinkyō FY1973, Tokyo: MOFA.
MOFA (1975) Waga gaikō no kinkyō FY1974, Tokyo: MOFA.
MOFA (1978) Waga gaikō no kinkyō FY1977 [The State of Our Diplomacy], Tokyo: MOFA.
MOFA (2004) Gaikō seisho 2004, Tokyo: MOFA.
MOFA (2006) Gaikō seisho 2006, Tokyo: MOFA.
MOFA (2007) Gaikō seisho 2007, Tokyo: MOFA.
MOFA (2008) Gaikō seisho 2008, Tokyo: MOFA.
MOFA (2009) Gaikō seisho 2009, Tokyo: MOFA.
MOFA (2010a) Gaikō seisho 2010, Tokyo: MOFA.
MOFA (2010b) Nippon gaikō monjo: Taiheiyō-sensō dai-ni satsu [Documents on Japanese Foreign Policy: The Pacific War, Second Volume], Tokyo: MOFA.
MOFA (2011) Gaikō seisho 2011 [The Diplomatic Blue Book], Tokyo: MOFA.
National Institute for Defence Studies (NIDS) (2009) Higashi-Ajia senryaku gaikan 2009 [East Asia Strategic Review], Tokyo: NIDS.
NIDS (2011) Chūgoku anzen-hoshō repōto 2011 [China Security Report], Tokyo: NIDS.
Nihon keizai shimbun (2013), 'Bōei-shō, shūdan-teki jiei-ken "kaigai-hahei ni tusnagarazu"' [Collective self-defence will not lead to troop deployment overseas, Defence Minister], 17 August; accessed at http://www.nikkei.com/article/DGXNASDE17001_X10C13A8NNE000/, 19 August 2013.
Nihon keizai shimbun (2014) 'Anpo kankyō "yori shinkoku ni"' [Security Environment Becomes Even More Severe], 5 August, p. 1.
Noda Y. (2011) 'Waga seiken kōsō' [My policy plan], Bungei shunjū [Literary Times], September, pp. 94–103.
Sadakata M. (2011) 'Higashi-Ajia chiiki-shugi no kanōsei to Nippon gaikō' [The Possibility of East Asian Regionalism and Japanese Diplomacy], Nagoya-daigaku hōsei ronshū [Nagoya University Law Papers] 239: 203–25.
Searle, J. (1995) The construction of social reality, London: Penguin.
Sekai (2009) '"Ajia no naka no Nippon" to shite anzen-hoshō seisaku wo kōchiku shinakereba naranai' [The need to establish defence policy for Japan in Asia], July, pp. 138–43.
Seki S. (1999) 'Introduction', in S. Seki (ed) Kindai Nippon gaikō shisō-shi nyūmon [Introduction to Diplomatic Thought in Modern Japan], Kyoto: Minerva, Introduction.

Schiff, J. (2008) '"Real"? As if! Critical reflections on state personhood', *Review of International Studies* 34(2): 363–77.
Takeuchi Y. (1979), 'Kindai no chōkoku' [Overcoming modernity] in T. Kawakami, et al. (eds) *Kindai no chōkoku*, Tokyo: Fuzan shobō, pp. 273–347.
Takeuchi Y. (1993) *Nihon to Ajia* [Japan and Asia], Tokyo: Chikuma gakugei bunko.
Tamaki K. (2013) 'Shoki ASEAN no seichō to Nippon: futatsu no tai-Nichi atsuryoku' ('Early Development of ASEAN and Japan: Two Pressures on Japan'), *Ajia-taiheiyō tōkyū (Asia-Pacific Research)* 20: 269–76.
Tanaka A. (1997) *Anzen hoshō: Sengo 50-nen no mosaku* [*National Security: 50 Years of Postwar Contemplation*], Tokyo: Yomiuri shimbun.
Tobe R. (1999) 'Ugaki Kazushige, "Ugaki Kazushige nikki"' [Ugaki Kazushige diaries], in S. Seki (ed) *Kindai Nippon gaikō shisō-shi nyūmon*, Kyoto: Minerva, chapter 15.
Wakamiya Y. (2006) *Wakai to nashonarizumu* [*Reconciliation and Nationalism*], Tokyo: Asahi shimbunsha.
The Washington Post (2013) 'Transcript of interview with Japanese prime minister Shinzo Abe', 20 February; accessed at http://www.washingtonpost.com/world/transript-of-interview-with-japanese-prime-minister-shinzo-be/2013/02/20/e7518d54-7b1c-11e2-82e8-61a46c2cde3d_story.html, 22 February 2013.
Wight, C. (2004) 'State agency: social action without human activity?' *Review of International Studies* 30(2): 269–80.
Yamamuro S. (2001) *Shisō-kadai to shite no Ajia: Kijuku, rensa, tōki* [*Asia as a Thought-Issue: Focal Point, Linkage, Project*], Tokyo: Iwanami shoten.
Yoon K. C. (1997) *Nippon kokumin-ron: kindai Nippon no aidentitī* [*Japanese Nation: Identity in Modern Japan*], Tokyo: Chikuma shobō.

Shimane Prefecture, Tokyo and the territorial dispute over Dokdo/Takeshima: regional and national identities in Japan

Alexander Bukh

Abstract This paper joins the debate on Japan's territorial dispute with South Korea over the Dokdo/Takeshima islets. Informed by the ontological security framework of analysis, this paper seeks to explain the decision to adopt the 'Takeshima Day' ordinance by the Shimane Prefectural Assembly and the subsequent ascendance of 'Takeshima' to the fore of Japan's identity construction vis-à-vis the Korean 'other'. In this paper, I distinguish between two processes: one that led to the adoption of the ordinance and another that resulted in the entrenchment of 'Takeshima' in Japan's identity construction vis-à-vis the Korean 'other'. The paper argues that the former process should be understood within the context of Shimane Prefecture's distinct identity construction vis-à-vis Tokyo, while the latter can be attributed to recent changes in Japan–Korea relations unrelated to the territorial dispute per se.

Introduction

Since the early 1950s, the Japanese Government has maintained the position that Korean occupation of the Takeshima islets (Korean name Dokdo)[1] is illegal, but well into the 2000s this territorial issue remained on the fringes of Japan's South Korea policy and related debates. In recent years though, the dispute has become one of the central issues in domestic debates regarding Japan's relations with its neighbor. Shimane Prefecture, which administered Takeshima between 1910 and 1945 and which, according to Japan's official position, continues to hold administrative rights to the islets, was the main agent behind this recent transformation: it was the passage of a 'Takeshima Day' ordinance by the Prefectural Assembly in 2005 that drew national attention to the territorial dispute (Nakajima 2007: 22).

The importance of the ordinance in igniting domestic debate is rather obvious. In 2005, prior to the Takeshima Day initiative, only 13% of the respondents in a *Yomiuri Shimbun* poll believed that Takeshima was an important issue in Japan's relations with South Korea. Only a year later, however, more than half of the respondents said that they were interested in the dispute (cited in Nakajima 2007: 1). In the most recent poll on the issue conducted by the Cabinet Office, over 90% of respondents said they knew about the Takeshima issue and over 70% stated that they were interested in it (Cabinet Office 2013b).

During the same period, there has been a sharp increase in the number of academic and quasi-academic publications devoted to the dispute. For example, one of Japan's major magazine articles' search engines, *Ōya Bunko*, gives only 82 hits for a keyword search of 'Takeshima' and 'problem' for the period between 1951 and 2004, and more than 500 hits for a similar search conducted only for the years 2005–2012. Furthermore, in 2008, for the first time Japan's Ministry of Foreign Affairs (MOFA) published a pamphlet devoted to the Takeshima issue. The 'Takeshima corner' on MOFA's website has become an instant hit with domestic internet users (Itō 2008: 2). From 2006, Japanese civic school textbooks introduced references to the Takeshima problem into their narratives and in 2008, the revised middle school teaching guidelines specified the Takeshima problem as a topic that needs to be taught to students (Itō 2008: 1).

If, following the post-structuralist branch of International Relations (IR) constructivism, we construe narratives on 'others' as the main building blocks in the discursive identity construction of the national 'self', we can plausibly conclude that today 'Takeshima' has emerged as one of the main symbols in Japan's identity construction vis-à-vis the South Korean 'other'. However, what accounts for the Takeshima Day initiative and the subsequent rise of 'Takeshima' to the fore of Japan's identity discourse on the Korean 'other'? In IR, post-structuralist constructivism focuses mostly on broad discursive formations of 'othering' (e.g. Tamaki 2010). Thus, it mainly explores how certain issues are interpreted through the existing identity discourse, rather than tracing the processes and the agents that facilitate the emergence of these issues as identity signifiers. This is not to say that the broader constructivist scholarship does not pay attention to the processes that lead to the emergence of a certain dominant identity. However, it tends to focus on national-level actors such as key politicians, Cabinet members, media and public intellectuals as agents in Japan's identity construction (e.g. Berger 1998; Bukh 2009; Catalinac 2007; Hagström, 2014; Suzuki 2005; Tamaki 2010). They rarely pay attention to such actors as prefectures or other sub-state actors in these processes.

Therefore, it is not surprising that the 'Takeshima Day' ordinance and the subsequent prominence of Takeshima in Japan's South Korea-related discourse have been dealt with mainly by scholars guided by more conventional theoretical frameworks. A structural realist take on the issue argues that the end of the cold war and the demise in the United States' ability to provide hegemonic stability in the region that followed the end of the bipolar confrontation have pushed Japan and Korea to take more assertive positions on the territorial dispute. In contrast, agent-level materialist accounts suggest that material resources associated with the islets (such as fisheries and gas) are the main factors behind this preoccupation with tiny islets that cannot sustain human habitation. Finally, an ideational account attributes the sudden interest in Takeshima to the recent rise in nationalism in Japan. These three conventional arguments are not mutually exclusive and have appeared in various combinations in the academic publications devoted to the dispute (e.g. Emmers 2010; Nakajima 2007; Schoenbaum 2008; Weinstein 2006). Thus, similar to the constructivist scholarship on Japan's identity, the extant academic literature on the Takeshima dispute does not pay much attention to the agency of Shimane Prefecture. Either explicitly or implicitly, it locates the passage of the 'Takeshima Day' ordinance within broad, national-level (e.g. Emmers 2010; Nakajima 2007) or international-level (e.g. Weinstein 2006) transformations.

This paper seeks to contribute not only to the literature on Japan's relations with Korea but also to the broader constructivist literature on Japan's identity formation. Drawing on a wide range of primary sources, it offers a more nuanced interpretation of Shimane Prefecture's activism and the sudden ascendance of 'Takeshima' to the fore of Japan's identity construction vis-à-vis the Korean 'other'. The argument developed in this paper is twofolded. First, this paper argues that 'Takeshima Day' ordinance was neither an expression of nationalism nor driven by material factors, but should be understood in the context of Shimane Prefecture's identity constructed vis-à-vis Tokyo. Second, the paper suggests that the subsequent entrenchment of 'Takeshima' in Japan's discourse on the Korean 'other' can be attributed to recent changes in Japan–Korea relations, unrelated to the territorial dispute per se.

Both of the abovementioned processes are analyzed through the prism of ontological security. In sociology, ontological security is seen as a fundamental prerequisite for individual's ability to exercise agency. In a nutshell, ontological security refers to stability and continuity in the individual's self-identity (Zarakol 2010: 6). Building on sociological work by Anthony Giddens and others, the IR ontological security approach extrapolates the argument to the state level. Thus, in IR, ontological security refers to states' need for a stable cognitive environment, which is achieved by developing a cognitive 'cocoon' (or cognitive apparatus) through which they interpret their everyday reality and regularize their social life (Mitzen 2006: 342–343). This cognitive stability is neither given nor static but continuously reproduced through states' actions and affirmed by others (Zarakol 2010: 6). Thus, ontological security is a social phenomenon. It is produced and reproduced through routinized relations with significant 'others' (Mitzen 2006: 345–346; Steele 2008: 6–8).

For the purposes of this paper, the suggestion that routinized relationships are manifestations of states' cognitive apparatus (in other words, their identity) that produce and reproduce its ontological security is important for two reasons. First, if we extrapolate the notion of cognitive security to other, non-state but nevertheless social entities, such as a prefecture, we can trace certain repetitive actions by the leaders of these entities to their collective identity. Namely, these repetitive actions can be seen as an integral part of their routinized relations with significant 'others' aimed at sustaining the stability of their collective self-identity. Second, unlike other IR theories of identity, the emphasis on routinized relationships as a central element in sustaining certain identity constructs offers important indications about possible sources of identity change. Namely, if ontological security is sustained through routinized relationships, then in order to understand certain transformations in collective identity discourses, we must explore possible disruptions in the routinized relationships that have sustained this identity. In other words, changes in identity discourses can be seen as adjustment measures aimed at restabilizing the cognitive environment through accommodation of changes in relationships.

The following section will explore the process of Shimane Prefecture's Takeshima-related identity formation and the routinized relations between Shimane and Tokyo that continuously reproduced this identity. This will be followed by analysis of the recent disruptions that occurred in Japan's routinized relations with the Korean 'other' and the role of 'Takeshima' in stabilizing these relations.

Takeshima, Tokyo and Shimane Prefecture

The early days

In the early post-war period, the positions and policies of the central government and Shimane Prefecture on Takeshima were almost identical. In the late 1940s and early 1950s, Tokyo insisted on inclusion of the islets within Japan's territory (Lee 2011: 62–63). At the same time, Shimane Prefecture was lobbying the central government and the occupation authorities to lift restrictions on access to Takeshima and adjacent waters. These petitions originated from a strong sense of urgency to secure fishing grounds for Shimane-based fishermen under limitations imposed by the 'MacArthur Line', and a sharp increase in population brought by the collapse of the Empire and the subsequent return of many Japanese from the former colonies (Oki Fishing Union 1951; Shimane Prefectural Assembly 1951). This sense of urgency was further exacerbated by Korea's unilateral imposition of the 'Rhee line' in 1952 and the subsequent detention of Japanese fishing vessels that crossed this line, and confiscation of their catches and boats. Most of the vessels were detained in waters far from Takeshima and only a small fraction of them belonged to Shimane Prefecture (Fukuhara 2012: 70–71; Shimane Prefecture 1967: 226–227). However, this further reduction in the fishing areas available to Japanese fishermen enhanced the sense of urgency related to finding new fishing grounds for Shimane fishermen and resulted in new petitions demanding the government to secure rights to Takeshima and 'rich fishing grounds' around it (Shimane Prefecture 1967: 231–232).

This persistence of Takeshima-related activism can be traced to the efforts of a local political heavyweight, Nakagawa Hidemasa. Nakagawa actively promoted the Takeshima cause, initiated petitions and continuously campaigned for a non-compromising position on the islets (Sugihara 2011). Nakagawa was a member of the ruling Liberal Democratic Party (LDP) and during two decades in prefectural politics, he served as the Chairman and Vice Chairman of the Prefectural Assembly (Shimane Prefectural Assembly 2004b). Nakagawa was elected from Oki Island, which, according to Shimane legislature administers Takeshima, owned the Oki Ferry that connected the island with the mainland and served as the chairman of the Oki Fishing Union (Sugihara 2011). Existing documents do not allow us to make a definitive statement on whether Nakagawa's activism was driven solely by demands from Oki fishermen and their desire to exploit the perceived riches of Takeshima waters. It is possible that such factors as Nakagawa's personal sense of righteousness, pursuit of material benefits or nationalism may also have played a certain role in his devotion to the Takeshima issue. Nevertheless, throughout his career Nakagawa played a central role in keeping the issue on the prefectural political agenda (Sugihara 2011).

Contrastingly, in the early 1960s, Tokyo's position on the islets experienced a drastic change, when the so-called 'Korean lobby' – a loose association of business executives and strongly anti-communist conservative politicians that formed around former Prime Minister Kishi Nobusuke – emerged as the key collective decision-maker in designing Japan's Korea policy (Roh 2008: 74–174). In the process of bilateral negotiations that culminated in the conclusion of the Treaty on Basic Relations and full normalization of relations in 1965, the ruling LDP and the government came to view the rights to Takeshima as secondary to the common struggle with communism and to the potential economic benefits of closer relations with South Korea (Roh 2008: 127–140). During the negotiations, the ruling elites even considered the possibility of a joint ownership of the islets (*Asahi Shimbun* 1963: 1).

In strong contrast, Shimane Prefecture's position on Takeshima remained unchanged and it actively opposed any possible compromise (Oki Association of Town and Village Assemblies 1963). It is in this context of diverging positions on the importance of the territorial dispute that Shimane's Takeshima-related identity, based on a sense of victimhood and abandonment by Tokyo, started to take shape. The emergence of this identity was further exacerbated by Tokyo's uncompromising position in the territorial dispute with the Soviet Union over the Northern Territories. Japan's normalization talks with the Soviet Union in the mid-1950s, which revolved around the territorial dispute, drew widespread attention and were extensively covered by the Japanese media. Therefore, it is not surprising that policy manifestations of Shimane Prefecture's Takeshima-related identity came to be influenced by the dynamics of the Northern Territories dispute. Both the sense of abandonment and the influence of the Northern Territories dispute can be witnessed in the 1963 proposal by a number of Prefectural Assembly members to establish an Alliance for Securing the Territorial Rights to Takeshima. The main purpose of the Alliance was to create a prefecture-level movement against the central government's Takeshima-related compromise in its negotiations with Seoul (Shimane Prefectural Assembly 1965). Judging by the name, the proposed structure and activities envisioned in the proposal, it was strongly influenced by the Alliance for Achieving the Return of the Northern Territories, established on Hokkaido in the same year under the leadership of Hokkaido Governor Machimura Kingo, another prominent member of the LDP. Similar to Hokkaido, the Shimane Alliance was to be headed by the governor of Shimane Prefecture and had an executive body comprised high-level prefectural politicians. Its purpose was also identical to the Hokkaido Alliance. According to the proposal, the Shimane organization was to act as an advocacy agent aimed at mobilizing prefectural residents and the broader public in Japan and at exercising direct and indirect pressure on the government 'not to abandon' territorial rights to Takeshima (Shimane Prefectural Assembly 1965). The exact reasons for the eventual failure to establish the Shimane Alliance are unclear, but it is highly plausible that pressure from LDP headquarters played a role: it was interested in consolidating the 'Northern Territories' related grassroots organization under the 'four islands' banner but wanted to keep the Takeshima issue away from public attention (e.g. Nanpō dōhō engokai 1965).

Consolidation of Shimane's identity

The 1965 normalization of Japan's relations with the Republic of Korea created a turning point in Shimane's relations with Tokyo, firmly entrenching the antagonism over Takeshima between the two governments and consolidating Shimane's distinct prefectural identity.

Based on the interviews and memoirs of both Japanese and Korean politicians and bureaucrats involved in the bilateral negotiations that led to the conclusion of the 1965 Treaty, Roh (2008: 175–234; see also Nakasone 2012: 160–162) argues that the sides reached a secret agreement related to Takeshima. This agreement has shaped both governments' actions related to the dispute over the following decades. According to this agreement, the dispute was to be shelved and both governments would continue to hold their respective interpretations regarding ownership of the islets, but would maintain the status quo and avoid escalation of the dispute.

The 1965 Treaty was accompanied by a bilateral fisheries agreement that was designed to offer a solution to practical issues that stemmed from competing claims over the islets. The agreement established a Joint Regulation Zone and led to the abolishment of the restrictions on Japanese fishermen imposed by the Rhee line. The Zone also included waters around Takeshima and enabled fishermen from both countries to engage in fishing activities there (Roh 2008: 10–11).

From the perspective of Japan–Korea relations, this was probably an ideal solution to a dispute that both sides did not perceive as important to their respective national interests, but over which neither could afford to yield to the other's demands for domestic political reasons. On the other hand, Tokyo's prioritization of economic and political cooperation with South Korea over demanding the return of Takeshima further facilitated the embedding of 'Takeshima' as a symbol of Shimane's victimhood in its prefectural identity. Well into the 1970s, the prefecture's actions were limited to submitting petitions that demanded the establishment of territorial rights over Takeshima and safe fishing in surrounding waters (Shimane Prefecture 1979a). Despite the relatively low profile of these actions, Shimane's confrontational relations with Tokyo over Takeshima gradually turned into a routine, according to which the former demanded governmental attention to the territorial issue while the latter ignored these demands. Since Nakagawa Hidemasa retired from politics in the mid-1970s (Sugihara 2011), Takeshima activism has not been driven by any particular individual. Furthermore, Shimane's fisheries-related grievances to a great extent were addressed by the establishment of the Joint Regulation Zone. However, Takeshima-related activism which initially was an expression of material interests turned into a social routine that reproduced Shimane's identity as a victim of Tokyo's policies and enhanced its ontological security.

In 1977, following the USA and the Soviet declarations of 200-mile exclusive fishery zones, Japan and Korea declared 12-mile territorial waters and 200-mile exclusive fishery zones. In this context, the question of territorial rights to Takeshima surfaced again in the domestic debates in both counties and resulted in a number of exchanges of rival claims and denouncements. Tokyo was eager to subdue the tensions and promptly announced the exclusion of Korea and China from the application of the 200-mile rule. In April 1978, however, Korea proclaimed a 12-mile territorial waters zone around the islets. In 1978 and 1979, Japan and Korea negotiated access of Japanese fishing vessels to the 12-mile area. It is unclear whether any kind of agreement was reached but the dispute disappeared from the bilateral agenda (Kajimura 1997: 471–473).

In contrast, Shimane Prefectural authorities escalated their Takeshima campaign. In 1977, they established a special committee with the purpose of developing prefectural policy related to the 200-mile exclusive economic zone (EEZ) (Shimane Prefecture 1979a) and even planned to send a ship to inspect Takeshima. This plan was eventually cancelled under the pressure from Tokyo (Ishida 2001). Nevertheless, prefectural authorities further expanded their activities. In April 1979, Shimane established a Prefectural Council for Facilitating the Solution of the Takeshima Problem. Similar to the Alliance envisioned in the 1963 proposal, its purpose was to coordinate the Takeshima-related activities of the various prefectural bodies such as the prefectural government, municipal authorities and fishing unions, and to engage in petitioning and educational activities (Shimane Prefecture 1983).

The establishment of the Council can be seen as the starting point of the prefecture's expansion of symbolic, often educational, activities aimed at manifesting its victimhood vis-à-vis Tokyo's inaction. These activities included publication and distribution of pamphlets that argued Japan's rights to the islets, and construction of road signs that called for the return of Takeshima. They were directed mainly at prefectural residents with the purpose of 'raising residents' awareness and deepening their understanding' of the Takeshima problem (Shimane Prefecture 1983).

What accounts for this escalation in prefectural activities and the shift towards educational activities directed at prefectural residents as manifestations of its prefectural identity? There is no doubt that the heightened tensions around the EEZ and territorial waters facilitated prefectural engagement. Thus, it may seem that prefectural activism was stimulated by material losses endured by its fishing industry that resulted from Korean exclusion of Japanese fishermen from the 12-mile zone around Takeshima. In June 1978, Shimane Prefecture published a report that supports this conclusion. The report estimated the prefectural losses from the Korean application of territorial sea rule to waters around Takeshima at 320 million yen (cited in Fukuhara 2012: 48).

Closer scrutiny, however, suggests that these material losses were more of a tool in the prefecture's demonstration of the injustice brought about by Tokyo's negligence, rather than its chief motivation. For example, certain anecdotal evidence suggests that the exclusion policy was not enforced by the Korean authorities (Fukuhara 2012: 72; Kajimura 1997: 472). More importantly, official statistical data on fish and squid catches in Shimane Prefecture in the late 1970s and early 1980s show that even if Shimane's fishermen may have been excluded from waters around Takeshima, the impact of these measures on Shimane's fishing industry was rather negligible (Chūgoku Regional Agricultural Administration Office 1984: 18).

Thus, it can be plausibly argued that Shimane's activism was more of a response to Tokyo's accommodating policies and the perceived abandonment of the Takeshima issue rather than driven by material losses sustained as a result of Korean actions. Furthermore, Tokyo's Northern Territories policy during the same period also played an important role in stimulating this escalation in Shimane activism. The Northern Territories campaign started in the late 1960s, but in the late 1970s the LDP-led central government embarked on an extensive domestic campaign aimed at consolidating public opinion around the 'Northern Territories' issue. The need to educate the public about the 'Northern Territories' was the main rationale for this campaign (Bukh 2012). In 1978, for the first time MOFA published its 'Our Northern Territories' booklet, which provided detailed explanations of the illegality of the Soviet occupation and Japan's inherent rights to the four islands. During the same period, the government had also built a number of 'Northern Territories' related facilities, including the 100 million yen observatory-cum-museum on Hokkaido's Nosappu Cape, and in 1981, the Diet enacted a national Northern Territories Day.

Contrastingly, Tokyo's policy on Takeshima continued to adhere to the principles of the abovementioned secret pact. This could be witnessed not only in the generally compromising stance it took during the frictions in the late 1970s but also in its continuous desire to keep the Takeshima issue away from the domestic discourse. The history of Shimane Prefecture's Northern Territories related 'citizens assembly' is rather illustrative of this policy. Starting from the early 1970s onwards, each of Japan's prefectures was encouraged to establish a 'Citizens Assembly to Demand the Return of the Northern Territories'. Shimane Prefecture refused to establish an organization devoted solely to the return of the Northern Territories and demanded a permission to include Takeshima in the name and scope of activities as a pre-condition for establishing its own prefectural 'citizens assembly'. Well into the 1980s, however, the government refused and the permission to establish such an organization was granted by the Internal Affairs Agency only in 1987 (Nagai 2012: 5).

Arguably, it was this discrepancy in Tokyo's policy on territorial disputes that further deepened the sense of victimhood and abandonment among the prefectural elites. At the same time, Tokyo's Northern Territories campaign also provided an important point of reference for the ways Shimane Prefecture could manifest its identity and enhance its ontological security. The correlation between the two campaigns can be observed in the resemblance of the names and missions of the bodies in charge of the educational campaigns, in the published materials and in other symbolic measures, such as the erection of road signs and monuments. This resemblance is particularly noticeable in the Takeshima and Northern Territories pamphlets published, respectively, by Shimane Prefecture and MOFA. The two publications are almost identical in form and content. Both texts state that the territory in question is Japan's 'inherent territory'; both provide a brief outline of Japan's legal and historical rights; both describe the economic activities conducted by Japanese prior to the seizure of the territory; and both outline the estimated richness of the islands' marine resources (MOFA 2008; Shimane Prefecture 1979b). As such, it can be argued that Shimane's educational campaign in the late 1970s and 1980s was not only provoked but also inspired by Tokyo's Northern Territories-related campaign. While the latter was an integral part of Tokyo's attempt to consolidate the public opinion against the USSR, Shimane's campaign was another manifestation of its prefectural identity that further secured its self-perception as a victim of Tokyo's negligence.

The 'Takeshima Day' ordinance

In the mid-1980s, the social routines that sustained Shimane Prefecture's sense of victimhood and abandonment retreated to its previous pattern of annual resolutions and petitions issued by Shimane and ignored by Tokyo. The territorial dispute flared up again in the mid-1990s when both Japan and Korea ratified the United Nations Convention on the Law of the Seas (UNCLOS), and this flare-up culminated in the 2005 Takeshima Day ordinance, which brought the territorial dispute to the center of public attention.

One of the most widespread interpretations of the roots of the 'Takeshima Day' ordinance, one which dominates the Japanese publications devoted to the issue, explains this action through a materialist lens. It argues that it was dissatisfaction with the new fishing agreement of 1998, adopted as part of the bilateral attempts to maintain the status quo on Takeshima, that prompted the Shimane Prefecture to enact the ordinance (e.g. Hosaka and Tōgō 2012: 109).

Similar to 1978, however, the actual impact of the new fishing agreement on Shimane's fishing industry is rather questionable. The rules that regulate fishing activities in the new Provisional Zone that replaced the Joint Regulation Zone remained largely unchanged. The main difference between the two agreements is in the scope of the area where both Korean and Japanese fishermen can engage freely in fishing activities and where jurisdiction is determined by the state flag principle. Unlike its predecessor, the area covered by the newly enacted Provisional Zone cuts quite deeply into Japan's EEZ and includes the Yamato Bank, an important area for the crab fishing industry in west Japan (Takaya 1998).

The extent and nature of the actual impact of the new fishing agreement on the fisheries in west Japan is a rather complicated question. Officials from Shimane Prefecture's Fishery Division suggest that it has brought both benefits and harm to the prefecture's fishermen (Interviews 1 and 2).

Importantly, however, the negative impact has been felt mostly in the crab industry. The latter occupies quite an important place in the neighboring Tottori Prefecture's fishing industry (Tottori Prefecture 2008) but is relatively insignificant for Shimane, where the number of fishermen engaged in crab catching is very limited (Interviews 1 and 2) and the number of crab catching vessels is less than a dozen (Shimane Prefecture 2011). The negligibility of the material factor in the 'Takeshima Day' ordinance is further underscored by the fact that in the early 2000s, the prefecture perceived problems related to the new fishing agreement and the territorial dispute as separate issues, and addressed them in separate petitions submitted to different governmental agencies (Shimane Prefecture 2002: 1, 44). It was only from 2006 onwards, after the passage of the 'Takeshima Day' ordinance, that Shimane started to include references to the new fishing agreement in its Takeshima-related campaign, and the two issues came to be presented as interrelated in the prefecture's petitions and other activities (e.g. Shimane Prefecture 2006). Thus, it can be plausibly argued that similar to the late 1970s, material losses associated with the new fishing agreement were more of a tool in Shimane's campaign rather than its cause.

To a large extent, the 'Takeshima Day' ordinance was an integral part of Shimane Prefecture's routinized relations with Tokyo aimed at securing its prefectural identity constructed around the Takeshima dispute. Similar to the late 1970s, however, certain important developments in the 1990s and early 2000s brought about this escalation from low-profile annual petitions to a 'Takeshima Day' enactment in Shimane's manifestations of its identity. All of these developments were directly or indirectly related to the Northern Territories dispute.

One of these developments was the conflict over the nature of Japan's fisheries relations with South Korea between Shimane and Hokkaido prefectures.

In the early 1980s, rapid developments in the Korean fishing industry and the expulsion of Korean vessels from the Soviet EEZ resulted in a rapid increase in Korean fishing activities in waters near Hokkaido. In response, Hokkaido fishing unions issued calls to the central government to abolish the Exclusive Fishing Area exemption for Korean fishermen adopted in 1977 and implement the 200-mile exclusive zone vis-à-vis Korea. Fishermen based in western Japan, including those in Shimane, opposed this measure, as they would suffer most from exclusion from Korean waters if the reciprocal exemption were abolished. The simultaneous negotiations between Japan and Korea and among the Japanese fishing unions over the desired amendments to the fishing agreement continued without much progress until 1996, with western Japan fishermen eventually agreeing to the need for a 200-mile EEZ (Kataoka and Nishida 2007).

Arguably, however, this conflict between western Japan and Hokkaido fishermen heightened Shimane's elites' dissatisfaction with the preferential treatment given to Hokkaido in the context of the 'Northern Territories' dispute and enhanced their sense of victimhood and injustice.

Another important development was the escalation in the Korean Government's activities related to the disputed islets. Thus, in 2002, stimulated by Korean Government plans to establish a national park on the disputed islets, the 'League of Shimane Prefectural Assembly Members for Establishing Territorial Rights over Takeshima' was formed. This League reignited the Citizens Assembly for the return of the Northern Territories and Takeshima established in 1987 (Nagai 2012: 6). Importantly, however, the actions of Korean Government were interpreted through the cognitive lens of victimhood vis-à-vis Tokyo and received as another confirmation of Tokyo's duplicity in its Northern Territories and Takeshima-related policies. Thus, at a 'people's rally' devoted to both Takeshima and Northern Territories, organized by the League in November 2003, local politicians expressed their dissatisfaction with the government's negligence of the Takeshima issue. This dissatisfaction was voiced by one of the local LDP heavyweights, Jōdai Yoshiro, who later became one of the initiators of the Takeshima Day ordinance. At the Prefectural Assembly meeting that took place one day after the rally, he stated: 'Similarly to the Northern Territories Day, it is desirable to have a national Takeshima Day, as a tool in enhancing the national movement [for the return of Takeshima]' (cited in Nagai 2012: 6).

Less than a year later, the Korean Government took another symbolic action and announced the issuance of a memorial stamp devoted to the islets. This symbolic action served as an immediate trigger for a reaction from Shimane. Again, however, the actions of Korean Government were interpreted through the identity lens of Shimane's victimhood vis-à-vis Tokyo. Thus, in March 2004, the Prefectural Assembly adopted a Takeshima-related memorandum that made policy demands to the central government (Shimane Prefectural Assembly 2004a). Later, this memorandum became the basis for the Takeshima Day ordinance. Importantly, the main point of reference for this manifestation of prefectural identity was again the Northern Territories dispute, or, to be more precise, Tokyo's domestic policies related to that dispute. The centrality of Tokyo's Northern Territories related policies for the Assembly's demands is easily detectable in the text of the memorandum. Along with references to the Korean actions and demands from the government to submit the issue to the International Court of Justice, the memorandum demanded the establishment of an official organization under the Cabinet Office similar to the Northern Territories Measures Headquarters, the enactment of a national Takeshima Day, inclusion of the Takeshima issue in history textbooks and enactment of government measures to create a 'national movement' (Shimane Prefectural Assembly 2004a).

In the summer of 2004, Shimane Prefectural Assembly members and Governor Sumita Nobuyoshi actively lobbied key members of the LDP to implement the demands voiced in this memorandum. LDP bosses, however, including future PM Abe Shinzō and the heavyweight Aoki Mikio, who was elected from Shimane and once headed one of the local fishing unions, turned down their demands, suggesting that the initiative should come from other Diet members from the Shimane constituency (Yokota 2005). At that time, the LDP likely did not see any reason to breach the 'secret pact' as it did not want to further aggravate Japan's relations with Korea, which were already tense because of PM Koizumi's visits to the Yasukuni Shrine. For prefectural leaders, however, this dismissive attitude underscored the confrontational relationship between Tokyo and Shimane and arguably further enhanced the salience of Takeshima in Shimane Prefectural identity. Tokyo's refusal to enact a national Takeshima Day thus became the immediate reason for the decision to enact the prefectural 'Takeshima Day' ordinance (Sumita and Izawa 2005). In other words, the ordinance was a symbolic measure that further enhanced Shimane's ontological security based on the sense of victimhood and abandonment vis-à-vis Tokyo.

The ordinance was adopted in March 2005 and designated February 22, the day Takeshima was officially incorporated into Shimane Prefecture in 1905, as Takeshima Day. Neither the prefectural lawmakers who initiated the ordinance, nor probably the LDP elders who opposed it fully anticipated the extent of domestic attention and Korean reaction to the ordinance. Importantly, however, neither nationalism nor material interests played a particularly significant role in the 'Takeshima Day' ordinance. It was instead an integral part of Shimane Prefecture's routinized manifestations of its prefectural identity, constructed vis-à-vis Tokyo and, at the same time, informed and shaped by Tokyo's Northern Territories policy.

Japan's ontological security, the Korean 'other' and 'Takeshima'

Japan's identity and the Korean 'other'

The previous section argued that the 'Takeshima Day' ordinance was a manifestation of Shimane's identity, aimed at enhancing Shimane's ontological security related to this identity. The ordinance was initiated by a group of Shimane Prefectural lawmakers, mostly from the LDP, and enacted despite strongly negative attitudes from key party members and MOFA. Furthermore, it went against the existing government/LDP policy of maintaining the low posture in the Takeshima dispute stipulated by the 1965 'secret pact'. While Koizumi's administration ignored the first Takeshima Day and was keen on preventing the ordinance from causing further damage to bilateral relations (Nagai 2012: 8), South Korea's fierce reaction and wide media coverage brought Takeshima to the center of public attention. Over the following years, the Takeshima issue turned into a valuable political asset, which came to be exploited by politicians from across the political spectrum.

What accounts for this sharp increase in the symbolic value of Takeshima and its firm entrenchment in Japan's public discourse? It is beyond doubt that the rise in tensions with China over the Senkaku/Diaoyu islands played an important role in stimulating public interest in the territorial dispute with Korea. Furthermore, similar to the dispute over the Senkaku/Diaoyu islands (Koo 2009), Japan's political elites, in this case, both from the LDP and the Democratic Party of Japan (DPJ), who suffered from legitimacy deficit, exploited Takeshima to enhance their credentials. These two factors, however, do not account fully for the entrenchment of 'Takeshima' in the domestic discourse, for a number of reasons. First, public interest in Takeshima has surpassed the dispute over the Northern Territories (Cabinet Office 2013a, 2013b). Furthermore, the centrality of Takeshima in the domestic discourse remained intact under the Abe administration. So far, PM Abe has taken a relatively low-profile stance on the territorial dispute with South Korea and the opposition has not attempted to contest this policy. Thus, neither the tensions over the Senkakus/Diaoyu nor the political exploitations of 'Takeshima' can fully explain its continuous salience in the domestic discourse. Arguably, the symbolic importance of 'Takeshima' can be traced to the discursive role it assumed in Japan's identity construction vis-à-vis the South Korean 'other'.

This discursive role of 'Takeshima' is related to the recent transformations that occurred in Japan's relations with South Korea and their impact on Japan's identity. In order to fully understand the importance of these transformations, we need to review the role of Korea in modern Japan's identity. The discursive construction of Japan's identity vis-à-vis Asia in general and the Korean 'other' in particular has been thoroughly examined in a number of excellent works (e.g. Atkins 2010; Koyasu 2003; Tamaki 2010; Tanaka 1995; Tei 1995). Due to limited space, I will refrain from repeating the whole range of arguments made by these scholars. Instead, the remaining part of this section will summarize their most pertinent conclusions and review them from the perspective of ontological security.

Modern Japan's identity construction vis-à-vis Korea evolved around two somewhat contradictory discourses of Pan-Asianism and a Japanese version of Orientalism. The former was based on the notion of a certain horizontal affinity between Japan and the rest of Asia based on racial sameness (Saaler and Koschmann 2007). In the context of Japan's relations with Korea, this notion of sameness manifested itself in the *naisenittai* (Japan and Korea as one body) paradigm. Contrastingly, Japanese Orientalism construed Japan as spatially located in Asia but temporally superior to its Asian neighbors and coeval with the West (Tanaka 1995). In this sense, Korea's position as a 'primitive self' (Atkins 2010) in Imperial Japan's identity corresponded to the broader role of the Orient in this construct. Japan's colonization of Korea and the wide range of colonial policies aimed at subjugating and 'civilizing' the Korean people, but also providing them with a certain measure of equality within the Empire, can be seen as products of this dual identity. For example, the assimilation policies pursued by the colonial authorities can be seen as embodying both the sense of Japanese superiority vis-à-vis the 'peripheral' Korea and the belief that cultural and racial sameness of the two people will enable their merge into one nation (e.g. Caprio 2009). A similar argument can be made about the economic relations during the colonial period. These were not driven purely by the pursuit of profit for Japan and its economic development, but included subsides and protection of Korean industries (e.g. Cummings 1997: 162–174; Kimura 1995). From the perspective of ontological security, these routinized relations reinforced Japan's identity constructed vis-à-vis the Korean 'other' and enhanced its contradictory self-identity as the guide and teacher but also as culturally and racially equal member of the *naisen* (Japan and Korea) body politic.

Japan's defeat in the Asia-Pacific War and the subsequent domestic and international transformations resulted in an almost complete disappearance of the horizontal thread from Japan's identity construction (Oguma 2007). Among the conservative elites, it was to a certain extent replaced with a cold war affinity based on the common struggle against communism (Roh 2008: 42–43). This horizontal identity thread, however, was quite thin as the authoritarian nature of the Korean regime precluded the emergence of a deeper political identification with Japan's former colony (e.g Ōhira 1964).

Conversely, the hierarchical identity thread was only slightly modified. Thus, in the post-war years, democratic, industrialized, prosperous and 'westernized' Japan was constructed in opposition to unruly, authoritarian, impoverished and 'Asian' Korea, in need of Japan's guidance and assistance (for a detailed analysis, see Tamaki 2010; Tei 1995). In the 1950s and 1960s, the state-level relations between Japan and South Korea remained tense, with Takeshima one of the central issues of contention. The hierarchical thread of Japan's identity maintained its salience and provided the sole cognitive framework for interpreting Japan's relations with its former colony. As an example, the unilateral declaration of the Rhee Line in 1952, which effectively placed Takeshima within Korean waters, simply confirmed to Japanese leaders the unruly nature of Korea (Tamaki 2010: 115).

Normalization of Japan–Korea relations became possible only after the 1961 military coup in South Korea. Unlike his predecessor, the leader of the coup, Park Chung Hee, viewed Japan's economic assistance as vital for Korean development and embarked on developing closer ties with Japan soon after seizing power. Most importantly, Park's behavior also reconfirmed the hierarchical identity construct and contributed to Japan's ontological security: this time, however, it was not the 'unruly Korea' that the Japanese leaders saw but one in need of guidance and assistance. Thus, Park's admission of the superiority of Japanese civilization and humility, when conversing with Japanese politicians in the aftermath of the 1961 *coup d'etat*, made the latter both welcome him as a person that speaks their language and identify him with Japanese Meiji era reformers (Huh 2013). In other words, in the eyes of LDP bosses, Park's behavior reconfirmed Korea's position as a 'primitive self': not dissimilar to a Japan of the past but not equal to a Japan of the present.

In the decades that followed the normalization of bilateral relations, economic relations between the two countries and in particular Korean dependency on Japanese capital and technology have played an important role in sustaining Japan's ontological security (Tamaki 2010: 162–163). A persistent trade imbalance between the two countries and the continuous efforts of Korea to catch up with Japan (James 2001) reminded Japanese leaders of Japan's own earlier relations with the West and its own modernization process (e.g. Nakasone 1983). This further enhanced Japan's ontological security, resting as it did on the notion of Japan's superiority to Korea.

Japan's relations with Korea in 2000s and 'Takeshima'

As the structure of economic relations between the two countries did not experience any drastic changes, Japan's superiority to Korea and the related ontological security vis-à-vis its former colony was maintained and continuously reaffirmed until the mid-2000s. Besides economy and trade, the stability of Japan's identity was also maintained and reaffirmed in other areas of bilateral relations. For example, anti-Japanese protests in Korea related to issues such as the 'comfort women' and visits by Japanese politicians to the Yasukuni shrine reaffirmed Korean emotionality and unruliness to the Japanese (e.g. Yamano 2005). The popularity of the Korean cultural wave that swept Japan in the early 2000s did not undermine Japan's ontological security but actually reinforced it. Namely, the reception of Korean television dramas in Japan was mediated through the sense of nostalgia for Japan's past, which the audience readily discovered in these cultural products (Iwabuchi 2002: 159). Thus, the Korean wave was interpreted through the extant ontological apparatus and was received as another routine in Japan's relations with Korea, reaffirming the latter's temporal position behind Japan.

Recently, however, bilateral relations have experienced some fundamental transformations, most importantly in the economic realm, which replicated the change that occurred in fisheries relations in the 1980s but on a much larger scale. South Koreans have become wealthier and closer to Japan in terms of per capita gross domestic product (GDP). In 2012, the IMF predicted that by 2017, South Korea will even become richer than Japan in terms of GDP per person at purchasing power parity (*The Economist* 2012). Most importantly, however, the dominance of global markets by key Japanese companies in certain important industries has been threatened or in some cases even undermined by Korean companies. For example, in 2009, the Korean Posco overtook Japan's Nippon Steel to become the world's third largest steel producer. In electronics, Samsung and LG have overtaken the Japanese giant Sony. Korean car-makers who until the 1990s were dependent on Japanese engines have recently been 'gobbling up' global market share at the expense of Japanese car industry (Prestowitz 2012). Even in terms of pop cultural exports, Korean products have come to rival those of Japan and in many countries, particularly in Asia, gained dominance in local markets (e.g. *The Economist* 2010).

Combined with Korea's vibrant democracy and proactive diplomacy, these dramatic changes in Japan–Korea economic relations, and their relative positions in the global economy, disrupted the century-long routine in Japan–Korea relations, and could not be accommodated in the existent cognitive framework. They have destabilized the hierarchical identity construct and have come to pose a direct threat to Japan's ontological security.

In this context of Japan's growing ontological insecurity vis-à-vis Korea, the emergence of 'Takeshima' in the domestic discourse has had a stabilizing effect on Japan's identity. The narrative on Takeshima has shifted the focus away from the significant changes that took place in bilateral relations and recreated a somewhat modified but nevertheless hierarchical construction of the Japanese 'self' vis-à-vis the Korean 'other', overriding the abovementioned disruptions. Korean emotionality and lack of respect for international law were reemphasized through the narratives of Koreans' reaction to the dispute and the history of Korea's occupation of the islets (e.g. Shimojō 2004; Yamamoto 2007: 73–108). The narrative on Korean nationalistic education in relation to Dokdo (e.g. *Yomiuri Shimbun* 2010) and the overwhelming presence of 'Dokdo' in Korean society (e.g. Wakita 2013: 101) also became important instances in the reconstruction of hierarchical difference through which 'non-nationalistic' Japanese national identity is constructed as superior. Travelogues of Japanese visitors to Korean Dokdo/Takeshima-related sites remind the domestic audience that Korea is a coarse, uncivilized nation engaged in collective lying (e.g. Furuya 2012).

Moreover, the linkage between the territorial dispute and fisheries issues between Japan and Korea has enabled further deepening of the hierarchical construct. The emphasis on damage to its fishing industry and to marine resources in the context of the territorial dispute, as well as the argument that they stem from differences in fishing practices, has been the central element of Shimane Prefecture's campaign and has been widely debated in the national press. Here, illegal and excessive Korean fishing, and fishing practices that lack consideration for the environment are narrated in opposition to law-abiding Japanese fishing practices and environmentally friendly fishing regulations (e.g. *Asahi Shimbun* 2009; *Yomiuri Shimbun* 2006). In other words, the rapid growth of the Korean fishing industry, which can be seen as an integral part of its overall economic development, has been turned into a narrative that actually reaffirms Japan's superiority and stabilizes its ontological security.

Importantly, the collapse of the Tokyo/Shimane divide and the entrenchment of Takeshima in Japan's national identity following the Takeshima Day ordinance have transformed Shimane Prefecture into an important agent of national ontological security. While the prefecture continues to demand wide-ranging policy changes from Tokyo, its Takeshima-related events are attended by MPs from most parties, including the LDP, and there is little difference in central and prefectural governments' narratives of the dispute. Thus, routinized manifestations of prefectural identity were incorporated and transformed into manifestations of national identity that continuously reaffirm Japan's hierarchical position vis-à-vis its former colony, and contribute to its ontological security.

Conclusions

This article has argued that 'Takeshima' has emerged as an important signifier in Shimane Prefecture's regional identity, in the context of Tokyo's reluctance to engage the territorial dispute with South Korea and simultaneous extensive domestic campaigning related to the Northern Territories dispute. In the four decades that passed since the conclusion of the 1965 Treaty, this identity in which Shimane was constructed as the victim of Tokyo's negligence was routinized in Shimane's antagonistic relations with Tokyo over Takeshima. Tokyo's Northern Territories policies during the same period both stimulated and shaped Shimane's actions aimed at securing this identity. Actions by the Korean Government and tensions in bilateral relations served as immediate triggers for escalation in Shimane's Takeshima-related activism. However, Seoul's policies were interpreted through the identity lens of Shimane's victimhood vis-à-vis Tokyo and led to actions aimed at sustaining the ontological security associated with this identity. The 'Takeshima Day' ordinance was one such manifestation. It was not driven by either nationalism or material interests as often argued, but it constituted an integral part of Shimane's routinized relations with Tokyo that reproduced Shimane's identity constructed vis-à-vis the center.

Furthermore, this paper has argued that the entrenchment of the Takeshima issue in Japan's domestic discourse should be treated separately from the passage of the 'Takeshima Day' ordinance. The symbolic importance of 'Takeshima' in Japan's discourse on the Korean 'other' can be traced to recent changes in bilateral relations. Namely, the entrenchment of Takeshima stemmed from the disruption to a more than century-old routine of Japan's relations with Korea characterized by the economic, political and cultural dominance of the former. This routine was informed by the cognitive apparatus that served as the basis for Japan's identity construction vis-à-vis the Korean 'other' and at the same time continuously reproduced and reinforced it. The fundamental economic changes that took place in bilateral relations, combined with political and social changes in South Korea, have undermined this cognitive apparatus and threatened Japan's ontological security. 'Takeshima', it was argued, came to perform a stabilizing role in Japan's identity construction, confirming its superiority to Korea and through this contributing to Japan's ontological security.

The process of national identity formation outlined in this paper carries important ramifications for the study of national identity in IR. Scholarship on national identity usually focuses on national-level elites (e.g. government officials, politicians, prominent scholars and journalists) as agents that craft national identities through their writings and actions (e.g. Bukh 2009; Hopf 2002; Neumann 1999; Tamaki 2010). Furthermore, the ideas espoused by these agents are often presented as being an integral part of, or identical to, the final product, namely, the discursively constructed national identity. This paper offers a fundamentally different depiction of a process of national identity construction. Focusing on 'Takeshima' as a signifier in Japan's identity construction vis-à-vis the South Korean 'other', it argued that the process of its rise to prominence in the identity discourse can be seen as an upward diffusion of a prefectural identity into a national one, which occurred despite strong opposition from political leaders and a complete lack of attention from other important agents of national identity construction. Furthermore, it suggested that while the former has transformed into the latter, the two should not be treated as identical. While references to the illegality of Korean occupation of the islets did feature in the prefectural narratives, the prefectural identity was constructed in opposition to Tokyo and the latter's inaction and duplicity. It was only after the disappearance of the Shimane/Tokyo divide that Shimane became an agent of Japan's national identity, stabilizing and reproducing the construct through narratives on Takeshima and the Korean 'other'.

Acknowledgements

I am most grateful to Dr Linus Hagström for his insightful comments on the earlier drafts of this article and for all the time and effort he devoted to this special issue project. I also thank my VUW colleagues, Prof. Oguma Eiji, Prof. Iwashita Akihiro, Dr Taku Tamaki and the anonymous reviewer for their comments on the early draft of this article.

Funding

Research conducted for this article was partially funded by Academy of Korean Studies [grant number AKS-2011-R 56].

Note

1. The name of the islets constitutes an integral part of the dispute. Since this paper is devoted to analyzing the Japanese side of the dispute, the Japanese name will be used throughout the text. This is done, however, solely for purposes of convenience and should not be interpreted as an expression of support for Japan's claims.

References

Asahi Shimbun. (1963) Takeshima, Nikkan Kyōyū An Mo Aru' [Takeshima: there is also a proposal for joint ownership], morning edition, 10 January, p. 1.
Asahi Shimbun. (2009) 'Ken Dokuji no Fuku Kyōzai o Haifu' [Prefecture distributes its own supplimentary teaching material], *Asahi Shimbun*, morning edition, 22 May, p. 4.
Atkins, E. T. (2010) *Primitive Selves: Koreana in the Japanese Colonial Gaze, 1910–1945*, Berkley, CA: University of California Press.
Berger, T. (1998) *Cultures of Antimilitarism: National Security in Germany and Japan*, Baltimore, MD: Johns Hopkins University Press.
Bukh, A. (2009) *Japan's Identity and Foreign Policy: Russia as Japan's 'Other'*, London: Routledge.
Bukh, A. (2012) 'Constructing Japan's "Northern Territories": domestic actors, interests, and the symbolism of the disputed islands', *International Relations of the Asia-Pacific* 12(3): 483–509.
Cabinet Office. (2013a) *Hoppōryōdo Mondai ni Kan Suru Tokubetsu Seron Chōsa [Special public opinion poll on the Northern Territories problem]*, Tokyo: Cabinet Office, accessed at http://www8.cao.go.jp/survey/tokubetu/h25/h25-hoppou.pdf, 7 July 2014.
Cabinet Office. (2013b) *Takeshima ni Kan Suru Tokubetsu Seron Chōsa [Special public opinion poll on Takeshima]*, accessed at www8.cao.go.jp/survey/tokubetu/h25/h25-takeshima.pdf, 29 September 2013.
Caprio, M. (2009) *Japanese Assimilation Policies in Colonial Korea, 1910–1945*, Seattle, WA: University of Washington Press.
Catalinac, A. (2007) 'Identity theory and foreign policy: explaining Japan's responses to the 1991 Gulf War and the 2003 U.S. War in Iraq', *Politics & Policy* 35(1): 58–100.
Chūgoku Regional Agricultural Administration Office. (1984) *Shimane Ken Gyogyō no Ugoki [Shimane Prefecture's fishing industry]*, Matsue: Statistics and Information Department, Agricultural Administration Office.
Cummings, B. (1997) *Korea's Place in the Sun*, New York, NY: W.W. Norton.
The Economist. (2010) 'Hallyu, yeah!', online edition, e-published on 25 January, accessed at http://www.economist.com/node/15385735, 24 July 2013.
The Economist. (2012) 'A Game of Leapfrog', online edition, e-published on 28 April, accessed at http://www.economist.com/node/21553498, 24 July 2013.
Emmers, R. (2010) 'Japan–Korea relations and the Tokdo/Takeshima dispute: the interplay of nationalism and natural resources', *RSIS Working Paper*. Singapore: S. Rajaratnam School of International Studies, Nanyang Technological University.
Fukuhara, Y. (2012) 'Gyogyō mondai to ryōdo mondai no kōsaku' [The interplay of fishing and territorial disputes]', *Shimane Journal of Northeast Asian Research* 23: 65–78.
Furuya, T. (2012) *Takeshima ni Itte Mita [I went to Takeshima!]*, Tokyo: Seirindo.

Hagström, L. (2014) 'The "abnormal" state: identity, norm/exception and Japan', *European Journal of International Relations*, published online before print, March 27, accessed at http://ejt.sagepub.com/content/early/2014/03/19/1354066113518356.abstract, 10 October 2014.

Hopf, T. (2002) *Social Construction of International Politics*, Ithaca, NY: Cornell University Press.

Hosaka, M. and Tōgō, K. (2012) *Nihon no Ryōdo Mondai:Hoppō Yontō, Takeshima, Senkaku shotō [Japan's Territorial Problems: Northern Territories, Takeshima, the Senkaku Islands]*, Tokyo: Kadokawa Shoten.

Huh, M. M. (2013) 'Bak Jung Hui, il jeonggyaek deul e meori sugyeo 'seonbyae nim deul dowa jusipsio" [Park Chung Hee, bowing his head to Japanese politicians asking 'seniors, please help"], *Donga*, 22 April, accessed at http://news.donga.com/Newsletter/3/all/20130422/54604083/1, 20 January 2013.

Ishida, R. (2001) *Shimane Prefectural Assembly Interpolations*, Matsue: Shimane Prefectural Assembly.

Itō, H. (2008) *Gakkō Kyōiku to Takeshima Mondai' [School education and Takeshima problem]*, accessed at http://www.pref.shimane.lg.jp/soumu/web-takeshima/H20kouza.data/H20kouza-ito.hiro1.pdf, 20 May 2013.

Iwabuchi, K. (2002) *Recentering Globalization: Popular Culture and Japanese Transnationalism*, Durham, NC: Duke University Press.

James, W. (2001) 'Trade relations of Korea and Japan: moving from conflict to cooperation?', *East-West Center Working Papers* 11: 7, accessed at http://www.eastwestcenter.org/sites/default/files/private/ECONwp011.pdf, 10 September 2013.

Kajimura, H. (1997) 'The question of Takeshima/Tokdo', *Korean Observer* 28(3): 423–75.

Kataoka, C. and Nishida, A. (2007) 'Nichūkan gyogyō kankeishi II [History of fisheries relationship among Japan, Korea and China 2]', *Nagasaki Daigaku Suisan gakubu kenkyū hōkoku* 88: 137–59.

Kimura, M. (1995) 'The economics of Japanese imperialism in Korea, 1910–1939', *The Economic History Review* 48(3): 555–74.

Koo, M.G. (2009) 'The Senkaku/Diaoyu dispute and Sino-Japanese political-economic relations: cold politics and hot economics?', *The Pacific Review* 22(2): 205–32.

Koyasu, N. (2003) *'[Ajia] Wa dō Katararetekitaka' [How has 'Asia' been narrated]*, Tokyo: Fujiwara shoten.

Lee, S. (2011) 'Territorial disputes in East Asia, the San Francisco Peace Treaty of 1951 and the legacy of US security interests in East Asia', in S. Lee and H.E. Lee (eds) *Dokdo: Historical Appraisal and International Justice*, Danvers: Brill., pp. 41–71.

Mitzen, J. (2006) 'Ontological security in world politics: state identity and the security dilemma', *European Journal of International Relations* 12(3): 341–70.

MOFA [Ministry of Foreign Affairs]. (2008) *10 Issues of Takeshima*, Tokyo: Northeast Asia Division.

Nagai, Y. (2012) 'The process of establishing Takeshima day in Shimane Prefecture', *Hiroshima Journal of International Studies* 18: 1–18.

Nakajima, K. (2007) 'Is Japanese maritime strategy changing? An analysis of the Takeshima/Dokdo issue', *USJP Occasional Papers*. Cambridge, MA: Program on US–Japan Relations, Harvard University.

Nakasone, Y. (1983) 'Interpolations at budget commission, house of representatives on 19 September 1983', *National Diet Library*, accessed at http://kokkai.ndl.go.jp, July 9 2014.

Nakasone, Y. (2012) *Sengo Nihon Gaikō [Japan's Postwar Diplomacy]*, Tokyo: Shinchosha.
Nanpō dōhō engokai. (1965) *Nihon Ryōdo no hanashi [A Talk on Japan's Territories]*, Tokyo: Nanpō dōhō engokai.
Neumann, I. (1999) *Uses of the 'Other': the East in European Identity Formation*, Manchester: Manchester University Press.
Oguma, E. (2007) 'The postwar intellectuals' view of "Asia"', in S. Saaler and V. Koschmann (eds) *Pan-Asianism in Modern Japanese History: Colonialism, Regionalism and Borders*, London: Routledge, pp. 200–13.
Ōhira, M. (1964) 'Nikkan kaidan ni kan suru shūgiin honkaigi ni okeru Ōhira Masayoshi gaishō no hōkoku'[Foreign Minister's Ohira Masayoshi report on Japan–Korea talks to the House of Representatives], 19 March 1964', *World and Japan* accessed at http://www.ioc.u-tokyo.ac.jp/~worldjpn/, 8 July 2014.
Oki Association of Town and Village Assemblies. (1963) *Takeshima no Ryōdoken Kakuho ni Kan Suru Chinjōsho [Petition Related to Securing Takeshima Territorial Rights]*, Matsue: Shimane Prefectural Library, Takeshima collection.
Oki Fishing Union. (1951) *Takeshima Gyoku no Sōgyō Seigen no Kaijohō ni Tsuku Chinjō [A Petition to Lift the Operation Restrictions in the Takeshima Fishing Zone]*, Matsue: Shimane Prefectural Library, Takeshima collection.
Prestowitz, C. (2012) 'Korea as number one', *Foreign Policy*, accessed at: http://prestowitz.foreignpolicy.com/posts/2012/06/07/korea_as_number_one?wp_login_redirect=0, 24 July 2013.
Roh, D. (2008) *Takeshima Mitsuyaku [The Takeshima Secret Pact]*, Tokyo: Soshisha.
Saaler, S. and Koschmann, V. (2007) *Pan-Asianism in Modern Japanese History: Colonialism, Regionalism and Borders*, London: Routledge.
Schoenbaum, T. J. (2008) *Peace in Northeast Asia*, Cheltenham: Edward Elgar Publishing.
Shimane Prefecture. (1967) *Shinshū Shimane Ken shi [New history of Shimane Prefecture]*, Matsue: Shimane Prefecture.
Shimane Prefecture. (1979a) *Kensei no Ayumi Showa 51–53 [Prefectural Politics 1976–1978]*, Matsue: General Affairs Division.
Shimane Prefecture. (1979b) *Takeshima*, Matsue: Shimane Prefectural Council for Facilitating the Solution of Takeshima Problem.
Shimane Prefecture. (1983) *Kensei no Ayumi Showa 54–57 [Prefectural Politics 1979–1982]*, Matsue: General Affairs Division.
Shimane Prefecture. (2002) *Teian/Yōbōsho [Proposals and Demands]*, Matsue: Shimane Prefecture Prefectural Administration Documents Division.
Shimane Prefecture. (2006) 'Takeshima no ryōdoken no sōki kakuritsu ni tsuite' [Regarding swift establishment of territorial rights to Takeshima]', in *Kuni he no jūten yōbō [Key priority demands to the central government]*, Matsue: Shimane Prefecture Prefectural Administration Documents Division, accessed at http://www.pref.shimane.lg.jp/admin/seisaku/housin/jyuuten/h19-jyuutenn.data/01takeshima.pdf, 7 July 2014.
Shimane Prefecture. (2011) *Shimane Ken Tōkeisho [Statistical data of Shimane Prefecture]*, Matsue: Shimane Prefectural Statistics Association.
Shimane Prefectural Assembly. (1951) *Dai 135 Kai Shimane Kengikai Ketsugiroku [Records of 135th Shimane Prefectural Assembly Resolutions]*, Matsue: Shimane Prefecture.
Shimane Prefectural Assembly. (1965) *Takeshima no Ryōdoken Kakuho ni Kan Suru Kenmin Undō Suishin Yōkō-an [An Outline of Proposal to Promote Prefectural Citizen's Movement for Securing Territorial Rights to Takeshima]*, Matsue: Shimane Prefecture.

Shimane Prefectural Assembly. (2004a) *Takeshima no Ryōdoken Kakuritsu ni Kansuru Ikensho* [*Memorandum on Establishing Territorial Rights to Takeshima*], Matsue: Shimane Prefecture.
Shimane Prefectural Assembly. (2004b) *Shimane Kengikai Rekidai Gichō/ Fukugichō Ichiran* [*List of Shimane Prefectural Assembly's Chairmen and Vice-Chairmen*], accessed at http://www.pref.shimane.lg.jp/gikai/gityou/gityou-2.html, 7 July 2014.
Shimojō, M. (2004) *Takeshima was nikkan dochira no monoka* [*Is Takeshima Japanese or Korean?*], Tokyo: Bungei Shunjū.
Steele, B. (2008) *Ontological Security in International Relations*, London: Routledge.
Sugihara, T. (2011) 'Zoku Takeshima no gyogyouken no hensen ni tsuite' [Continued: transformations in Takeshima fishing rights]', *Web Takeshima*, accessed at http://www.pref.shimane.lg.jp/soumu/web-takeshima/takeshima04/takeshima04-1/takeshima04-230701.html, 15 March 2013.
Sumita, N. and Izawa, M. (2005) '50 nen ni watari seifu, media ni mushi sareta shimanekenmin no takeshima he no omoi o kike' [Listen to Shimane residents thoughts about Takeshima after 50 years of being ignored by the government and the media]', *Sapio*, 17(13): 21–3.
Suzuki, S. (2005) 'Japan's socialization into Janus-faced European international society', *European Journal of International Relations* 11(1): 137–64.
Takaya, H. (1998) Ōhaba Jōho Shi, Dakyō [Compromise After Significant Concessions], *Asahi Shimbun*, morning edition, 25 September, p. 1.
Tamaki, T. (2010) *Deconstructing Japan's Image of South Korea: Identity in Foreign Policy*, London: Palgrave Macmillan.
Tanaka, S. (1995) *Japan's Orient*, Berkley, CA: University of California Press.
Tei, T. (1995) *Kankoku no Imeji* [*The Image of Korea*], Tokyo: Chuō kōron shinsha.
Tottori Prefecture (2008) *Nikkan Zantei Suiki Oyobi Waga Kuni Haitateki Keizai Suiki ni Okeru Gyogyō Chitsujo no Kakuritsu ni Tsuite* [*Petition Regarding Establishment of Fishery Related Order in Japan–Korea Provisional Zone and Japan's EEZ*], submitted to MOFA, MLIT and MAFF, obtained from Tottori Prefecture's Tokyo office on 28 February 2013.
Yamamoto, K. (2007) *Nihonjin ga ikenai nihonryōdo* [*Japanese Territories That Cannot be Visited by Japanese*], Tokyo: Shōgakkan.
Yamano, S. (2005) *Kenkanryū* [*Hating the Korean Wave*], Tokyo: Shinyūsha.
Yokota, H. (2005) 'Takeshima no hi jōrei seitei no butai ura' [The backstage of Takeshima Day ordinance]', *Shukan Asahi*, 10 June, p. 170.
Yomiuri Shimbun. (2006) 'Kokka Senryaku wo Kangaeru' [Thinking about national strategy]', *Yomiuri Shimbun*, morning edition, 25 May, p. 4.
Yomiuri Shimbun. (2010) Nikkan 100 Nen' [100 years of Japan–Korea relations], *Yomiuri Shimbun*, morning edition, 24 August 2010, p. 3.
Wakita, Y. (2013) 'Kongo no nikkankankei to rekishi ninshiki mondai' [The future of Japan–Korea relations and the problem of historical consciousness]', *Rippō to Chōsa* 337: 88–102.
Weinstein, M. (2006) 'South Korea-Japan Dokdo/Takeshima dispute: toward confrontation', *The Asia-Pacific Journal: Japan Focus*, accessed at http://www.japanfocus.org/-Michael-Weinstein/1685#sthash.6C4w5qmN.dpuf [10 September 2013].
Zarakol, A. (2010) 'Ontological (in) security and state denial of historical crimes: Turkey and Japan', *International Relations* 24(1): 3–23.

Interviews

(1) Interview with unnamed official from Shimane Prefecture Fisheries Division, Oki branch on 29 January 2013 at Shimane Prefecture's Oki Branch, Oki Island, Shimane Prefecture.
(2) Interview with unnamed officials from Shimane Prefecture Fisheries Division on 30 January 2013 Shimane Prefectural Government, Matsue, Shimane Prefecture.

The North Korean abduction issue: emotions, securitisation and the reconstruction of Japanese identity from 'aggressor' to 'victim' and from 'pacifist' to 'normal'

Linus Hagström and Ulv Hanssen

Abstract After Kim Jong-il's confession in 2002 that North Korean agents had abducted thirteen Japanese citizens in the 1970s and 1980s, North Korea has become the most detested country in Japan, and the normalisation of bilateral relations has been put on the back burner. The abduction issue has taken precedence in Japan even over North Korea's development of nuclear weapons and long-range missiles. It has also grossly overshadowed the atrocities for which Imperial Japan was responsible in the 20th century. Why has there been such strong emphasis on an issue that could be disregarded as comparatively 'less important'? This article understands the ascendency of the abduction issue as the epitome of an identity shift under way in Japan – from the identity of a curiously 'peaceful' and inherently 'abnormal' state, to that of a more 'normal' one. The differentiation of North Korea as 'abnormal' emphasises Japan's own (claim to) 'normality'. Indeed, by incarnating the perils of Japan's own 'pacifist' 'abnormality', which has been so central to the collective sense of Japanese 'Self' in the post-war period, the abduction issue has become a very emotional argument for

Japan's 'normalisation' in security and defence terms. The transformation from 'abnormal' to 'normal' is further enabled by Japan trading places with North Korea in the discourse, so that Japan is defined as 'victim' (rather than former aggressor) and North Korea as 'aggressor' (rather than former victim). What is at stake here is the question whether Japan is 'normalising' or 'remilitarising', and the role of the abduction issue discourse in enabling such foreign and security policy change.

Introduction

In the past decade, North Korea has remained at the top of Japan's political agenda. Yet it is not North Korea's development of nuclear and missile capability that has enjoyed the most enduring political attention, as a rational agent model might suggest, but rather the abduction of seventeen Japanese citizens by North Korean agents in the 1970s and 1980s.[1] This 'abduction issue' has also grossly overshadowed the fact that Imperial Japan systematically violated the human rights of the Korean people during Japan's colonial period (1910–1945), not least by forcefully displacing millions of Koreans to work in the Japanese military and in mines, brothels and factories (Cumings 2007: 259–60). Why has the abduction issue remained a top priority of successive Japanese governments, and why has it continued to trump other seemingly vital matters in bilateral and regional affairs? How can its puzzling ascendency in Japan be understood?

Samuels (2010) and Williams and Mobrand (2010) tackle similar questions, although their scopes are broader in that they also undertake comparisons with Pyongyang's abduction of South Korean nationals. Samuels (2010: 389) concludes that differences in the way in which the abduction issue has evolved in Japan and South Korea 'defy systematic structural explanation in either the international or domestic arenas'. Yet he explains the rise of the abduction issue in Japan by a general 'rightward drift in Japanese politics' and a '"mainstreaming" of the right' (Samuels 2010: 369): 'It was not until hard line LDP leaders with a demonstrated antipathy for North Korea consolidated power that the abductee issue was elevated in the national discourse' (Samuels 2010: 386–7). Williams and Mobrand (2010: 511) conclude similarly that '[t]he incremental moves further to the right along the domestic political continuum have contributed to the hardening of Tokyo's stance on the abductions issue'. They infer that the abduction issue was deliberately used to promote a right-wing agenda (Williams and Mobrand 2010: 520), but also that is has 'assumed a life of its own' (Williams and Mobrand 2010: 532).

These interpretations overlook the fact that the abduction issue was 'elevated in the national discourse' *immediately* after Kim Jong-il's abduction confession on 17 September 2002 – a date simply known in Japan as '9/17' – during the premiership of Koizumi Jun'ichirō (2001–2006), who did not necessarily harbour a 'demonstrated antipathy for North Korea'.

We agree that there is a relationship between a 'rightward shift', or, more precisely, the increased saliency of a certain identity discourse that could be identified as 'right-wing' and the abduction issue, but we argue that the relationship is constitutive rather than causal (cf. Wendt 1998). An already completed identity shift did not *cause* increased interest in the abduction issue; instead, the abduction issue is deeply entangled in an ongoing reconstruction of Japanese identity. In other words, rather than being causally independent, the two phenomena are mutually constitutive.

In this article the discourse on the 'abduction issue' is understood as one important vehicle for reconstructing Japanese identity, from that of a curiously 'peaceful' and inherently 'abnormal' state, to that of a more 'normal' one. Such ascriptions of identity are understood here as social constructions, which emerge as an effect of boundary production vis-à-vis difference, or distinctions between Self and Other (Campbell 1998 [1992]; Rumelili 2004). The article argues that the securitisation of both North Korean and Japanese 'abnormality' is crucial to this identity reconstruction – securitisation being defined as the social construction of an existential threat, 'requiring emergency measures and justifying actions outside the normal bounds of political procedure' (Buzan, Wæver, and de Wilde 1998: 23–4). This securitisation, in turn, is driven by Japan trading places with North Korea in the discourse, so that Japan becomes 'victim' (rather than former aggressor) and North Korea 'aggressor' (rather than former victim).

The process is mediated by the diffusion of emotions related to the abduction issue in Japanese society, particularly anger and sympathy. The literature on emotions in international studies argues that such diffusion is crucial for the internalisation of identities 'below the level of consciousness' (Ross 2006: 210). Moreover, representation in widely circulated narratives is seen as key to how emotions 'acquire a collective dimension' and become shared by entire communities (Bleiker and Hutchison 2008: 130). Indeed, Hutchison (2010: 67) argues that some extreme, 'traumatic', occurrences can be experienced as 'so disturbing' that 'Self's' understanding of the world and 'Self's' own place in it is destabilised. Such events are then often followed by 'a push to restore or reconfigure collective identity' along conservative lines (Hutchison 2010: 68). Lynn (2006: 502) argues that the abduction issue is precisely such a 'vicarious trauma', in which repeated media representations of North Korea as 'evil and strange' have 'fostered a sense of unity based on a common sense of indignation and fear'. By emphasising how certain emotions related to the abduction issue have come to define what is seen as 'true' about both Japan and North Korea, this article transcends rationalist accounts, which assume a clear distinction between objective reason and subjective passion (cf. Mouffe 2000).

What is at stake when Japan is inter-subjectively defined as 'abnormal', 'pacifist' or 'normal'? Most fundamentally, the literature associates such identity constructions with distinct foreign and security policies (Berenskoetter 2010), and a 'pacifist' identity is believed to enable and constrain action in a different way from the identity of a 'normal' country. In other words, in light of different identity constructions, distinct foreign and security policies are made conceivable/thinkable, communicable/resonant and indeed coercive/dominant (Holland 2013).

The aim of this article is (1) to analyse the role of the abduction issue discourse in shifting the balance between 'abnormality' and 'normality' in Japanese identity construction; and (2) to discuss how the emerging balance enables changes in Japan's foreign and security policy. The article will not summarise the Japanese abduction debate exhaustively, but only reconstruct the dominant discourse, as it has appeared in widely circulated books and popular monthlies and weeklies, in particular the vocal opinions of influential policy makers and organisations devoted to the issue.

The first section serves to establish the ascendancy of the abduction issue in Japan over the past decade. It demonstrates how emotions have been mobilised to construct a *collective* understanding of the issue and to restrict alternative understandings. The second section argues that this ascendancy enables a shift from the 'pacifist' 'abnormality', which has been so central to the collective sense of Japanese 'Self' in the post-war period, to 'normality,' making the 'normalisation' of Japanese foreign and security policy conceivable to policy makers, communicable to an larger audience, and possibly even coercive as a preferred way of acting.

The ascendancy of the abduction issue

In 2012, ten years after Kim Jong-il confessed that North Korean agents had abducted thirteen Japanese nationals in the 1970s and 1980s, and agreed to let five abductees return to Japan, opinion polls showed that 96 per cent of the Japanese had 'heard about the issue and know its contents', while only 0.2 per cent had 'never heard about the issue' (Cabinet Office 2012). While the North Korean nuclear and missile issues are focal points in the international North Korea debate, the abduction issue has captured the interest of the Japanese public much more powerfully than any of those traditional security issues. Moreover, while the Japanese interest in the nuclear and missile issues has ebbed and flowed in conjunction with particular events, such as nuclear tests and missile launches, interest in the abduction issue has been stable since 2002, consistently hovering just below 90 per cent (see Figure 1).

Strong interest in the abduction issue, moreover, has coincided with a sharp increase in hostile sentiments toward North Korea. After 9/17 the Japanese 'dislike rate' toward North Korea rose almost 20 percentage points (from 63 per cent in August 2002 to 82 per cent in January 2003), but more importantly, it has remained in the 80 per cent range ever since (see Figure 2). Again, how can this puzzling ascendancy of the abduction issue be understood?

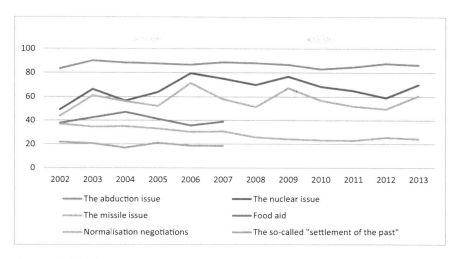

Figure 1. Which North Korea related topics are you interested in? The graph is a compilation of results of the Cabinet Office's annual survey between 2002 and 2013 (Cabinet Office 2002–2013).

The diffusion of sympathy and anger

There is consensus that constant lobbying efforts by Kazokukai (Association of the Families of Victims Kidnapped by North Korea) and its support organisation Sukūkai (National Association for the Rescue of Japanese Kidnapped by North Korea) have been instrumental in placing the abduction issue on the Japanese political agenda since their establishment in the

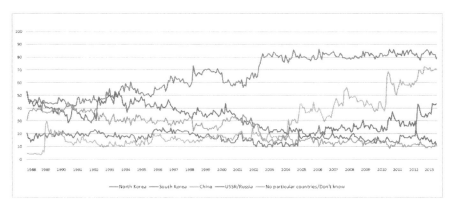

Figure 2. Pick up to three countries which you dislike. Compiled from *Jiji seron chōsa* [*Jiji Public Opinion Survey*]. Jiji Press has conducted opinion polls monthly since 1960 asking respondents to 'pick up to three countries which you dislike [*kirai*]' (Jiji Tsūshinsha 1988–2013).

late 1990s (Hasuike 2009: 89; Hirasawa 2004: 145; Samuels 2010: 367–8). These organisations were not fully recognised before 9/17, but after that watershed event Kazokukai in particular began to be showered with attention and sympathy, and its campaigns went increasingly unchallenged. Some analysts have even talked of Japan's North Korea policy as having been, or facing the risk of being, 'kidnapped' (Samuels 2010) or 'abducted [*rachi*]' (Vogel 2004: 11; Wada 2004) by these pressure groups, or by the abduction issue itself.

The mirror image of surging public sympathy for Kazokukai was outbursts of antipathy toward North Korea – for abducting Japanese citizens in the first place; for claiming that eight of the abductees were dead; and for the apparent flaws in the information that it revealed about those deaths. Public anger was soon also directed against (1) the politicians, bureaucrats and scholars who had advocated the normalisation of relations with North Korea while doubting or denying that abductions had occurred; (2) the government, which for so long had failed to detect, much less prevent, the abductions; and (3) the mainstream media, which had not connected vital pieces of information linking North Korea to the disappearances of Japanese citizens.

Immediately after 9/17, the Japanese media – particularly the weekly and monthly magazines associated with the political right – initiated a campaign to track down and expose those understood as having obstructed progress on the abduction issue. In an essay in the national newspaper *Sankei shimbun*, the respected author Sono Ayako (2002) called for full exposure of the 'North Korea sympathisers'. Her call was heard, and in November 2002 a commentator in *Bungei shunjū* exclaimed: 'now is the perfect time to publicise ... the names of these politicians, scholars and members of the cultural elite and to examine what they have said about North Korea and what actions they have taken' (Ishii 2002). Before long, meticulous examinations of 'improper' comments and actions of alleged North Korea sympathisers began to thrive in Japan's weeklies and monthlies. The articles went by such titles as '[Those] pretending not to know about the abduction incident: [we] won't forget your heartlessness! (Araki and Ishikawa 2002); 'The death throes of the North Korea clique: rip out the double-talking tongues of these guys!' (Inagaki 2002); and 'The politicians, bureaucrats and debaters who have stood by and watched eight [abductees] die: atone for your great sins through death' (*Shūkan bunshun* 2002).

In the lynch mob atmosphere after 9/17, some of those represented as having obstructed the abduction issue were physically punished – a tendency that even gained a degree of public support. In 2003 former Liberal Democratic Party (LDP) Secretary General Nonaka Hiromu, who had been an advocate of food aid to North Korea in the 1990s, was harassed for days as sound trucks affiliated with right-wing groups circulated outside his house. Although Nonaka arguably even retired from politics as a result of this (Samuels 2010: 371), the problems continued. After his retirement he received a metal piece believed to be a bullet in the post, and a right-wing organisation claimed responsibility (*Japan Times Online* 2003). Bullets were also sent to Chōsen sōren (the General Association of Korean Residents in Japan) – Pyongyang's de facto embassy in Tokyo – and shots were fired at a bank affiliated with the organisation (Samuels 2010: 370).

A couple of months earlier a time bomb was found in the garage of then Deputy Foreign Minister Tanaka Hitoshi, who had secretly brokered the 2002 meeting between Koizumi and Kim. Tanaka was much criticised for prioritising normalisation of bilateral relations with North Korea over the abduction issue and for his cold relations with the families of the abductees (e.g. Sakurai 2008: 66; cf. Tanaka 2009: 132). The bomb did not explode, but the incident nonetheless sent a strong message that North Korea was outside the confines of normal diplomacy. Soon after, then Tokyo Mayor Ishihara Shintarō publicly stated that Tanaka 'had it coming', elaborating that Tanaka 'deserves to die for his treachery [*baikoku kōi wa banshi ni atai suru*]' (*Asahi shimbun* 2003). Moreover, according to the Tokyo Metropolitan Government, more than 50 per cent of the 538 calls, e-mails and faxes it received in response to the incident were supportive of Ishihara's remarks (47 News 2003).

In the emerging narrative people and institutions understood as having obstructed a yet undefined solution to the abduction issue were represented as 'traitors [*kokuzoku*]' (Hirasawa 2002b: 38), 'the North Korea clique [*Kitachōsenzoku*]' (Inagaki 2002: 74), 'fools possessed by the North [*Kita ni tsukareta orokamono*]' (Inagaki 2002), 'North Korea lackeys [*bichōka*]' (Kakiya 2002: 100), 'enemies of the rescue [*dakkan no teki*]' (Nishioka and Hasuike 2004: 82), and suchlike. Waseda University Professor Shigemura Toshimitsu (2002: 17) wrote immediately after 9/17 that the acts of the politicians who did not condition the normalisation of bilateral relations on a solution to the abduction issue 'should probably be considered treacherous [*baikokuteki*]', and, further: 'The crimes of the people who have forsaken the Japanese people's call for a rescue are huge ... but even more unforgivable are the people who insisted that the abductions did not exist' (Shigemura 2002: 18).

For instance, in 1999, diplomat and former Director General of the Ministry of Foreign Affairs (MOFA) Asian Affairs Bureau Makita Kunihiko commented that Japan should not sacrifice normalisation with North Korea for the sake of 'a mere ten people [*tatta no jūnin*]' (*Sankei shimbun* 2012). At the time the remark did not stir much controversy, but after 9/17 it has been widely circulated and criticised as telling of MOFA's past neglect of 'national interests' (Sakurai 2008: 31), and its greed for normalisation at all costs (Araki and Ishikawa 2002: 88–9). Ishihara even remarked that 'if this had been the ancient time of respectable, loyal retainers [*matomona gishi*], such a traitor [*baikokudo*] would have been killed' (Nishimura and Ishihara 2002: 31). The 'betrayal narrative' has also been used as a threat against forces seeking to relax some of the tough measures already in place vis-à-vis North Korea. For example, Sukūkai leader Nishioka Tsutomu (2009: 132) warned in 2009 that 'any action toward the removal of governmental sanctions is nothing less than a betrayal [*uragiri*] that will complicate the rescue of the abductees'.

The sanctioning of non-conformity became particularly palpable in the mass condemnation of Hirasawa Katsuei in 2004. Hirasawa was a powerful figure in the incumbent LDP and one of the fiercest Japanese critics of the North Korean regime after 9/17. Frustrated with the lack of progress after the Japanese government refused to keep its alleged promise to send the five returning abductees back to North Korea in 2002, Hirasawa eventually accepted a request to establish secret negotiations with North Korean interlocutors and held meetings in December 2003 and March 2004 (Hirasawa 2004).

When news of the talks leaked, there was a public outcry against Hirasawa for taking diplomacy into his own hands and for using the abduction issue for narrow political gains. Hirasawa was eventually forced to step down as vice minister for internal affairs and communications and secretary general of Rachi giren (the Diet Members' Union for the Early Rescue of Japanese Abducted by North Korea), where his solo diplomacy was branded as a 'betrayal' which 'damaged our trust-based relationship with Kazokukai and Sukūkai' (Wakamiya 2004: 244–5).

Hirasawa had nurtured close ties with the families; he had designated the abduction issue as 'the nation's top priority' even before 9/17 (Hirasawa 2002a: 91); as a National Police Agency bureaucrat, he had personally led raids on Chōsen sōren; he saw the North Korean regime collapse as 'the only way to completely resolve the abduction issue' (Hirasawa 2004: 131); and he had himself anathematised people whom he perceived as North Korea-friendly. He had thus been instrumental in whipping up the anger which now turned against him. Although Hirasawa probably had secret authorisation from Koizumi to engage in the unofficial talks (Hirasawa 2004: 15, 91; Wakamiya 2004: 217, 240), and although the talks arguably led to a breakthrough which saw the return of the returnees' children just two months after his last meeting, he was attacked and ostracised for his firm belief that sanctions alone will not lead to a resolution, and hence that diplomacy is requisite.[2]

The diffusion of conformism

As anger reverberated in Japan, those who had sought improved ties with North Korea, allegedly at the expense of resolving the abduction issue, were told to 'disappear from the view of the Japanese people' (Kakiya 2002: 100) because they 'didn't have the qualification to talk about contemporary history or present developments' (Inagaki 2002: 82) or 'the qualification to comment on the Korea problem' (Shigemura 2002: 21). Many left-wing commentators accepted defeat either by altering their stances or by shunning the abduction debate altogether. In the words of one triumphant hard-liner: 'Kim Jong-il's abduction apology brought "death" ['*shi*' *o motarashita*] upon some North Korea experts and debaters' (Shigemura 2002: 18). Former Kazokukai Secretary General Hasuike Tōru, who was ousted from Kazokukai in 2010 for his increasingly conciliatory stance vis-à-vis North Korea, remarked that the political left had 'faced a shock and fallen silent' (Hasuike, Ikeda, Suzuki, and Mori 2009: 86).

On 7 October 2002 Social Democratic Party (SDP) party leader Doi Takako said that her party had raised the abduction issue in talks with the Korean Workers' Party. Yet, she admitted, 'we can't say that we pursued [the issue] sufficiently', and she apologised to the families of the abduction victims (*Yomiuri shimbun* 2002a). *Yomiuri shimbun* subsequently ran an editorial stating that 'no matter what [the SDP] is saying now, they cannot be trusted' (*Yomiuri shimbun* 2002b). After 9/17 the SDP suffered defections and internal strife and it fared miserably in the subsequent Lower House elections in November 2003. Even Chōsen sōren apologised as its past comments related to the abduction issue came under increased scrutiny. On 27 September 2002, it issued an open apology in its affiliate newspaper *Choson sinbo*, admitting that its denials of the abductions were 'acts unbecoming to journalists [*jānarisuto ni totte wa arumajiki kōi*]' (*Choson sinbo* 2002). The Diet Members' Union for Japan−North Korea Friendship (Nicchō yūkō giren) was also practically disbanded after 9/17 when its members were branded as 'traitors and "Pro-North" agents' (Lynn 2006: 500).

The LDP also got its share. The then Sukūkai acting chairman, Nishioka (2002: 231), denounced the alleged servility and ignorance of LDP members, remarking sarcastically, 'what country are our government and ruling party working for? Why doesn't the LDP just put up a sign reading "The Korean Workers' Party − Japan Branch Office"?' (Nishioka 2002: 223). After 9/17 more centrist and right-wing politicians also became the targets of criticism, and politicians and political parties have since gone out of their way to emphasise their devotion to the abduction issue. For example, all prime ministers have made it one of their first priorities upon assuming office to visit the families personally, and both Prime Minister Abe Shinzō of the LDP and his predecessor Noda Yoshihiko of the Democratic Party of Japan are seen wearing Kazokukai's blue ribbon badge on most public occasions.

Indeed, before the Lower House election in 2009 Kazokukai and Sukūkai issued a survey questionnaire to all 1374 candidates (demonstrating the privileged status of these organisations) and 87 per cent of the respondents (response rate: 77.3 per cent) agreed that the abduction issue was a 'top priority of the government' (Sukūkai 2009). Even more than 10 years after 9/17 it is virtually impossible for Japanese policy makers with any aspirations to dismiss the abductions as a second-tier issue. Conversely, when Abe Shinzō was elected the LDP president and prime minister in 2006, he was widely regarded as a one-issue politician squarely focusing on the abduction issue (Son 2010: 183).

The Japanese government has also largely accommodated Kazokukai and Sukūkai's various policy requests. First, after 9/17 it instituted a position of special advisor to the prime minister for the abduction issue – upgraded in 2006 to minister for the abduction issue. Second, it has gradually strengthened the sanctions regime vis-à-vis North Korea, describing the abduction issue as one 'important factor' among others (Headquarters for the Abduction Issue 2011). Third, in multilateral talks on the North Korean nuclear and missile issues, it has consistently clung to the policy of withholding all economic and diplomatic incentives until the 'abduction issue' has been resolved (Hagström 2009). Fourth, in 2004 the Japanese Diet passed the Law to Prevent Designated Ships From Visiting Japanese Ports (e-Gov 2004) – widely understood as a measure to prevent North Korean 'mystery ships', allegedly used to carry out the abductions, from entering Japanese waters. Moreover, in 2006 all North Korean ships were banned from Japanese ports (Edström 2012: 34–7). Fifth, in 2006 the Diet passed another law, obligating the government to 'make maximum efforts to resolve the abduction issue', to 'deepen our people's awareness' of the issue, and to cooperate with the international community in 'deterring' human rights abuses by North Korea (e-Gov 2006). Sixth, the government has continued to pursue domestic campaigns as well as campaigns to increase awareness of the abduction issue abroad. Seventh, in 2006 the government established a Headquarters for the Abduction Issue. Eighth, Tokyo sticks with the premise that all the abductees unaccounted for are still alive. Ninth, when North Korea in May 2014 agreed to reinvestigate the cases of missing Japanese who are possibly in North Korea, Tokyo presented Pyongyang with a list of 470 missing people whose disappearances might be related to North Korean abductions. Since it operates with the exact same figures, this was almost certainly the list produced by the Investigating Committee on Missing Japanese Probably Related to North Korea (COMJAN) – a pressure group with close ties to Sukūkai, led by former Sukūkai Secretary General Araki Kazuhiro.[3]

Japan's mainstream media have also been criticised for not taking the abduction issue seriously before 9/17, and they have since sought to redeem themselves by giving the families much attention (Hasuike and Ōta 2009: 102–103). The left-leaning *Asahi shimbun*'s allegedly 'soft' stance on the abduction issue was subject to particularly fierce criticism. The newspaper's database reveals that in the four and a half years between the establishment of Kazokukai in March 1997 and 9/17, *Asahi* printed just four articles containing the words 'Kazokukai' and '*rachi* [abduction]'. In contrast, in the four and a half years after 9/17 the same search words yielded 741 articles. In fact, *Asahi shimbun* (2002) reacted instantly to 9/17 by characterising the abductions as 'completely unacceptable acts that are tantamount to acts of terrorism' [*tero kōi ni hitoshiku, totemo yurusu koto ga dekinai*]'. Although it warned against using the issue 'as a reason to implement sanctions against North Korea and close the window for normalisation negotiations', it also stressed that 'as the abduction issue has clearly shown, North Korea is a dangerous country for the citizens of Japan', quoting one bereaved family member as saying that Kim's admission was like 'getting a sentence as cruel as hell' [*jigoku no yōna zankokuna saiban o uketa*]'.

Another illuminating example of the media's increasing sensitivity to the abduction issue came in 2006. In the first nine months of that year, NHK, Japan's national broadcasting organisation, had devoted one third of its roughly 2000 North Korea-related broadcasts to the issue (Clarke 2006). However, then (and current) Prime Minister Abe ordered it to increase the coverage in international radio broadcasts. Although the order sparked a debate about the freedom of the media in Japan (*Japan Times Online* 2007), NHK did not resist. Moreover, 46 per cent of the public agreed with the order (35 per cent opposed it), and 85 per cent of the supporters argued that it was necessary 'because the abduction issue is important' (*Asahi shimbun* 2006).

Historian Ōta Masakuni (2004: 60) remarks critically that 'the media ... one-sidedly promote only Kazokukai, Sukūkai or commentators who, without a single objection, agree [with these organisations]'. One commentator even labels the lack of criticism in the mainstream media the 'Kazokukai taboo in the media world' (Takashima 2006: 88). Hasuike (2009: 89) similarly notes that the media 'have tabooed reporting which might anger the families of the victims because such reporting would turn public opinion into an enemy [*yoron o teki ni mawashite shimau*]. In that respect, the words and actions of the victims' families have become a sanctuary [*sankuchuari*]'. In fact, the media have continued to pay close and mostly uncritical attention to the opinions of the families, even regarding matters unrelated to the abductions.

Ōta warns that 'the more we become conformed and united as one nation based on a cunning form of frenzied nationalism, the further away we stray from the path leading to a natural solution [to the abduction issue]. Rather, the only option which awaits us [on our current path] is war' (Hasuike and Ōta 2009: 54). In a similar vein, Rikkyo University Professor Ishizaka Kōichi (2004: 72) observes that 'comments that benefit "the criminal" North Korea have become taboo. An atmosphere has been created which does not allow alternative arguments'. At the same time, these comments themselves epitomise the limits to the diffusion of conformism, because they show that a critical approach was possible, albeit not widespread.

What the abduction issue discourse enables

Although there is near-consensus among scholars that Japan has punched below its weight in international affairs in the post-war period – and that it has therefore been 'abnormal', or an 'anomaly' – there is dissensus as how to understand this state of affairs (Hagström, forthcoming). According to one line of thinking, 'pacifist' norms or a culture of 'antimilitarism' were institutionalised in Japan after the war as a way of checking the 'aggressiveness' of the 1930s and 1940s (Berger 1993, 1998; Katzenstein and Okawara 1993; Katzenstein 1996). The foremost example of such norms/culture is Article 9 of the Japanese Constitution, which relinquished Japan's sovereign right to wage wars and to use force or the threat of force 'as means of settling international disputes', and which established that 'land, sea, and air forces, as well as other war potential, will never be maintained' (Cabinet Office 1947).

Many agree that the Japanese people started to adhere to an inward-looking 'one-country pacifism [*ikkoku heiwa shugi*]' after the war (Togo 2012). Yet domestically Japan was generally seen as 'victim' rather than 'aggressor'. While the political left regarded it as a victim of the faulty decisions of a small military clique and the US dropping of atom bombs on Hiroshima and Nagasaki, the political right saw Japan as victim of 'victor's justice' and emasculation under US occupation, epitomised par excellence by the US-imposed 'Peace Constitution' and Article 9. One could thus argue that an allegedly 'pacifist' or 'antimilitarist' identity was founded on both 'victim' narratives and 'victimiser' ones, although by the 1960s the former had allegedly become dominant (Buruma 2009 [1994]; Orr 2001: 3).

At the same time, one might question the notion of a 'pacifist' or 'antimilitarist' identity to begin with. Diametrically opposed stances in the realm of defence and security policy have provided the clearest line of division between the two poles in Japan's post-war political landscape. To simplify somewhat, the political left favoured unarmed neutrality and criticised the Japan–US alliance and the Self-Defense Forces (SDF) since their establishment in the early 1950s, while the political right wanted to keep or further upgrade Japanese defence. Yet both positions shared the notion that Japan is 'abnormal'; to the centre-left Japan was (or aspired to become) legitimately exceptional, and to the right it was illegitimately deviant. The Yoshida Doctrine (1954) arguably epitomised the careful balancing of these two extremes, and Japanese self-restraint was perpetuated through the institutionalisation of Article 9, a security framework centred on the SDF, and the security treaty with the USA (Soeya 2005). Yet, concomitant with the diffusion of anger and conformism surrounding the abduction issue, this balance has become severely disrupted, and the scale has begun to tilt heavily in favour of the political right.

From 'pacifist'/'abnormal' to 'normal'

An 'abnormality' narrative also permeates discourse on the abduction issue, thereby connecting it to a broader political agenda. The political right presents the abduction issue as the gravest infringement on Japanese sovereignty in the post-war era, and the one concrete instance where post-war Japan's 'abnormal' security posture most certainly has resulted in the loss of Japanese lives at the hands of a foreign country (Hasegawa 2003). 9/17 revealed once and for all that leaving Japan's 'security and existence' at the mercy of the 'peace-loving peoples of the world', as stated in the Japanese Constitution, is exceedingly naïve.

This is the very bottom line of Prime Minister Abe's 2006 book (Abe 2006: 44–66). LDP politician Hirasawa Katsuei (2004: 133) explicates this logic: 'If Japan had been a normal state [*futsū no kokka*], we would certainly have been able to prevent the abductions. We would also have been able to rescue them'. Araki Kazuhiro (2005: 11) similarly claims that 'our country, which has continuously allowed the North Korean abductions, can be characterised as abnormal [*ijō*]'. In this sense, 'the entire post-war structure has obstructed a solution of the abduction issue' (Araki 2009: 141). Kyoto University Professor Nakanishi Terumasa (2002: 49) argues that 9/17 dragged Japan into a period of 'real crisis [*hontō no kiki*]' for the first time since the war, but he rejoices that it is therefore 'about to wake up from its delusion [*meimō*]' (Nakanishi 2002: 46), and 'make a clean break [*ketsubetsu*] with the mistaken past of the post-war era' (Nakanishi 2002: 49).

With the securitisation of Japan's alleged 'abnormality', Japan's 'normalisation' in the form of constitutional reform and preparations for a more solid national defence have entered the realm of the politically possible (e.g. Kakiya 2002: 114). For example, Yokota Sakie, the mother of Yokota Megumi who was abducted at the age of thirteen in 1977, has been credited with the statement that 'Japan does not deserve to be called a nation if it remains shamefully incapable of rescuing all of the abductees'; it needs to become 'normal' through 'revision of its post-war "peace" constitution' (Sakurai 2012). Former Tokyo Governor Ishihara Shintarō also referred precisely to Yokota Megumi in a more recent plea for revision of the Japanese Constitution:

> Even though Yokota Megumi and more than 200 other people were abducted and killed, and even though there was evidence [proving this], Japan was unable to demand their return by taking a tough stance vis-à-vis North Korea. Thanks to [*okage de*] Article 9 they were abandoned to die. If it weren't for that [Article 9], Japan could have got them back by threatening to go to war unless North Korea send them back. (*Asahi shimbun* 2012)

Most succinctly, Araki (2009: 142) describes the constitution as a 'cap on the bottle', which prevents Japan from pursuing its national interests, arguing that 'one can even say that *not* using the army [to rescue the abductees] is unconstitutional' (Araki 2005: 160, italics added).

Sukūkai leader Nishioka (2009: 137), in turn, has called on the SDF to devise plans for rescue operations in case of an emergency or a sudden change on the Korean Peninsula. After the North Korean shelling of Yeonpyeong Island in 2010, Kazokukai and Sukūkai convened a meeting where, addressing Japanese lawmakers, an outraged Kazokukai Secretary General Masumoto Teruaki made a similar proposal: 'We request legal reforms, including reform of the SDF law, in order to rescue the Japanese who are in North Korea' (Sukūkai 2010). Just three days later, then Prime Minister Kan Naoto met with the families and hinted that he would take steps precisely to allow the SDF to 'rescue the abductees in North Korea in case of a contingency' (Reizei 2010). However, Chief Cabinet Secretary Sengoku Yoshito quickly retracted Kan's remarks, saying 'there is absolutely no such plan'. He speculated that Kan had meant that Japan needs to undertake 'mental exercises' on how to cope with a possible contingency in North Korea (Kyodo News 2010).

The abduction issue has even been used in arguments for arming Japan with nuclear weapons, a position held, for example, by all Sukūkai leaders since 1997. Then Tokyo Governor Ishihara also brought up the issue of Japanese nuclear armament in the context of the abduction issue by saying that if Japan had had such capability 'North Korea wouldn't have taken so many of our citizens' (McNeill 2011).

From 'aggressor' to 'victim'

Japan is not the only country whose 'abnormal' status has been securitised in the abduction issue discourse. The title of Araki's book from 2005 catches the ambiguity in that it can be interpreted as referring to both Japan and North Korea: *Abductions: The Essence of an Abnormal State* [*Rachi: ijōna kokka no honshitsu*] (Araki 2005). North Korea's 'abnormality', moreover, both serves to emphasise Japan's (claim to) 'normality' and becomes a rationale to 'normalise' Japan's security policy. North Korea's 'abnormality' is epitomised by a 'cruelty beyond imagination [*sōzō o zessuru yōna gyakutai*]'. More concretely, this is a country 'where 200,000 people, or 1 per cent of the population, are put in labour camps, and which not only [carries out] abductions, but also enforces person glorification despite a wretched economic situation in which people are starving to death. The Kim Jong-il regime ... is abnormal even compared to China and other countries under communist rule' (Araki 2005: 11).

The abduction issue is again very central. When Kazokukai and Sukūkai surveyed 1159 Lower House candidates in 2003 (response rate: 84.8 per cent), 93 per cent considered the abductions as acts of 'terrorism' [*tero*] (Sukūkai 2003). Two months before becoming prime minister in 2006, Abe also wrote that 'the abductions were carried out as a part of North Korea's international terrorism [*kokusai tero*]' (Abe 2006: 52). Since Abe's first stint as prime minister in 2006–2007, moreover, the Ministry of Defense's annual white papers have continued to characterise the abductions with the exact same sentence, calling them a 'major threat to the lives and security of the Japanese public' (Ministry of Defense 2006–2013).

Many observers have noted how the securitisation of the North Korean abduction of Japanese nationals has transformed both the collective understanding of North Korea and Japanese self-understanding. Former bureaucrat Tanaka Hitoshi (2009: 217), for instance, has argued that 'the abduction issue changed the obligatory post-war perception of Japan as an "assailant" [*kagaisha*] into one where Japan is a "victim [*higaisha*]"'. Moreover, leftist historian Wada Haruki (2004: 251) wrote, 'in Japan–North Korea relations the abduction issue is everything. Settling the past history of colonial rule is no longer an issue. Japan's past as an assailant [*kagaisha*] is now forgotten or justified, and Japan is now only the victim [*higaisha*] in the relationship with North Korea'. Historian Ōta commented similarly that the abduction issue has come to be dominated by groups and elements who are 'dissatisfied with Japan being called an "assailant" [*kagaisha*] when it comes to colonial rule and aggressive warfare, but now find relief in that Japan has become a "victim" [*higaisha*]' (Hasuike and Ōta 2009: 54).

There are many examples of this tendency. For example, following 9/17, former *Asahi shimbun* journalist Inagaki Takeshi (2002: 75) asserted that Japanese colonial rule 'cannot be placed in the same category as [North Korea's] state crimes'. Military analyst Kakiya Isao (2002: 102) also criticised the notion of 'placing the abductions, which are a state crime, side by side with the Japanese colonial period which was a legitimate act'. The abductions are fresher in memory and better documented than Imperial Japan's colonisation of Korea (1910–1945), whose imprint on history has been blurred partly by the passage of time and partly due to the quasi-legal annexation treaty of 1910. Moreover, the abductees, particularly Yokota Megumi, approximate 'ideal victims', in the language of criminology, because the offender can be construed as almost 100 per cent 'evil', and the victims as 100 per cent 'innocent' (Christie 1986). The continued use of young Yokota Megumi as a rallying point in the abduction issue discourse is also instructive from a feminist viewpoint, because young women are typically represented as objects of male protection, enabling more robust security and defence policies (Repo 2008).

The way in which Japan has been reconstructed as 'victim' and North Korea as 'aggressor' shows how the abduction issue discourse reinforces Japanese post-war victim narratives. In Lynn's (2006: 497) words, the abductions 'provided an opportunity for Japan to wear the mantle of victimhood' after years of being 'cast as the former aggressor'. Together with the emotional securitisation of Japan's 'abnormality', this reconstruction serves to enable the abandonment of 'pacifism' as we know it, and to further the 'normalisation' of Japanese foreign and security policy. Relatedly, it also serves to enable a 'correct understanding of history [*tadashii rekishi ninshiki*]' (Kakiya 2002: 114) and the abandonment of Japan's alleged 'atonement mentality [*shokuzai ishiki*]' (Nakanishi 2002: 53).

Since the securitisation of the abduction issue broadly serves to question post-war Japan's ability to protect, it also enables a 'protector narrative' on the more radically rightist fringes of the debate. Here, the challenge of handling problems on the Korean Peninsula justifies the Japanese dispatch of troops there in the past, present and future. According to Araki (2005: 163–4), 'we have to topple the Kim Jong-il regime with our own hands and we have to rescue the abductees, not only the Japanese ones, but also the South Korean and other abductees as well. Moreover we have to save the 20 million North Koreans ... Actually, it is no exaggeration to say that this is our duty as one of the leading countries of the world'. Similar remarks were made at the 2009 symposium on 'Abductions and National Defence' [*rachi to kokubō*], where Araki appeared together with Kazokukai's Masumoto and the former chief of staff of Japan's Air Self Defense Force, General Tamogami Toshio (*Nikkan berita* 2009).

Conclusions and implications

Identity issues have been central to both the analysis and the conduct of Japan's international relations in the post-war period. Scholars have debated how to describe what country Japan *is*, and there have been animated political disputes around the question of what country Japan *should aspire to become*. To summarise, nearly everyone – both policy makers and scholars – has agreed that Japan has been 'abnormal' in its foreign and security policy, and that the 'pacifist' provisions of the 1947 Constitution are key to that 'abnormality'. However, where the political left has generally hoped that Japan would become a 'pacifist' example for others to follow, the political right has bemoaned that it would or *should* eventually have to 'normalise' its foreign and security policy, or 'remilitarise' (Hagström forthcoming).

Many observers interpreted tendencies in the 2000s precisely as Japan's 'normalisation' or 'remilitarisation', including the rise to prominence of right-wingers such as Abe, intensifying quarrels between Japan and its neighbours, and, relatedly, the increasing conspicuousness of radical right-wing rhetoric in Japanese society. This article has demonstrated that the abduction issue is one important context where such arguments have been heard. Although the abduction issue discourse does not in itself equal Japan's 'normalisation' or 'remilitarisation', it can be understood as a vehicle for renegotiating Japanese identity; indeed, through the diffusion of emotions, the issue has been securitised and collectivised in such a way that a policy of 'normalisation'/'remilitarisation' has become both conceivable and communicable. The silencing of dissent could, moreover, forebode such a policy becoming coercive (cf. Holland 2013: 44).

The abduction issue discourse is constitutively connected to identity change not only in that the differentiation of North Korea as 'abnormal' emphasises Japan's (claim to) 'normality'; the abductions are also taken to epitomise the perils of Japan's own alleged 'abnormality', namely the 'pacifism' which has been so central to the collective sense of Japanese Self in the post-war period, and the securitisation of which is an argument for the country's 'normalisation' in security and defence terms. As this article has shown, the transformation from 'abnormal'/'pacifist' to 'normal' is enabled by Japan's trading places with Korea in the discourse, so that Japan becomes the unambiguously 'peaceful' 'victim' (rather than the former aggressor) and North Korea the unmistakably 'threatening' 'aggressor' (rather than the former victim) – hence, an archetypal Other.

The discourse on the abduction issue is *constitutively* connected to identity change in that it has materialised in a context where the increased saliency of a certain identity discourse identified as 'right-wing' was already under way. Yet the role of the abduction issue in propelling this development should not be underestimated; as a kind of national 'trauma' it has further unsettled Japanese understandings of Self in relation to the world, and strengthened calls for a renegotiation of national identity along conservative lines. Hence, we think it would have been unlikely that this kind of discourse could have emerged, and had equally profound effects on Japanese identity, one, two or three decades earlier.

While securitisation is again defined as the social construction of threats, which justifies 'actions outside the normal bounds of political procedure' (Buzan, Wæver, and de Wilde 1998: 23–4), in Japan's case it is present political practice that is defined as outside the bounds of 'normality'. Since the securitisation of this practice paradoxically justifies not some state of emergency, but rather actions understood to be 'normal', obviously the dichotomy between 'normality' and 'abnormality' is very problematic in the first place. Although the Japanese political right often emphasises the necessity to 'normalise' Japan and to accelerate changes in the country's foreign and security policy, perhaps it is not surprising that they seem to be aiming for the unique and superior rather than the 'normal' defined as 'average' (Hagström forthcoming).

The objection can be anticipated that the abduction issue discourse just represents fringe opinions in Japanese society. It is correct that many of the participants in the debate are well-known right-wingers and that others do not necessarily draw exactly the same implications from the abduction issue for Japan's foreign and security policy as they do. However, this article has demonstrated how the issue has been *collectivised*; how most Japanese have come to share strong feelings – of anger toward North Korea and the Japanese who presumably obstructed a solution to the abduction issue, and of sympathy toward the families; and how the boundaries of this collective understanding have become so tightly guarded as to make physical sanctions toward 'dissenters' seem both reasonable and justified, and, as the case of Hirasawa illustrated, to end effectively any freewheeling initiatives toward North Korea that do not fall into line with established practice.

The role of the abduction issue in the reconstruction of Japanese identity is arguably the reason why few Japanese challenge the prioritisation of the issue over the missile and nuclear issues, or object that it seems much less serious than Imperial Japan's forceful displacement of hundreds of thousands of Koreans in the first half of the 20th century. This is also why it is difficult to expect Japan to make a constructive contribution to the solution to the North Korean nuclear issue, for example by providing much sought-after economic incentives, or make any unilateral concessions in the bilateral talks with North Korea (cf. Hagström 2009). Indeed, since North Korea is defined as 'evil' it is very much fraught with peril for Japanese policy makers in charge to change approach to the abduction issue.

At the same time, Abe, if anyone, may have the right-wing credentials necessary to withstand a political backlash were he to alter Japan's North Korea policy. He might also be more willing to do so now that Japan's 'normalisation' is already well underway and a reinterpretation of Article 9 has begun to look politically inevitable. Bilateral talks in Stockholm in May 2014 produced an agreement that Japan will ease unilateral sanctions in return for a North Korean reinvestigation of potential Japanese abductees. However, the big question is: What will Abe do when North Korea presents its results which are almost inevitably bound to be unsatisfactory? Too few abductees will be interpreted as North Korean insincerity; too many as North Korean inhumanity. Little will change unless unpopular decisions are made. The sad implication is that the abduction issue will almost certainly remain unresolved.

Acknowledgements

For useful comments on earlier drafts of this article, we would like to express our sincere gratitude to Robert Boynton, Alexander Bukh, Amy Catalinac, Anthony DiFilippo, Björn Jerdén, Karl Gustafsson, Sebastian Maslow, Paul O'Shea, Hidekazu Sakai, Jens Sejrup, Michael Strausz, Shogo Suzuki, Marie Söderberg, Taku Tamaki, Cecilia Åse and one anonymous reviewer.[4]

Notes

1. North Korea claims that it abducted 13 Japanese nationals; five were returned in 2002 and eight are dead. The Japanese government's official figure has since 2006 been seventeen, but in June 2014 it presented North Korea with a list of 470 persons whose whereabouts are unknown, and whose disappearances might be linked to North Korean abductions. Of these 77 were 'strongly suspected' to have been abducted.
2. Linus Hagström's interview with Hirasawa Katsuei, Tokyo 10 December 2013.

3. E-mail correspondence with Murao Tatsuru of COMJAN, 16 June 2014.
4. Unless otherwise indicated, all Internet pages referred to in this article could be accessed on 19 June 2014.

References

47 News (2003) '"Sanpi hobo dōsū" to to: atarimae hatsugen no hankyō' [Tokyo Metropolitan Government (says) 'support and opposition almost equal': 'deserved' statement reverberates], 12 September; accessed at http://www.47news.jp/CN/200309/CN2003091201000220.html
Abe, S. (2006) *Utsukushii kuni e* [Toward a Beautiful Country], Tokyo: Bungei shunjū.
Araki, K. (2005) *Rachi: ijō na kokka no honshitsu* [Abductions: The Essence of an Abnormal State], Tokyo: Bensei shuppan.
Araki, K. (2009) 'Seifu wa "kikoku" "kaiketsu" de wa naku, "kyūshutsu" o kakageyō' [The government must pursue 'rescue', not 'return' and 'solution'], *Seiron* 2 (February): 138–47.
Araki, K. and Ishikawa, M. (2002) 'Rachi jiken ni shiranpuri: anatatachi no hijō wa wasurenai!' [(Those) pretending not to know about the abduction incident: (we) won't forget your heartlessness], *Seiron* 12 (December): 82–93.
Asahi shimbun (2002) 'Kanashisugiru rachi no ketsumatsu: henka unagasu seijōkakōshō o' [The way too tragic conclusion of the abductions: (carry out) normalisation talks that will spur change], 18 September; accessed through Asahi Kikuzō at https://database.asahi.com/library2/
Asahi shimbun (2003) '"Tanaka saigikan, banshi ni atai suru", Ishihara tochiji ga gikai tōben' ['Deputy director-general Tanaka deserves to die', Tokyo governor Ishihara explains at the Diet] 25 September; accessed at http://www.asahi.com/special/abductees/TKY200309250310.html
Asahi shimbun (2006) 'Shitsumon to kaitō: Asahi shimbunsha yoron chōsa' [Questions and answers: Asahi newspaper publishing company public opinion survey], 14 November; accessed through Asahi Kikuzō at https://database.asahi.com/library2/
Asahi shimbun (2012) '"Rachi higaisha, 9 jō no okage de mikoroshi" Ishihara Shintarō shi' [Mr Ishihara Shintaro: 'Thanks to Article 9 (we) let the abduction victims die without helping'], 10 December; accessed at http://www.asahi.com/politics/update/1210/TKY201212100332.html, 18 September 2013.
Berenskoetter, F. (2010) 'Identity in international relations', in R. Denemark (ed) *The International Studies Encyclopedia*, Oxford: Wiley-Blackwell.
Berger, T. U. (1993) 'From sword to chrysanthemum: Japan's culture of antimilitarism', *International Security* 17(4): 119–50.
Berger, T. U. (1998) *Cultures of Antimilitarism: National Security in Germany and Japan*, Baltimore and London: Johns Hopkins University Press.
Bleiker, R. and Hutchison, E. (2008) 'Fear no more: emotions and world politics', *Review of International Studies* 34(S1): 115–35.
Buruma, I. (2009) [1994] *The Wages of Guilt: Memories of War in Germany & Japan*, London: Atlantic.
Buzan, B., Wæver, O. and de Wilde, J. (1998) *Security: A New Framework for Analysis*, Boulder, CO: Lynne Rienner.
Cabinet Office (1947) *The Constitution of Japan*, accessed at http://www.kantei.go.jp/foreign/constitution_and_government/frame_01.html
Cabinet Office (2002–2013) *Gaikō ni kan suru yoron chōsa* [Public Opinion Survey on Diplomacy], Tokyo: Cabinet Office; accessed at http://www8.cao.go.jp/survey/index-gai.html

Cabinet Office (2012) 'Kitachōsen ni yoru nihonjin rachi mondai ni kan suru tokubetsu yoron chōsa [Extraordinary public opinion survey on the North Korean abduction of Japanese [citizens]), Tokyo: Cabinet Office, 19 July; accessed at http://www8.cao.go.jp/survey/tokubetu/h24/h24-rachi.pdf

Campbell, D. (1998) [1992] *Writing Security: United States Foreign Policy and the Politics of Identity*, Manchester: Manchester University Press.

Choson sinbo (2002) 'Henshūbu kara no oshirase' [Notification from the editorial staff], 27 September.

Christie, N. (1986) 'The ideal victim', in D. D. Koski (ed) (2003) *The Jury Trial in Criminal Justice*, Durham, NC: Carolina Academic Press, pp. 154–60.

Clarke, T. (2006) 'Can NHK keep the air free?' *Japan Times Online*, 26 December; accessed at http://www.japantimes.co.jp/text/fl20061226zg.html

Cumings, B. (2007) 'Why memory lingers in East Asia', *Current History* 106 (September): 257–62.

Edström, B. (2012) 'From carrots to sticks: Japanese sanctions towards the DPRK', Institute for Security & Development Policy, Asia Paper (August); accessed at http://www.isdp.eu/images/stories/isdp-main-pdf/2012_edstrom_from-carrots-to-sticks.pdf.

e-Gov (2004) *Tokutei senpaku no nyūkō no kinshi ni kan suru tokutei sochihō* [Special Legal Measures Concerning the Port Ban on Particular Ships], Tokyo: Government of Japan; accessed at http://law.e-gov.go.jp/htmldata/H16/H16HO125.html

e-Gov (2006) *Rachi mondai sono hoka Kitachōsen tōkyoku ni yoru jinken shingai mondai e no taisho ni kan suru hōritsu* [Law Concerning the Handling of the Abduction Issue and Other Human Rights Violations by the North Korean Authorities], Tokyo: Government of Japan; accessed at http://law.e-gov.go.jp/htmldata/H18/H18HO096.html

Hagström, L. (2009) 'Normalizing Japan: supporter, nuisance, or wielder of power in the North Korean nuclear talks', *Asian Survey* 49(5): 831–51.

Hagström, L. (forthcoming) 'The "abnormal" state: identity, norm/exception and Japan', *European Journal of International Relations*, published online before print, 27 March 2014, doi:10.1177/1354066113518356.

Hasegawa, K. (2003) *Kitachōsen no saishū ketsumatsu* [The Final Outcome for North Korea], Tokyo: PHP.

Hasuike, T. (2009) *Rachi: sayū no kakine o koeta tatakai e* [Abductions: Toward a Battle That Overcomes the Fences of Left and Right], Tokyo: Kamogawa shuppan.

Hasuike, T., Ikeda, K., Suzuki, K. and Mori, T. (2009) *Rachi 2: sayū no kakine o koeru taiwashū* [Abductions 2: A Compilation of Dialogues That Overcome the Fences of Left and Right], Tokyo: Kamogawa shuppan.

Hasuike, T. and Ōta, M. (2009) *Rachi Tairon* [Abduction discussion], Tokyo: Ōta shuppan.

Headquarters for the Abduction Issue (2011) *Measures Taken Against North Korea*, Tokyo: Headquarters for the Abduction Issue; accessed at http://www.rachi.go.jp/en/ratimondai/syousai.html

Hirasawa, K. (2002a) *Nihon yo kokka tare* [Japan, be a nation!], Tokyo: Kōdansha.

Hirasawa, K. (2002b) 'Kokuzoku gaimukanryō: Tanaka Hitoshi no bōsō' [The traitor MOFA bureaucrats: Tanaka Hitoshi's reckless behaviour], *Shokun!* 11 (November): 38–46.

Hirasawa, K. (2004) *Rachi mondai: Kitachōsen gaikō no arikata o tou* [The Abduction Issue: Questioning the State of Our North Korea Diplomacy], Tokyo: PHP.

Holland, J. (2013) 'Foreign policy and political possibility', *European Journal of International Relations* 19(1): 49–68.

Hutchison, E. (2010) 'Trauma and the politics of emotions: constituting identity, security and community after the Bali bombing', *International Relations* 24 (1): 65–86.
Inagaki, T. (2002) 'Koitsura no "nimaijita" o hikkonuke! Kitachōsenzoku no danmatsuma' [Rip out the 'double-talking tongues' of these guys! The death throes of the North Korea clique], *Shokun!* 12 (December): 74–88.
Ishii, H. (2002) 'Shinchōha chishikijin: muhansei mōgenroku' [The North Korea-friendly intellectuals: a record of (their) insensitive, careless remarks], *Bungei shunjū* 11 (November): 160–7.
Ishizaka, K. (2004) 'Kokkō seijōka o hakaritsutsu kitachōsen shakai to kakawaru michi o' [Taking a road that involves North Korean society while aiming at normalisation of relations], *Ronza* 8 (August): 70–5.
Japan Times Online (2003) 'Nonaka sent 5 cm piece of metal: police think it may be a bullet: rightists claim responsibility', 12 September; accessed at http://www.japantimes.co.jp/text/nn20030912a3.html
Japan Times Online (2007) 'State sued for ordering NHK abduction reports', 7 March; accessed at http://www.japantimes.co.jp/text/nn20070307a6.html
Jiji Tsūshinsha (1988–2013) *Jiji seron chōsa* [Jiji Public Opinion Survey], Tokyo: Jiji Tsushinsha.
Kakiya, I. (2002) '"Eikyū hozonban": "bichō" katachi no kitachōsen raisan, geigō hatsugenshū' ['The permanent edition': a compilation of the opportunistic and North Korea-worshipping comments of the 'North Korea lackeys'], *Seiron* 12 (December): 100–14.
Katzenstein, P. J. (1996) *Cultural Norms and National Security: Police and Military in Postwar Japan*, Ithaca and London: Cornell University Press.
Katzenstein, P. J. and Okawara, N. (1993) 'Japan's national security: structures, norms, and policies', *International Security* 17(4): 84–118.
Kyodo News (2010) 'Japan not eyeing dispatch of SDF to Korea in case of contingencies', 13 December; accessed at http://www.thefreelibrary.com/Japan+not+eyeing+dispatch+of+SDF+to+Korea+in+case+of+contingencies.-a0244167273
Lynn, H. G. (2006) 'Vicarious traumas: television and public opinion in Japan's North Korea policy', *Pacific Affairs* 79(3): 483–508.
McNeill, D. (2011) 'Japan must develop nuclear weapons, warns Tokyo governor', *The Independent*, 8 March; accessed at http://www.independent.co.uk/news/world/asia/japan-must-develop-nuclear-weapons-warns-tokyo-governor-2235186.html
Ministry of Defense (2006–2013) *Defense of Japan*, Tokyo: Ministry of Defense; accessed at http://www.mod.go.jp/e/publ/w_paper/index.html
Mouffe, Chantal (2000) 'Politics and passions: the stakes of democracy', *Ethical Perspectives* 7(2–3): 146–50.
Nakanishi, T. (2002) 'Kitachōsen no kaku kara kokka to kokumin o mamoreru no ka' [Can we protect our nation and people from the North Korean nuclear weapons?], *Seiron* 12 (December): 46–56.
Nikkan berita (2009) '"Rachi to kokubō" de shinpojiumu Kazokukai jimukyokuchō Masumotoshi, Tokutei shissōsha chōsakai daihyō Arakishira' [Kazokukai Secretary General Masumoto and representative from the Commission on Missing Japanese Probably Related to North Korea, Araki, (participate in) the symposium on 'Abductions and National Defence'], 3 March; accessed at http://www.nikkanberita.com/read.cgi?id=200903031356022
Nishimura, S. and Ishihara, S. (2002) 'Kitachōsen 1: yatta na!! Ada o utte yaritai! "Rachi sasatsu" o yare!' [North Korea 1: (they) killed (them)!! (We) want to

take revenge! Carry out an 'abduction investigation!'], *Shokun!* 12 (November): 24–37.
Nishioka, T. (2002) *Rachi kazoku to no 6 nen sensō: teki wa Nihon ni mo ita* [(My) Six-Year Long Battle Together with the Abduction Families: There Were Enemies Also in Japan], Tokyo: Fusōsha.
Nishioka, T. (2009) 'Nani o tamerau! Nihon dokuji no tsuika seisai o dankō seyō' [What are (you) waiting for?! Let's carry out additional sanctions unilaterally], *Seiron* 2 (February): 128–37.
Nishioka, T. and Hasuike, T. (2004) 'Tanaka Makiko no bōgen ga "Kita" o ri suru' [Tanaka Makiko's wild remarks benefit 'the North'], *Shokun!* 1 (January): 82–92.
Orr, J. J. (2001) *The Victim as Hero: Ideologies of Peace and National Identity in Postwar Japan*, Honolulu: University of Hawaii Press.
Ōta, M. (2004) 'Hankitachōsen hōdō o hitobito wa reisei ni miteita: media wa kakuitsutekina rachi kyanpēn kara dasseyo' [People calmly watched the anti-North Korea coverage: media, break away from the standardised abduction campaign], *Ronza* 8 (August): 58–63.
Reizei, A. (2010) 'Chōsen hantō yūji no sai ni, jieitai ni yoru hōjin kyūshutsu wa kanō ka?' [Is it possible to rescue Japanese (citizens) with the SDF during an emergency on the Korean Peninsula?], *Newsweek Japan*, 7 December; accessed at http://www.newsweekjapan.jp/reizei/2010/12/post-236.php
Repo, J. (2008) 'A feminist reading of gender and national memory at the Yasukuni Shrine, *Japan Forum* 20(2): 219–43.
Ross, A. A. G. (2006) 'Coming in from the cold: constructivism and emotions', *European Journal of International Relations* 12(2): 197–222.
Rumelili, B. (2004) 'Constructing identity and relating to difference: understanding the EU's mode of differentiation', *Review of International Studies* 30(1): 27–47.
Sakurai, Y. (2008) *Watashi wa Kimu Jon Iru to no tatakai o yamenai: beichū no yūwa seisaku ni mo makenai* [I won't stop my battle against Kim Jong-il: nor will (I) give in to the appeasement policy of the US and China], Tokyo: Bungei shunjū.
Sakurai, Y. (2012) 'Needed: revision of Japan's Constitution to resolve the North Korean abduction issue', *Sakurai Yoshiko Official Website*, 6 November; accessed at http://en.yoshiko-sakurai.jp/2012/11/06/4964
Samuels, R. J. (2010) 'Kidnapping politics in East Asia', *Journal of East Asian Studies* 10(2): 363–95.
Sankei shimbun (2012) 'Dai 2 bu 9.17 o kenshō suru (4) "seijōka" ariki no seifu, Abe shi wa kaya no soto' [Part 2: verifying 9/17 (4) government insistent on 'normalization' (with North Korea) (kept) Abe out of the loop], 20 September; accessed at http://sankei.jp.msn.com/politics/news/120920/plc12092009570008-n1.htm
Shigemura, T. (2002) *Saishin Kitachōsen dētabukku* [The newest data book on North Korea], Tokyo: Kōdansha.
Shūkan bunshun (2002) 'Hachinin o mikoroshi ni shita seijika, kanryo, genronnin: isshi motte daizai o shase' [The politicians, bureaucrats and debaters who have stood by and watched eight (abductees) die: atone for your great sins through death], *Shūkan Bunshun* 4(38): 38–41.
Soeya, Y. (2005) *Nihon no 'midoru pawā' gaikō* [Japan's 'middle power' diplomacy], Tokyo: Chikuma shobō.
Son, K. Y. (2010) 'Constructing fear: how the Japanese state mediates risks from North Korea', *Japan Forum* 22(1/2): 169–94.

Sono, A. (2002) 'Shinchoha chishikijin: muhansei mogenroku' [The North Korea friendly intellectuals: a record of (their) insensitive, careless remarks], *Bungei shunju* 11(November): 160.

Sukūkai (2003) 'Heisei 15 nen shūgiin senkyo rikkōhosha ankēto kekka' [Results from the questionnaire (distributed to) the candidates in the Lower House election of 2003], accessed at http://www.sukuukai.jp/H15enquete/

Sukūkai (2009) 'Rachi mondai ni kan suru sōsenkyo zenrikkōhosha tōsensha ankēto kekka hōkoku' [Announcement of the results from the questionnaire about the abduction issue (distributed to) all the candidates and elected candidates in the general election]; accessed at http://www.sukuukai.jp/H21enquete_result/

Sukūkai (2010) 'Kitachōsen no Kankoku hōgeki ni kōgi shi rachi higaisha kyūshutsu ni banzen no sonae o motomeru kinkyū shūkai hōkoku' [Report from the extraordinary meeting which protested against North Korea's shelling of South Korea and demanded emergency preparations for the rescue of the abduction victims], 7 December; accessed at http://www.sukuukai.jp/mailnews/item_2416.html

Takashima, N. (2006) *Rachi mondai de yugamu Nihon no minshushugi: ishi o nageru nara watashi ni nageya* [Japan's democracy which is distorted due to the abduction issue: if (you) are going to throw stones, throw them at me], Tokyo: Supēsu kaya.

Tanaka, H. (2009) *Gaikō no chikara* [The power of diplomacy], Tokyo: Nihon keizai shimbun shuppansha.

Togo, K. (2012) 'Japanese national identity: evolution and prospects', in G. Rozman (ed) *East Asian National Identities: Common Roots and Chinese Exceptionalism*, Stanford, CA: Stanford University Press, pp. 147–68.

Vogel, S. (2004) 'Rachi mondai ni gaikō o "rachi" saseru na' [Don't let diplomacy become 'abducted' by the abduction issue], *Newsweek Japan*, 23 July, p. 11.

Wada, H. (2004) 'Rachi sareta kokuron o dasshite' [Break free from the abducted public opinion], *Sekai* 1 (January): 248–61.

Wakamiya, K. (2004) Shinsō: Kitachōsen rachi higaisha no kodomotachi wa ikanishite Nihon ni kikan shita ka [The truth: how the children of the abduction victims were returned to Japan], Tokyo: Asuka shinsha.

Wendt, A. (1998) 'On constitution and causation in International Relations', *Review of International Studies* 24(5): 101–18.

Williams, B. and Mobrand, E. (2010) 'Explaining divergent responses to the North Korean abductions issue in Japan and South Korea', *The Journal of Asian Studies* 69(2): 507–36.

Yomiuri shimbun (2002a) 'Rachi mondai: Doi shamintōshu ga chinsha, "tsuikyū fujūbun"' [The abduction issue: SDP leader Doi apologises, '(we) did not pursue (the abduction issue) sufficiently'], 8 October; accessed thorugh Yomidasu Rekishikan at https://database.yomiuri.co.jp/rekishikan/

Yomiuri shimbun (2002b) 'Rachi mondai: Doi, shamintōshu ga chinsha, "rachi" meguru kako wa kienai' [The abduction issue: SDP leader Doi apologises, but the past surrounding the 'abductions' won't go away], 11 October; accessed thorugh Yomidasu Rekishikan at https://database.yomiuri.co.jp/rekishikan/

The rise of the Chinese 'Other' in Japan's construction of identity: Is China a focal point of Japanese nationalism?

Shogo Suzuki

Abstract Since 1945, the United States (US) has served as a focal point of both Left-wing and Right-wing Japanese nationalism. Both sides argued that the US was an arrogant hegemon that unjustly robbed Japan of its autonomy, and prevented Japan from achieving its own ideal national identity. Both sides frequently demanded that Japan should be more 'resolute' and resist unfair demands emanating from the US. In recent years, however, both camps are increasingly using the same rhetoric to criticise the Japanese government's China policy. China is also being depicted as an overbearing state that unfairly browbeats Japan into making diplomatic concessions. Given the similarities between the portrayal of China and the US, has China now become a nationalist focal point for *both* the Japanese Left and Right? Utilising constructivist insights, this article seeks to shed light on this question, by examining how the Japanese Right and Left portray China, and explores the implications for Japan's China policy.

Introduction

The recent squabbling between China and Japan over the ownership of the disputed Senkaku/Diaoyu Islands has plunged Sino-Japanese relations into another cycle of mistrust and tension. There have been all too familiar anti-Japanese outbursts throughout China, which even resulted in the attack of the Japanese ambassador's vehicle. In Japan, politicians from both the Liberal Democratic Party (LDP) and the Democratic Party of Japan (DPJ) responded by making repeated statements that China would, and should, be dealt with in a 'resolute manner (*kizen to shita taido*)', a term that has effectively come to denote a tougher stance towards China.

This determination to deal with China in a 'resolute manner' is usually understood to mark a departure from Japan's perceived 'subservient' diplomacy (often known as *yowagoshi gaikō* or 'kowtow diplomacy', *dogeza gaikō*) vis-à-vis China, and is something that has become increasingly prominent in Japanese debates pertaining to Sino-Japanese relations. China is depicted as an irrational or arrogant state that frequently tries to intimidate the 'weak' Japanese state into making diplomatic concessions. In 2010, Prime Minister Kan Naoto came under heavy fire for his 'diplomatic defeat' when the captain of the fishing boat that had collided with a Japanese Coast Guard vessel was released and deported back to China (*Asahi* 2010c: 4). That such criticisms are not solely aimed at criticising the DPJ government can be discerned from the fact that certain LDP politicians have also been charged with 'fawning' to Beijing (Yamagiwa 2006: 76–89). In contrast, politicians seen to be 'tough' on China have been praised, regardless of their party political affiliations: for instance, then DPJ leader Maehara Seiji's statement that the People's Republic of China (PRC) was a 'realistic threat' was highly praised by the *Yomiuri Shimbun*, which stated that it was important to 'demonstrate a *resolute* posture [towards China] in order to protect [Japanese] national interests (*Yomiuri* 2005: 3, emphasis added). Such discourses have conventionally been seen as typical of the Japanese Idealist Right,[1] which has long been resentful of Japan's perceived diplomatic weakness and the post-Second World War international order that has kept Japan this way (Suzuki 2011). The Japanese Left, in contrast, has traditionally tended to see China as a 'victim' of Japanese past aggression, and rarely regarded the PRC as a country that Japan had to stand up to. If anything, China's special status as one of the key victims of Japanese imperialism meant that Beijing's wishes had to be given special consideration, and ultimately accommodated.

There are signs that this traditional status quo may be changing, however. While it is true that the Japanese Right (particularly its Idealist wing) remains the more vociferous party demanding that Japan opposes the 'high-handed' PRC, there are increasing calls from the Japanese Left that Japan adopt a more 'resolute' attitude towards Beijing as well. Furthermore, the Left now increasingly depicts China in a similar fashion to that of the Right: as a bullying state that attempts to force Japan into making unjust compromises with China. Interestingly, these characterisations of China have certain parallels with how the United States (US) has been depicted by both the Right and Left camps in Japan. The US has frequently (if not exclusively) been a nationalist focal point for the Japanese Left and Right, and both sides have argued that the Americans have unjustly robbed Japan of its autonomy, and prevented Japan from achieving its own ideal national identity. Both sides frequently demanded that Japan should be more 'resolute' and resist unfair demands emanating from the US. Given the similarities between the portrayal of China and the US, has China now become a nationalist focal point for *both* the Japanese Left and Right? How do both sides portray China? Do the Left and Right's depictions of China share similar characteristics with their portrayals of the US? What are the implications for this for Japan's China policy?

This article attempts to provide some answers to this question by making use of a broadly constructivist framework which emphasises the role that 'Others' play in the formation of a social actor's identity (Bukh 2010; Suzuki 2007; Hagström, forthcoming; Neumann 1999). Constructivist scholars have noted that identities are shaped through the construction of 'Others' whose differences from the 'Self' are emphasised. This framework is particularly suited to our analysis for a number of reasons. First, this framework does not assume that identities and 'Others' are static, and as such allows us to examine the evolving dynamics of 'Othering' that is so integral to identity formation. Second, the theory does not assume the existence of a singular 'Other', which is in line with the fact that Japan's 'Others' have included states such as Russia and the US.

The findings of this article suggest a number of new developments that could have important implications for Sino-Japanese relations. First, it indicates that Japan's relations with China have become a nationalist focal point for both Left and Right, insofar as both sides demand that Japan resist China to protect Japanese national interests. In his study of Sino-Japanese relations in the 1980s, Ijiri Hidenori argued that the Japanese adopted 'a "low posture" because they retain their sense of guilt in relation to China for misdeeds during the Sino-Japanese War' (Ijiri 1996: 61). Japan's immoral past resulted in the emergence – at least among some quarters of the Left – of a 'victimising Self' and a 'victimised' Chinese 'Other'. This meant that being assertive towards the PRC would be deemed 'arrogant' and inappropriate for a country that owed the Chinese a large moral debt. The sense of a 'victimising Self' vis-à-vis China remains to this very day. However, it is increasingly clear that the PRC cannot be considered as an 'Other' that only serves to highlight Japanese aggressiveness and immorality.

Second, given nationalism's intimate connection to national identity, the convergence of the Left's and Right's images of China indicate that the PRC could be emerging as a 'common Other' in both sides' attempts to construct Japan's identity. This 'common Other' used to be the US, as both Idealists of the Right and Left agreed that the US was an arrogant hegemon that forced Japan to adopt policies that were in direct opposition to their respective images of a desirable Japanese 'Self'. Just as they did with the US, both the Left and Right use the Chinese 'Other' for different ends. The Idealist Right camp points to the PRC's use of the 'history card' and high-handed manner in territorial disputes to highlight Japan's 'weakness' and 'subservient' identity, thus pushing for their pet project of rearming Japan and embarking on a more independent security policy. China must be confronted as a matter of principle in order to overcome this 'emasculated' identity that has characterised the post-war Japanese state. The Left, in contrast, use a 'bullying China' to highlight Japan's 'moral' and 'peaceful' nature, thus emphasising the need for Japan not to stray off its post-1945 pathway of development. Whatever one's political colours may be, one thing seems certain: China has become a 'bullying Other' that Japan needs to be more assertive towards, and there is less need for Japan to pay attention to Beijing's 'amoral' demands. On the contrary, it is important for Japan to resist them.

The article proceeds as follows. It will first attempt to contextualise the Chinese 'common Other' between the Japanese Left and Right by briefly examining the case of the US. It will then examine how both the Left and Right camps have 'Othered' China in recent years. Particular attention is paid to the Japanese Left's evolving construction of the Chinese 'Other', which to date has remained relatively underexplored in the literature. The article does so primarily by examining various debates on Sino-Japanese disputes by both conservative and liberal Japanese newspapers and journal articles in the 1980s and 2000s. The 1980s is an interesting period, as political tensions between the two states began to emerge after the initial 'honeymoon period' that followed diplomatic normalisation in 1972. A comparison of how Japanese policies towards China were debated at times of bilateral controversies gives us some insight into the evolving constructions of China as an 'Other' in Japan's identity formation, and how this has informed Japanese foreign policy vis-à-vis China. Articles critical of China have typically been published by Idealist Right writers and politicians who may not always have represented the views of mainstream moderate conservatives in Japan. However, they are an important component of steadily growing voices critical of China and Japan's China policy, and their influence is arguably on the increase within the ruling LDP. They thus have the ability to shape – if not directly influence – Japan's future policies towards the PRC, and are therefore worthy of analysis in their own right. Newspapers are useful for two reasons. First, they can serve as 'opinion leaders' and play a crucial role in shaping the public's policy preferences (Shinoda 2007: 175; cf. Hagström and Williamsson 2009: 249). Second, insofar as newspapers must be able to sell (this pressure is arguably stronger today, given the increasing competition newspapers face from the digital media), they are also more likely to be sensitive to the 'general mood' of their targeted leadership. They are therefore a useful means to gauge broader public perceptions of Japan's China policy and perceptions of Japan's future identity.

Japan's national identity: some starting points

Like many other social actors, Japan has been ascribed multiple identities, and debates over national identity have tended to turn on a 'Left–Right' political axis. However, it has not always been clear as to what exactly these terms mean in the Japanese context. While an exhaustive and precise definition of the 'Right' and 'Left' lies beyond the scope of this article, it may be worth offering a brief 'working definition' of these two camps in the Japanese context.

Unlike many western democracies, where the 'Left' and 'Right' tend to diverge over the degree to which the collective should be responsible for the welfare of the individual (Downs 1957; Duverger 1954), in Japan, the political 'Right' and 'Left' have traditionally been differentiated on the basis of their attitudes towards rearmament and Article 9 of the Constitution. The Right can be broadly divided further into two branches, the Idealist and Moderate. The Idealist Right believes that the post-1945 political status quo made Japan 'abnormal', and that 'the true path towards normality is the removal of constitutional prohibitions on the use of force, ...the equalisation of roles in the Japan-US alliance and the eventual abrogation of the security treaty with the US' (Hughes 2004: 51). Notable individuals who are associated with this group include Kishi Nobusuke, Hatoyama Ichirō, and more recently Ishihara Shintarō. The moderates (such as Yoshida Shigeru, Takeshita Noboru, or Miyazawa Kiichi), on the other hand, are seen as more closely adhering to the Yoshida Doctrine, and regard the Japan–US security alliance as the main pillar of Japanese foreign/security policy and are more cautious about Japanese rearmament.

The Left can similarly be divided into Idealist and Moderate groups. The Idealist Left's ultimate goal was the upholding of Article 9, and they were thus committed to the idea of abandoning the Japan–US Security Alliance, and declaring unarmed neutrality (*hibusō chūritsu*). The Idealists, who were a powerful force in the then Japan Socialist Party and Japanese Communist Party, remained dominant in the Japanese Left until the end of the Cold War. Today, the previous views of the Idealist Left are increasingly seen as 'too anachronistic in an era of changing security challenges that demanded a more proactive response from Japan' (Hughes 2004: 54). Today, the Japanese Left is dominated by Moderates (which consisted of elements of the Rightist Socialist Party of Japan and the Democratic Socialist Party during the Cold War period), who are committed to liberal democracy and support (at least for the time being) the Japan–US Security Alliance.

The US as a common 'Other'

Since the end of the Second World War, debates on Japanese national identity have been frequently depicted as revolving around the issue of Japan's 'pacifist' identity and its security policy, with controversy raging over whether or not Japan should become a 'normal' state with an independent military, or carve out a niche for itself by closely adhering to the spirit of Article 9 of the Constitution (Berger 1996; Katzenstein 1998). While these discourses are (and continue to be) important, what is often missed is the fact that the fundamental issue undergirding these discussions has frequently been about constructing an identity of Japan as an 'autonomous state'. Whatever one's political colours were, debates surrounding Article 9 were intimately linked to a persistent fear that Japan had a 'weak' and 'subservient' identity that allowed it to be dominated by foreign powers.

The construction of a 'weak' 'self' entails the construction of a 'dominating' 'Other'. The multitude of Japanese 'Selves' in Japanese discourses means that there have been a number of important 'Others' (Bukh 2010). In the context of debates over Japan's 'subservient' identity, however, the US arguably served as a key focal point. This was perhaps inevitable, as the US played a crucial role in shaping Japan's postwar political development, and continues to be a major actor not only in Japan's security and foreign policy, but also in the international relations of the Asia-Pacific region.

Although we should be cautious in making sweeping generalisations, a number of characteristics seem to stand out in these discourses. First, Japan's security and foreign policy was believed to be excessively weak, and this was symbolised by Japan's heavy reliance on the US to provide for its security. This was seen as an embarrassment unbefitting an independent sovereign state. Furthermore, Japan's security dependence on the US was seen to result in an excessively deferential foreign policy to Washington (Ishihara 2012: 366). While it is easy to associate such aspirations for 'Japan to function as a truly independent sovereign state' with the Idealist Right (Hughes 2004: 51), it is important to note that some of these sentiments overlapped with the nationalism espoused by both the Moderate Right and the Idealist Left. Yoshida Shigeru, the architect of the so-called 'Yoshida Doctrine', believed that Japan should eventually possess its own independent military if it wanted to be a 'first-rate power (*ittōkoku*)' (Ōtake 2005: 88–89), and other politicians often perceived to be 'pro-America' (*shinbei*) have at times also demonstrated their nationalistic resistance to what they perceived as undue American pressure towards Japan (Kitaoka 2008: 287). For its part, the Idealist Left shared an interesting (and perhaps ironic) common desire for an 'autonomous' identity for Japan, albeit for very different reasons. The Idealist Left was, of course, less concerned with Japan's lack of an independent military. Their anger was rather directed towards Japan's conservative leaders' inability to assert an independent, pacifist path of development because of their servile attitude towards Washington. They consequently accused the US of restricting Japan's independence and of using it as a pawn in America's Cold War strategy, which forced it down the path of remilitarisation (Oguma 1998: 522–531).

Thus, whatever one's political colours, a common ground of debate about Japanese identity was Japan–US relations. The US was frequently seen by both the Right and Left camps as an overbearing, 'bullying' state

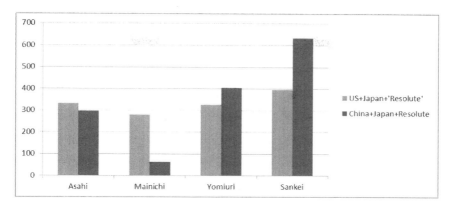

Chart 1. Comparison of the total number of articles (headlines and content) containing the words 'US', 'Japan' and 'Resolute'; and 'China', 'Japan' and 'Resolute', 1992–2012.

that denied Japan's sense of self-worth (Oguma 1998: 273–280). In this sense, then, Japan's relations with the US was (implicitly and explicitly) a focal point of Japan's post-war identity. Resisting America – in other words, taking a 'resolute stance' – was important to highlight Japan's identity either as a 'strong, independent power' and/or a 'pacifist state' that was fundamentally different from the US. At times, Japan's relations with the US could become a highly politicised issue that would feature prominently in political struggles, most notably in the violent demonstrations over the renewal of the Japan–US Security Treaty of 1960. This overlap between conservative and progressive camps arguably persists to this day. Chart 1 shows the number of articles that included the words 'Japan', 'America (*beikoku*)' and the word 'resolute (*kizen*)', which is a word frequently bandied about by critics whenever Japan is seen to have capitulated to foreign pressure, and is frequently used in the context of Sino-Japanese relations nowadays. It is particularly interesting to note that the more left-leaning *Asahi Shimbun* (333 articles) carried a higher number of articles and headlines than the conservative (but moderate and pro-American) *Yomiuri Shimbun*, and actually comes second behind the more hawkish *Sankei Shimbun* (395 articles), which is often seen as being representative of the Idealist Right voices who call for Japan to overcome the legacy of Japan's military defeat in 1945, remilitarise and establish a more equal relationship with the US.

The rise of China as Japan's 'Other': the case of the Japanese Idealist Right

Recent debates among the Idealist Right on how Japan should deal with China have interesting parallels with debates on Japan–US relations, and suggest that China is now an 'Other' with equal importance to America. The first similarity between China and the US is that they are seen to be perpetuating Japan's servile foreign policy. It is interesting to note that such voices were already visible at the time of the normalisation of Sino-Japanese diplomatic relations, when the Idealist Right criticised Prime Minister Tanaka Kakuei for rushing to establish relations with the PRC almost entirely on the latter's terms (Hoppens 2012: 48). Yet, it is arguable that the 'Othering' of China as an arrogant, overbearing state that robs Japan of its autonomy has increasingly become a particular pet project of the Japanese Idealist Right since the 1980s, when political disputes (particularly those stemming from the 'history issue') between China and Japan came to the fore. Commentators such as Nakajima Mineo (1986, 1987), for example, criticised the Japanese government for their 'deceitful (*giman teki*)' and 'servile (*hikutsu na*)' responses to Beijing's complaints against Prime Minister Nakasone Yasuhiro's visit to Yasukuni Shrine in 1985, which they considered to be undue Chinese interference in what was essentially a Japanese domestic matter. Despite the changes that have taken place within the Japanese Left (as we will see below) since the 2000s, this use of an arrogant 'Chinese Other' to call for the construction of a stronger, more independent Japan is still a tendency that is more prominent among the Idealist Right than the Left. This can be seen from Chart 1, which shows that the *Sankei Shimbun* carries by far the highest number of articles that contain the keywords 'Japan', 'China' and 'Resolute (*kizen*)'.

For the Idealist Right, the use of a Chinese 'Other' is useful because the rise of the PRC presents them with a 'window of opportunity' to call for their long-standing agenda of breaking free from the shackles of Japan's post-war political order. China's opaque military spending, coupled with increasing excursions of Chinese vessels and aircraft close to Japanese territory, has caused increasing anxiety in Japan. This of course dovetails with the Idealist Right's long-standing agenda of enhancing Japanese military power. Furthermore, Beijing's frequent (and often strategic) reminders that Japan should not forget their imperialist past has only fuelled the Idealist Right's antipathy towards the PRC, as the latter is seen as being part of a plot to perpetuate Japan's 'self-loathing' and keep it permanently weak (Suzuki 2011).

China also gets depicted as an immoral and inferior state with fundamentally different values from Japan, in a similar fashion to past representations of the US. Minister of Economy, Trade and Industry, Nakagawa Shōichi, for instance, has alluded to Beijing's lack of gratitude for Japan's help in constructing infrastructure. Nakagawa cited reports that sex shops had been allowed to set up shops in Beijing's Sino-Japanese Youth Exchange Centre (Nakagawa 2005: 37), thus insinuating that China throws gestures of friendship back in Japan's face by allowing immoral commercial activities to take place in a building built with Japanese money. China's economic growth is at times also derided as being 'unethical', because it is built on the basis of being good at making fake goods (Fukada and Kusano 2001: 199). Chinese foreign policy is also described as 'childish' and 'irrational' (Tanizawa 2005: 359). For instance, Beijing's range of sanctions announced in the wake of the 2010 Senkaku/Diaoyu incident were described as 'abnormal (*iyō*)' in a *Sankei* editorial (2010b). Although such views of the US are perhaps less visible today, representations of a similarly 'irrational' or 'morally inferior' America did exist in the not too distant past. During the height of Japan–US trade disputes in the late 1980s and early 1990s, the West (including the US) was described by the Idealist Right as 'racist' (Ikeda and Aida 1990: 130–139) or 'hysterical' (Ishihara 2012). There were also claims that the US trade deficit derived from negative qualities in American politics and society, such as 'undisciplined financial policies, falling quality of labour and [unrealistic] desires for a higher standard of living, which paid scant regard to resource [consumption] and trade deficits' (*Asahi* 1989: 5). Even then Prime Minister Nakasone got himself into trouble by indirectly suggesting in 1986 that the reasons for American 'decline' were to do with its multiethnic society Rowen (1986: a25), which implied that American society was somehow inferior compared to Japan.

The rise of China as Japan's 'Other': the case of the Japanese Left

It is arguable that the Japanese liberals have also 'Othered' China in the past, albeit for very different political reasons. Traditionally, the Japanese Idealist Left's political goals were the construction of a 'pacifist' Japan that had made a clean break from its imperialist past. It was Japan's servility vis-à-vis the US that was bringing Japan closer to rearmament. Any domestic and international attempts to revive the political institutions or the ideology of the pre-1945 era were therefore to be resisted. China provided an excellent 'Other' to this end. China served as a 'positive Other', as a state that had constructed an independent national identity. Intellectuals such as Takeuchi Yoshimi argued in 1948 that the Chinese had carved out a uniquely Chinese pathway to modernisation by successfully resisting western (and Japanese) imperialism. In contrast, Japan's servile, weak national identity had made it follow the path of slavish westernisation, which only ended in war and utter devastation (Hoppens 2012: 62). The Idealist Left also constructed a 'victimised' China that would help in the construction of a 'remilitarising' or an 'unrepentant' Japan. By doing so, the Idealist Left could remind the public of the dangers of remilitarisation, and resist American and conservative attempts to incorporate Japan into American hegemony (Yamamoto 1987: 49–50).

China's positive image as a state that resisted American domination was damaged when it invaded Vietnam in 1979. Many progressives expressed their dismay that China appeared to be behaving just like any other Great Power. As noted by Robert Hoppens (2014):

> Chinese nationalism was now seen as atavistic and dangerous, as threatening to plunge an emerging liberal international order back into a modernist state system governed by military force. Interestingly, this view of the PRC was very similar to that presented by conservatives.

These events, however, did not take away from the historical reality of Japan's invasion of China. Therefore, China's identity as the 'victimised Other' remained relatively stable in the context of Sino-Japanese relations. Indeed, even at times of political disputes between China and Japan, the Idealist Left was quick to criticise the way in which the Japanese government handled its China policy. During the 1982 textbook issue, for instance, the Idealist Left did not charge Beijing with interfering in Japanese domestic affairs, and instead saw the PRC's objections as reasonable (Rose 1998: 158–160). Even at times when the Idealist Left disagreed with Beijing's policies towards Japan, China's identity as a 'victim' remained intact. One particular instance was the 1987 *Kokaryō* Case, where the Osaka High Court ruled that the Republic of China in Taiwan had legal ownership of the *Kokaryō* student dormitory in Kyoto, as the 'building was not a diplomatic asset and therefore did not belong to [the People's Republic of] China, despite Japan's 1972 switching of diplomatic recognition from Taiwan to China' (Ijiri 1996: 73). Beijing complained that this went against the 1972 Sino-Japanese communiqué, and Deng Xiaoping warned against the rise of 'Japanese militarism' and foreign elements plotting to take over Taiwan once more (*Asahi* 1987a: 5).

Deng's remarks, however, were seen as interference with Japan's constitutional principle of the separation of judiciary, executive and legislative powers. It was met with some resistance, even within the Left. In an editorial that took the form of a letter to 'Respected Mr. Deng Xiaoping', the *Asahi Shimbun* explained that 'even the government cannot interfere with the legal process [in Japan]', and the separation of powers was 'adopted because of our own bitter experiences of being criticised for "militarism" when a small handful of those in power went out of control'. The editorial went on to state that 'if our two countries, with different societal systems, are to get on with each other on a long-term basis, we need to acknowledge each other's stances' (*Asahi* 1987a: 5).

However, the *Asahi* quickly became less critical of Beijing when the Chinese took offense at a Japanese diplomat's suggestion that Deng's lack of appreciation for Japan's political system was because he was misinformed by his aides and had 'become a man above the clouds (*kumo no ue no hito*)'. Beijing mistook the comment as implying that Deng had become senile, and claimed that the remarks were reminiscent of pre-1945 Japanese arrogance towards China. In their editorial on 6 June 1987, the *Asahi* (1987b: 5 emphasis added) seemed to take note of Deng's remarks when they wrote:

> ...we need to understand the weight of the problems [suggested by Deng]. The Japanese military inflicted huge damages in a total war that lasted eight years....perhaps we need to ask ourselves whether or not we are too insensitive (*donkan*) towards the pain still felt by *those we victimised*.

While the *Asahi* in principle agrees that China needs a better understanding of Japan's democratic system, we can see here that China's identity as the 'victimised Other' is strengthened once more, and the possibility that *Japan* may be the 'victim' of unreasonable Chinese demands is not seriously considered. The *Asahi* (1987c: 5) repeated this argument further in another editorial on 1 July 1987. While repeating its call for China to understand that Japan is a democracy, the newspaper argued:

> We need to reflect on whether or not we are arrogant [towards China]. Ever since Japan became strong economically, we have tended to receive international criticism for being 'ill-mannered'. Did we not start economic cooperation with China on the understanding that 'China hasn't asked for reparations from us, so we should cooperate with them as much as possible in order to show our gratitude'?

However, the tendency to construct a 'victimised' Chinese other may be changing among the Japanese Left. As Chart 1 indicates, the increasing mention of Japanese 'resoluteness' in Sino-Japanese relations in Left-leaning media outlets like the *Asahi Shimbun* may suggest that there is a gradual rise of a Chinese 'Other' that is seen as a threat to the consolidation of an independent Japanese 'Self', and that this 'Other' may no longer be something that is constructed exclusively by the Idealist Right. If the American 'Other' was depicted as an overbearing hegemon that denied Japan its rightful status as an independent, equal power, then China is now increasingly seen as an arrogant, even deranged country that thinks its rise to power entitles it to make unreasonable demands to Japan. The *Mainichi Shimbun* editorial, on 28 September 2010, described China's demand for compensation and an apology for detaining the fishing boat captain as both 'unreasonable (*rifujin*)' and 'astounding (*azen to saserareta*)' (*Mainichi* 2010b: 5; cf. *Sankei* 2010a). The *Asahi Shimbun* (2010a: 1) also stated that the PRC's behaviour resembled that of 'great power-ism (*taikoku shugi*)', a term closely associated with hegemonic behaviour.

These depictions stand in interesting contrast to those of the 1980s. One of the most prominent differences is that the PRC is no longer uncritically seen as the 'victim' of any disputes between China and Japan. In the 1980s, the PRC's complaints towards Japan were not seen as 'irrational', even though the Left did not always agree with them. China's special status as a 'victim' needed to be respected. Today, this appears to be less the case. Instead, Japan is being seen increasingly as a 'victim' of heavy-handed Chinese diplomacy, as the various debates surrounding the Senkaku/Diaoyu disputes of 2010 discussed in this article show.

Interestingly, this change can also be seen (albeit subtly) even in cases where Japanese politicians have clearly made insensitive or controversial remarks with regard to the 'history issue'. This frequently happens when there are debates surrounding the interpretation of Japan's imperialist past. When LDP Diet member and cabinet minister Okuno Seisuke stated in May 1988 that Japan had not intended to invade the Asia-Pacific in WWII (*Mainichi* 1988: 1), the *Asahi* (1988a: 3, 1988b: 5) pointed out that such remarks harmed post-war Japan's fundamental stance of showing remorse for victimising Asian states and peoples. It also warned readers that Japan's economic growth could have made Japan look arrogant.

However, when the then Air Defence Force Chief of Staff Tamogami Toshio (2008) claimed twenty years later that the Sino-Japanese War of 1931–45 was a result of a Chinese conspiracy, the Left-leaning media's views were subtly different. Tamogami had claimed that Japan had been dragged into a military conflict by Chiang Kai-shek, so it was *Japan* that was actually the victim. As can be expected, the Left-leaning media were highly critical of Tamogami's remarks, and disagreed with his interpretation of history. The bulk of their criticism, however, was directed towards 'the breakdown of civilian control', where the government was unable to control a military officer from making irresponsible remarks that would harm Japan's national interests. While these editorials did not endorse Tamogami's view of Japanese 'victimhood', neither did they go out of their way to reproduce *Chinese* victimhood as they had in the past, even though the Chinese government did express their 'shock and indignation' that a 'serving high-ranking military officer had openly distorted history' (*Zhongguo Wang* 2008). The *Mainichi* editorial of 28 December 2008, for instance, did not mention the need for Japan to pay special attention to Chinese feelings. The *Asahi* editorial on 2 November 2008 did note that the PRC and South Korea have been somewhat concerned about the Self-Defence Forces, but it concentrated more on the domestic political problems that allowed Tamogami to become Chief of Staff in the first place (*Asahi* 2008: 3; *Mainichi* 2008: 5).

The rise of a 'bullying' Chinese 'Other' in the Japanese Left

There are a number of factors that explain this construction of an 'arrogant' or 'bullying' Chinese 'Other' within the Left camp, which until recently tended to stick to a more 'victimised' Chinese 'Other'. With the end of the Cold War, the argument that the 'American Other' was dragging Japan into unnecessary rearmament for its own selfish 'strategic goals' became more difficult to sustain. Furthermore, the end of the East–West confrontation in Europe had the effect of shifting the focus onto Asia's own security issues. Japan was perceived as facing an increasing number of security challenges (such as China's military spending or the North Korean nuclear issue) as a result, and this meant that the construction of a 'peaceful' Japanese national identity in the form of an unarmed, neutral state came to be seen as both unrealistic and politically unappealing.

In addition to these changes in the international environment, societal change within Japan seems to have contributed to the emergence of a Chinese 'Other' different from the one that was constructed in the 1980s by the Idealist Left.[2] The end of the Cold War resulted in the collapse of the Idealist Left as a viable political force. Today, the diminished Japanese Left is dominated by Moderates who are committed to liberal democracy and support the Japanese Defence Force and the Japan–US Security Alliance (at least for the time being).[3] The Moderate Left does, to be sure, continue to be relatively sympathetic to China's 'victim' identity, even though the older generation that had feelings of guilt towards the Chinese is dying out. The Moderate Left also continues to demonstrate their resistance towards American 'domination', as seen from their opposition to US demands of 'burden sharing' during the so-called 'war against terror'. However, the 1989 Tiananmen Incident, China's nuclear tests in 1996, as well as the various disputes that have dogged Sino-Japanese relations means that there has been a growing sense that China is something fundamentally 'different' and antithetical to the Japanese 'Self'. Consequently, the Ideal Left's rosy depictions of China as an idealised, 'independent' 'Other' constructing its own brand of socialist development became less influential.

Furthermore, Takemi Keizō (2001: 89) notes the rise of a new generation of Japanese citizens 'who were born at a time when Japan was already rich and advanced', and 'neither share the older generation's inferiority complex towards the West, nor the sense of superiority towards Asia'. Takemi argues that, this new generation is less concerned about economic growth and other forms of materialism, and is committed to the ideals of 'freedom and democracy'. This means that they tend to be far more critical towards China and its various military or human rights policies than the older generations (Takemi 2001: 89). Thus, the Moderate Left's 'Chinese Other' has the following characteristics which reflect this change. First, PRC is seen as increasingly 'irrational', or as an entity that does not follow international rules and norms. Therefore, Japan's difficulties with its China policy are blamed on the PRC, because 'China is governed by the rule of men, rather than the rule of the law, and to make matters worse, it is a one-party dictatorship' (*Asahi* 2010d: 1). Even the *Asahi Shimbun*, which has long been a favourite target of the Japanese Idealist Right for allegedly being too 'pro-China' (e.g. Komori 2012), noted in the context of the 2010 Senkaku/Diaoyu dispute that Beijing's diplomacy was 'childish (*otonagenai gaikō*)' (*Asahi* 2010e: 3), and resembled that of an immature, 'probationary great power' which finds it hard to understand the 'common sense of the international community' (*Asahi* 2010d: 1; *Mainichi* 2010a: 5; also see *Mainichi* 2012: 5).

Second, China's perceived 'hard-line policies' vis-à-vis Japan have resulted in a growing sense that China engages in 'arrogant' or 'unreasonable' diplomacy to unfairly browbeat Japan. This depiction is similar to the Idealist Left's images of the US in the past, and highlights the common characteristics the Japanese Left and Right's American and Chinese 'Others' share. In the case of the Left, however, it is worth noting that the construction of a 'bullying' China means that the PRC cannot be seen simply as a weak 'victim' of Japan any longer.[4] Such thinking is visible even in issues surrounding the legacy of Japanese imperialism: while the Moderate Left continues to decry the Idealist Right's attempts to deny Japanese war crimes, there are increasing signs that even they are getting exasperated with what they see as Beijing's cynical attempts to use the 'history card' to pressurise Japan into accepting 'unreasonable' Chinese demands that would threaten Japan's national interests. In an editorial looking back on Sino-Japanese relations after Tokyo's purchasing of the Senkaku/Diaoyu Islands, the *Asahi Shimbun* (2013: 12) noted:

> What cannot be ignored is the fact that China is linking the Senkaku issue with the history issue....On 15 August [the day of Japan's surrender in 1945] the CCP newspaper *Renmin ribao* stated that the Senkaku issue was 'related to Japan's post-World War II territorial issues and that of the international order'. It appears that they are attempting to create the image of a Japan that opposes the post-War international order by illegally occupying the islands....The reason that China brings up 'history' is probably because it wants to link the Senkaku issue with Japan's invasion and colonial rule, and get the support of international opinion. Japan needs to carefully explain that the two are separate issues. On the other hand, we have to admit that Japan has allowed China to make these unreasonable claims (*rifujin na shuchō*). A typical example of this is Prime Minister Abe's remark that 'the definition of invasion has yet to be determined'....

The result is the construction of a Chinese 'negative Other' within the Left that shares interesting similarities with both the Idealist Right's image with China and the American 'Other'. The Idealist Left and Right previously shared a common nationalist agenda in that both sides agreed – to different degrees – that the US prevented Japan from exercising its rightful autonomy. If the Idealist Left's traditional agenda was to highlight a 'bullying American Other' to call for the construction of a more independent, pacifist Japanese 'Self', China has begun to complement the US as another 'bullying Other' that plays this role. China is no longer exclusively a 'weak victim' who can make moral demands on Japan. Instead, the PRC is attempting to browbeat Japan to submit to its 'unreasonable' demands, and this means that there is less need to be deferential to China. Rather, Japan should show a 'resolute' attitude in rejecting these demands, and demonstrate its autonomy.

There is another convergence with the liberals Left and the Idealist Right, primarily in the sense of 'Othering' China to emphasise Japan's 'democratic' or 'peaceful' nature. This is not exactly something new: during the Cold War, both the Japanese Right and Left made use of the Soviet 'Other' to emphasise these characteristics of Japan. As Alexander Bukh (2010: 33) notes with reference to the Right, '[t]he communist Soviet Union (as well as communist China, to a certain degree) presented an opportunity to rescue Japan's imperial history from the negative narrative of the left, which was engaged in fierce critique of Japan's recent history of authoritarianism, militarism, and imperialism'. The Soviets were seen as an unprincipled state, because they had 'betrayed' their neutrality pact with Japan to join the war at the last minute, and had caused much suffering to the Japanese through their internment of Japanese prisoners of war in Siberia. This characterisation of the Soviets as 'unethical' was shared by the Idealist Left as well, as Moscow's successive military interventions in Eastern Europe offended their support for national autonomy.

Yet, this shared 'Soviet Other' was never entirely stable, as the Idealist Left's views on the Soviet Union frequently oscillated, due to the latter's sympathies with socialism. We should also note that Japan's democratic values were less used as a key 'marker' of Japan's identity during this time. In contrast, the 'undemocratic' Chinese 'Other' is far more established among both the Right and Left camps in Japan today. Socialism and communism are no longer seen as attractive alternative ideologies, and the rising perception of China as a security risk to Japan has provided fertile ground for the emergence of an 'unethical Chinese Other'.

What kind of 'Self' is being constructed?

If China is described as an 'arrogant', 'high-handed' and 'irrational' 'Other', how does it contribute to the construction of the Japanese 'Self'? Given that the construction of a 'Self' rests on the basis of emphasising 'difference' with multiple 'Others', one obvious aspect of Japanese identity which features prominently is its 'weakness'. Japan is seen as excessively deferential to 'unreasonable' Chinese demands, and continues 'to suffer from China's interference in its internal affairs' (Yamagiwa 2006: 78). This damages Japan's own autonomy and makes China even more arrogant than before.

This identity is also emphasised to highlight policy failures that perpetuate Japan's weakness. Prime Minster Kan Naoto came under heavy criticism for his handling of the 2010 Senkaku/Diaoyu incident, and his successor Noda Yoshihiko similarly came under fire for being seen as excessively deferential to the PRC (*Sankei Nyūsu* 2013). Regardless of the validity of these claims, this demonstrates that it is now possible to score political points by criticising and highlighting the government's failures in its foreign policy towards China. This used to be the pet project of the Idealist Right, but it is important to note that the Left has also joined in criticising the government's allegedly 'weak' China diplomacy in more recent years, as epitomised by the chorus of criticisms surrounding Tokyo's handling of the 2010 Senkaku/Diaoyu dispute.

The political necessity to construct a 'weak' Japan means that the possibility of Japan coming out *better off* in its numerous diplomatic rows with China is (perhaps curiously) not often considered by both Left and Right: as noted above, the DPJ government's decision to release the Chinese captain came under sustained criticism as a 'total defeat' of Japanese diplomacy in 2010. However, it could also be interpreted that it was *Japan* that was the overall 'winner' in this diplomatic game, as it managed to secured an American statement that the Senkaku/Diaoyu Islands came under the remit of the Japan–US Security Alliance. This was arguably a positive development for Japan, which had long been dissatisfied with Washington's neutrality as regards the territorial ownership of the Islands (Hagström 2012: 286–287). One could also claim that China scored a diplomatic 'own-goal' by ending up looking like a revisionist power that would use forceful measures to solve any territorial disputes it has with its neighbours, and undoing the regional goodwill it had earned through its 'peaceful rise' strategy. The result was a growing perception that China's foreign policy had become more 'assertive', as well as Washington's 'pivot to Asia' policy, which aims to increase America's military and political influence in the region. Such alternative interpretations were ignored, however: instead, there was widespread condemnation of the Japanese government's 'naïve diplomacy (*amai gaikō*)' (*Asahi* 2010b: 3) that would 'diminish (*otoshimeru*)' the country (*Sankei* 2010b). This is indicative of a strong perception that Japan is a subservient country that allows itself to be bullied by the PRC.

Critiques of 'conciliatory' policies towards China are widespread, and not limited to times of political crises alone: the visit of a large delegation of DPJ lawmakers to China in December 2009 was attacked as 'tributary foreign policy (*chōkō gaikō*)', an obvious reference to China's hierarchical ordering of foreign policy where all non-Chinese states were seen as 'barbarous' and inherently inferior. It is clear that such discourses, while accusing Japanese politicians of making Japan look weak, are constructing and reproducing Japan's 'inferior' identity. It is also worth bearing in mind that criticising a party's/government's China policies does not favour one particular party, as the DPJ is not the only party that gets criticised by commentators who advocate a tougher line towards the PRC. Even Koizumi Jun'ichirō, who arguably took a 'strong' line against China by visiting Yasukuni Shrine in the face of Chinese protests, is criticised by Tokuoka Takao for his failure to demand an apology from Beijing when Chinese vice premier Wu Yi suddenly cancelled her meetings in Japan in 2005 (Tokuoka and Hosaka 2010: 141).

Another aspect of the Japanese 'Self' emphasised by both the Idealist Right and the Left is its moral righteousness. For a start, Japan's own identity as a state that 'behaves in accordance with international rules' is rarely questioned. The legality of Japan's claims to the Senkaku Islands is also taken for granted (*Sankei* 2010a), implying that Japan's refusal to accept 'unreasonable' Chinese claims of territorial ownership was a 'just' act. Another point of reference which points to Japan's superiority vis-à-vis China is its system of governance. During the 2010 Senkaku/Diaoyu dispute, Japanese editorials were keen to shore up this particular aspect of Japan's identity by depicting Japan as a country under the 'rule of law (*hōchi kokka*)'. An *Asahi* editorial pointed out that while China put enormous diplomatic pressure on Japan to release the Chinese captain, it was 'natural for Japan to solemnly undertake its own investigations, as it is under the rule of law' (*Asahi* 2010b: 3). Beijing's seemingly irrational overreaction to such Japanese policies, the same newspaper warned, would result in 'resentment growing among *rational* Japanese people'. While this characterisation is not necessarily intended to apply to the entire Japanese nation, it is nevertheless telling to see this quality juxtaposed next to an 'irrational' China (*Asahi* 2010a: 1). Thus, even for those who are less concerned about the political agenda of reconstructing a 'strong' Japan through remilitarisation, it is nevertheless important for Japan to resist Chinese political pressure and demonstrate Japan's autonomy vis-à-vis the PRC, because failure to do so is an affront to Japan's identity as a 'rational' or 'reasonable' identity.

Conclusion

In an article looking back on Sino-Japanese relations in 2012, the *Sankei Shimbun* noted: 'It is interesting that when critics debate how we should deal with China, their visions of Japan's image surface. The flourishing China debate is probably indicative of a lively debate about Japan's future as well' (Usui 2012). The findings of this study demonstrate that China is beginning to share interesting features with the US in this process. Just like America during the Cold War period, China is increasingly 'Othered' by both the Idealist Right and the Left as a 'bully' that denies Japan's ability to act as an independent state. It is also seen as an 'immoral' state that has fundamentally *different* values from Japan. With the end of the Cold War and growing acceptance of the Japan−US Alliance, China may have even surpassed the US to become *the* key 'common Other' used by both Left and Right for the formation of Japan's identity. The end of the Cold War and the rise of China means that the Japan−US 'social cleavage' that had long been influential in Japanese politics has ceased to exist. This means the US may no longer be the most prominent 'bullying Other' which provides a common rallying point for Japanese nationalism, even though anti-American nationalism continues to exist among both the Idealist Right and Left camps. While China has been a significant negative 'Other' for the Idealist Right for some time, an interesting shift of the image of the Chinese 'Other' has been taking place among the Japanese Left. Previously, the PRC served as an important 'victimised Other' that was used to consolidate a 'pacifist, democratic Japan', particularly among the Idealist Left. Now, it has gradually become a 'negative Other' which is undemocratic and unwilling to follow international rules. In short, even the Japanese Left − particularly the Moderate Left, who now constitute the mainstream of Japan's Left camp − are beginning to see the PRC as an entity that is negatively *different* from Japan, even though they are still aware of China's identity as a victim of Japanese imperialism.

The result of this is an increasing call for Japan to be 'resolute' and push back against China whenever there is a political dispute between the two states. What is worth noting here is that such calls for adopting a more assertive stance towards China actually seems to go against the long-standing consensus on Japan's foreign policy towards China. As Linus Hagström and Björn Jerdén have noted, there is nowadays a mutual understanding among Japanese political elites that the PRC *does* pose a long-term security threat to Japan. However, Tokyo has tended to accommodate China's rise and seek to integrate it into the international community, rather than to confront it. Part of this policy was motivated by Tokyo's desire to 'avoid straining an already sensitive relationship' (Hagström and Jerdén 2010: 737; cf. Jerdén and Hagström 2012). The construction of a 'bullying Chinese Other' could have implications for future Sino-Japanese relations, in the sense that we are likely to see Japanese politicians come under increased criticism for following this relatively moderate 'established' policy towards China. First, the calls for opposing China could mean that Tokyo will be less afraid of 'straining' Sino-Japanese relations further. The PRC is no longer a 'special case', whose claims to 'victimhood' have to be respected first and foremost. As we have seen, this dynamic is already visible: as seen from our discussions in this article, Japanese politicians are increasingly and persistently criticised for following this well-established policy of 'cautious engagement', and Japan is constantly seen to have 'lost out' to China. Second, the fact that both the Left and the Right have 'Othered' China in a similar way means that Sino-Japanese relations could become a focal point for Japanese nationalism(s). This suggests that there could be a greater scope for the politicisation of Sino-Japanese relations in

Japanese politics. Since both Left and Right camps agree that China is becoming an entity that 'bullies' Japan, both sides could use the 'Chinese Other' to criticise their opponents for not being 'resolute' enough to China, and score political points. This may indeed have been part of Ishihara Shintarō's motivation for deciding to purchase the Senkaku/Diaoyu Islands in his capacity as governor of Tokyo. By provoking a diplomatic row between China and Japan, Ishihara was able to pose as a nationalist capable of standing up to China, while simultaneously accusing the DPJ government of being too timid towards the PRC. Whatever Ishihara's true intentions may have been, what we do know is that his actions have had profound consequences. They have plunged China and Japan into their worst diplomatic standoff since 2005 – and if China continues to be 'Othered' as a high-handed, arrogant neighbour, we could be set to witness many more diplomatic standoffs between these two Great Powers of East Asia for some years to come.

Acknowledgements

The author gratefully acknowledges the financial support provided by the Asian Dynamics Initiative, University of Copenhagen, Denmark, for the researching of this article. Special thanks are also due to members of the Sino-Japanese Relations Research Network, as well as to Tadokoro Masayuki, for insightful comments and thoughts in improving this article.

Notes

1. My use of the term 'Idealist Right' is closest to what Christopher W. Hughes (2004: 51) has called 'Gaullist' thinking in Japan.
2. The Left's shifting position on China is not necessarily based exclusively on a (belated) realisation that China is now a threat to both the international community and Japanese national security and interests. The possibility of China as a threat increased sharply from the mid-1990s onwards in the more Left-leaning newspapers (*Asahi* and *Mainichi*). If the demands for Japan to be more 'resolute' towards China were undergirded by a fear of China's military power, we would have expected such discussions to emerge around the same time. However, this only happened from the 2000s onwards. As discussed later, this is most likely to be linked to the collapse of the Idealist Left in Japan, which took place in the late-1990s.
3. Unlike the Cold War period, it is not easy to distinguish between the Moderate and Idealist Left along party lines today. The DPJ, for instance, consists of former members of the LDP, DSP and Socialists, and this means that members of the same party may take different positions over certain issues. Furthermore, the decline of the Idealist Left means that Japanese party politics is increasingly fought over the 'middle ground', like in many liberal democracies. This also results in an increasing blurring between the Moderates on both the Right and Left camps.
4. Indeed, a 2012 survey conducted by Genron NPO (2012) for the Tokyo–Beijing Forum revealed that 41.9 per cent of Japanese viewed China's economic growth

References

Asahi Shimbun (1987a) 'Shasetsu: shōi o nokoshite daidō o motomeru', 10 May, p. 5.
Asahi Shimbun (1987b) 'Shasetsu: rekishi no chōbo ni yūkō no moji koso', 6 June, p. 5.
Asahi Shimbun (1987c) 'Shasetsu: kenka shite koso hajimete...', 1 July, p. 5.
Asahi Shimbun (1988a) 'Okuno hatsugen, sensō e no hansei aimai, jimin ni zokushutsu yurusu dojō', 14 May, p. 3.
Asahi Shimbun (1988b) 'Shasetsu: okuno jinin kara nani o manabu ka', 14 May, p. 5.
Asahi Shimbun (1989) 'Shasetsu: nichibei masatsu to nashonarizumu', 27 November, p. 5.
Asahi Shimbun (2008) 'Shasetsu: kūbakuchō kōtetsu zotto suru jeikan no bōsō', 2 November, p. 3.
Asahi Shimbun (2010a) 'Tensei jingo: senkaku shotō meguru "shuku shuku"', 22 September, p. 1.
Asahi Shimbun (2010b) 'Shasetsu: chūgoku senchō shakuhō, amai gaikō, nigai seiji handan', 25 September, p. 3.
Asahi Shimbun (2010c) 'Chūgokujin senchō shakuhō, yotō nai ni hihan: "haiboku da" yatō tsuikyū senkaku oki shōtotsu', 25 September, p. 4.
Asahi Shimbun (2010d) 'Tenseijingo: kyoryū to no tsukiai', 26 September, p. 1.
Asahi Shimbun (2010e) 'Shasetsu: nitchū gaikō, doronuma ni wa hairanakattaga', 31 October, p. 3.
Asahi Shimbun (2013) 'Shasetsu: senkaku ichinen, amari ni ōku o ushinatta', 7 September, p. 12.
Berger, T. U. (1996) 'Norms, identity, and national security in Germany and Japan', in P. J. Katzenstein (ed) *The Culture of National Security: Norms and Identity in World Politics*, New York: Columbia University Press, pp. 317–56.
Bukh, A. (2010) *Japan's National Identity and Foreign Policy: Russia as Japan's 'Other'*, London: Routledge.
Downs, A. (1957) *An Economic Theory of Democracy*, New York: Harper and Row.
Duverger, M. (1954) *Political Parties*, New York: Wiley.
Fukada, Y. and Kusano, A. (2001) 'Shinshutsu nippon kigyō wa mata nakasareru', *Bungei Shunjū* 79(11): 195–202.
Genron NPO (2012) Accessed at http://www.genron-npo.net/pdf/forum2012.pdf, 19 September 2013.
Hagström, L. (2012) '"Power shift" in East Asia? A critical reappraisal of narratives on the Diaoyu/Senkaku islands incident in 2010', *Chinese Journal of International Politics* 5(3): 267–97.
Hagström, L. (forthcoming) 'The "abnormal" state: identity, norm/exception and Japan', *European Journal of International Relations*, published online before print, 27 March 2014.
Hagström, L. and Jerdén, B. (2010) 'Understanding fluctuations in Sino-Japanese relations: to politicize or to de-politicize the China issue in the Japanese Diet', *Pacific Affairs* 83(4): 719–39.
Hagström, L. and Williamsson, J. (2009) '"Remilitarization", really? Assessing change in Japanese foreign security policy', *Asian Security* 5(3): 242–72.

Hoppens, R. (2012) 'Peace through historical revisionism: Yamamoto Shichihei on Sino-Japanese relations in the 1970s', *Sino-Japanese Studies* 19: 48–65.
Hoppens, R. (2014) 'The 1979 Sino-Vietnamese war and the transformation of Japan's relations with China in diplomacy and discourse', *Electronic Journal of Contemporary Japanese Studies* 14(2); accessed at http://www.japanesestudies.org.uk/ejcjs/vol14/iss2/hoppens.html, 14 August 2014.
Hughes, C. W. (2004) 'Japan's re-emergence as a "normal" military power', *Adelphi Paper* 368-9.
Ijiri, H. (1996) 'Sino-Japanese controversy since the 1972 diplomatic normalization', in C. Howe (ed.) *China and Japan: History, Trends, and Prospects*, Oxford: Clarendon Press, pp. 60–82.
Ikeda, M. and Aida, Y. (1990) 'Seiō no nihon tataki ni dō tsukiauka', *Chūō kōron*, August, pp. 130–9.
Ishihara, S. (2012) '"No" to ieru nippon: shin nichibei kankei no hōsaku' in *Ishihara Shintarō no shisō to kōi*, Vol. 2, Tokyo: Sankei Shimbun Shuppan.
Jerdén, B. and Hagström, L. (2012) 'Rethinking Japan's China policy: Japan as an accommodator in the rise of China, 1978–2011', *Journal of East Asian Studies* 12(2): 215–50.
Johnston, A. I. (2013) 'How new and assertive is China's new assertiveness?', *International Security* 37(4): 7–48.
Katzenstein, P. J. (1998) *Cultural Norms and National Security: Police and Military in Postwar Japan*, Ithaca: Cornell University Press.
Kitaoka, S. (2008) *Jimintō: seikentō no sanjūhachi nen*, Tokyo: Chūō Kōron Shinsha.
Komori, Y. (2012) 'Asahi shimbun no wakamiya yoshibumi shuhitsu no henkō o tadasu'; accessed at http://komoriy.iza.ne.jp/blog/entry/2875307/, 12 June 2013.
Mainichi Shimbun (1988) 'Okuno kokudochō chōkan ga "taisen de nihon ni shinryaku no ito nashi" to kokkai de kenkai', 10 May, p. 1.
Mainichi Shimbun (2008) 'Shasetsu: mizou 08 tamogami jiken yōnin suru seikai no fūchō koso...', 28 December, p. 5.
Mainichi Shimbun (2010a) 'Shasetsu: kakuryō kōryū teishi, reiseisa kaku chūgoku no taiō', 21 September, p. 5.
Mainichi Shimbun (2010b) 'Shasetsu: chūgoku no kyōkō sochi, rifujin na taiō wa yameyo', 28 September, p. 5.
Mainichi Shimbun (2012) 'Shasetsu: senkaku to nitchū tairitsu, taiwa kaiketsu ni zenryoku ageyo', 18 September, p. 5.
Nakagawa, S. (2005) 'Chūgoku keizai, koko ga honto ni shinpai da', *Shokun!* 5: 34–41.
Nakajima, M. (1986) 'Chūgoku ni jubaku sareru nippon: nitchū kankei to rekishi no kessan', *Shokun!* 18(3): 26–42.
Nakajima, M. (1987) *Chūgoku ni jubaku sareru nippon*, Tokyo: Bungei Shunjū.
Neumann, I. B. (1999) *Uses of the Other: 'The East' in European Identity Formation*, Minneapolis: University of Minnesota Press.
Oguma, E. (1998) '*Nihonjin no kyōkai: okinawa, ainu, taiwan, chosen shokuminchi shihai kara fukki undō made*, Tokyo: Shin'yōsha.
Ōtake, H. (2005) *Saigunbi to nashonarizumu: sengo nippon no bōei kan*, Tokyo: Kōdansha.
Rose, C. (1998) *Interpreting History in Sino-Japanese Relations: A Case Study in Political Decision-Making*, London: Routledge.
Rowen, H. (1986) 'Nakasone shot himself in the foot', *Washington Post*, 25 September, p. a25.

Sankei Shimbun (2010a) 'Shuchō: taichū shisei, senkaku no mamori kyōka ga kadai da', 14 September. Retrieved from the *Sankei Archives*, National Diet Library.

Sankei Shimbun (2010b) 'Shuchō: chūgokujin senchō shakuhō, dokomade kuni o otoshimerunoka', 25 September. Retrieved from the *Sankei Archives*, National Diet Library.

Sankei Nyūsu (2013) 'Meigen ka meigen ka: Abe shushō no 'wana' ni kakatta okada zen fuku sōri', 9 March 2013; accessed at http://sankei.jp.msn.com/politics/news/130309/stt13030918010001-n2.htm, 31 May 2013.

Shinoda, T. (2007) 'Becoming more realistic in the post-cold war: Japan's changing media and public opinion on national security', *Japanese Journal of Political Science* 8(2): 171–90.

Suzuki, S (2007) 'The importance of 'Othering' in China's national identity: Sino-Japanese relations as a stage of identity conflicts', *The Pacific Review* 20 (1): 23–47.

Suzuki, S. (2011) 'The strange masochism of the Japanese right: redrawing moral boundaries in Sino-Japanese relations', in G. D. Hook (ed.) *Decoding Boundaries in Contemporary Japan: The Koizumi Administration and Beyond*, Abingdon: Routledge, pp. 35–58.

Takemi, K. (2001) 'Shinrai kankei o dō kōchiku suruka', *Sekai* (685): 88–93.

Tamogami, T. (2008) 'Nippon wa shinryaku kokka de atta no ka'; accessed at http://www.apa.co.jp/book_report/images/2008jyusyou_saiyuusyu.pdf, 10 May 2009.

Tanizawa, E. (2005) *Jigyaku shikan mō yametai! Hannichi teki nihonjin e no kokuhatsujō*, Tokyo: Wakku Shuppan.

Tokuoka, T. and Hosaka, M. (2010) 'Kan Naoto dakara chūgoku ga tsukeagaru', *Bungei shunjū*, November, pp. 136–43.

Usui, S. (2012) 'Kaiko heisei 24 nen: rondan "chūgoku ron" hanazakari, ukabu nippon no arubeki sugata', *Sankei Shimbun*, 24 December. Retrieved from the *Sankei Archives*, National Diet Library.

Yamagiwa, S. (2006) 'Kane ni koronda ka, onna o dakasareta ka: bichū seijika hajikaki genkōroku', *WiLL*, September, pp. 76–89.

Yamamoto, T. (1987) 'Nakasone seiken ka no nitchū kankei: kōkaryō, ichi paasento, soshite yasukuni...', *Sekai* 504: 43–50.

Yomiuri Shimbun (2005) 'Maehara bei chū hōmon: sekinin seitō toshite no jikaku o hatashita', 14 December, p. 3.

Zhongguo Wang (2008) 'Tianmushen junxiong diandao heibai qiwen jiexuan: riben ceng shi qinlüe guojia ma', November 6; accessed at http://www.china.com.cn/military/txt/2008-11/06/content_16720689_3.htm, 22 October 2013.

Identity and recognition: remembering and forgetting the post-war in Sino-Japanese relations

Karl Gustafsson

Abstract In the 1990s, Japanese views of China were relatively positive. In the 2000s, however, views of China have deteriorated markedly and China has increasingly come to be seen as 'anti-Japanese'. How can these developments, which took place despite increased economic interdependence, be understood? One seemingly obvious explanation is the occurrence of 'anti-Japanese' incidents in China since the mid-2000s. I suggest that these incidents per se do not fully explain the puzzle. Protests against other countries occasionally occur and may influence public opinion. Nonetheless, the interpretation of such events arguably determines their significance. Demonstrations may be seen as legitimate or spontaneous. If understood as denying recognition of an actor's self-identity, the causes of such incidents are likely to have considerably deeper and more severe consequences than what would otherwise be the case. Through an analysis of Japanese parliamentary debates and newspaper editorials, the paper demonstrates that the Chinese government has come to be seen as denying Japan's self-identity as a peaceful state that has provided China with substantial amounts of official development aid (ODA) during the post-war era. This is mainly because China teaches patriotic education, which is viewed as the root cause of 'anti-Japanese' incidents. China, then, is not regarded as 'anti-Japanese' merely because of protests against Japan and attacks on Japanese material interests but for denying a key component of Japan's self-image. Moreover, the analysis shows that explicit Chinese statements recognising Japan's self-identity have been highly praised in Japan. The article concludes that if China recognises Japan's self-understanding of its identity as peaceful, Japan is more likely to stick to this identity and act accordingly whereas Chinese denials of it might empower Japanese actors who seek to move away from this identity and 'normalise' Japan, for example, by revising the pacifist Article Nine of the Japanese constitution.

Introduction

In the 1990s, Japanese views of China were relatively positive and China was rarely described as 'anti-Japanese'. This changed dramatically in the 2000s, when the number of respondents in opinion polls who 'dislike' or 'feel no affinity' with China increased substantially.[1] In addition, since around 2003–2004, China has frequently been described as 'anti-Japanese'. In the 1990s, China was only mentioned in 8 out of 81 Japanese parliamentary debates in which the word 'anti-Japan/anti-Japanese' (*han'nichi*) appeared. In contrast, between 2000 and 2012, China was discussed in 140 out of 235 such debates.[2] Among 25 books published up until 2002 that mention the word 'anti-Japan/anti-Japanese' in their titles none focused on China. Out of a total of 98 such books published since 2003, 40 dealt specifically with China and an additional 15 books focused on China among other states.[3] The same trend can be detected in editorials in Japan's two largest daily newspapers *Yomiuri Shimbun* and *Asahi Shimbun*. In the former, only 2 out of 22 editorials in the 1990s mentioning the word 'anti-Japan/anti-Japanese' concentrated on China compared to 58 out of 70 published since 2000.[4] In the latter, only 7 out of 38 editorials published in the 1990s discussed China. The corresponding figure for the period from 2000 to 2012 was 65 out of 89.[5] All these indicators, then, point in the same direction – China was hardly mentioned in the discourse on 'anti-Japanism' in the 1990s but dominated it completely in the 2000s. It has even reached the point where China is ascribed an 'anti-Japanese' identity.

These changes have occurred even though trade, economic interdependence, travelling between the countries and student exchanges have increased tremendously during the 1990s and 2000s (Hagström 2008/09: 226–229; Kokubun 2006; Koo 2009), and despite the fact that Japan has largely accommodated China's rise between 1978 and 2011 (Jerdén and Hagström 2012). Why have Japanese views of China deteriorated to the point that China is even ascribed an 'anti-Japanese' identity, despite these positive developments?

One seemingly obvious explanation is that 'anti-Japanese' incidents have repeatedly occurred in China. Three cases involving widespread demonstrations against Japan were especially striking due to their large scale: in the spring of 2005 over Japan's bid for a seat on the United Nations Security Council (UNSC), concerning the arrest of the captain of a Chinese fishing boat in disputed waters in autumn 2010 and regarding the Japanese nationalisation of three of the Diaoyu/Senkaku Islands in autumn 2012.

Even though such incidents certainly matter, I suggest that the incidents per se do not fully explain why the Chinese state has become so closely associated with the word 'anti-Japanese'. In addition, an explanation focused on the incidents per se fails to highlight the deeper implications of the labelling of China as 'anti-Japanese'. The interpretation of the causes of such protests and related acts need to be taken into account. The mere fact that demonstrations, violent or otherwise, against country A occur in country B does not necessarily need to have a profound impact on bilateral relations. It might be argued that vandals are responsible and that the violence is unrelated to the government of state B. It is also possible that protests in country B may be regarded as provoked by country A. In addition, demonstrations may be considered spontaneous emotional outbursts by a minority while the majority of the population holds less negative views or expresses those views in a nonviolent manner. Either way, the state does not necessarily need to be blamed and even if it is, the meaning and significance of such events remains open to interpretation. Country B does not necessarily need to be ascribed an identity as 'anti-country A'.

The article suggests that theories about recognition in international politics can help better explain why Japanese views of China have become increasingly negative to the extent that China has even come to be branded as 'anti-Japanese' in Japanese discourse. In Japan, China's patriotic education is regarded as the root cause of 'anti-Japanese' sentiments, which have exploded in 'anti-Japanese' demonstrations. This education is described as 'anti-Japanese' and believed to foster 'anti-Japanese' sentiments not merely because it contains detailed descriptions of Japanese wartime cruelty but also because it ignores Japan's post-war development as a peaceful state. China has thus come to be seen as 'anti-Japanese' not primarily because of protests against Japan and attacks on Japanese material interests, but because it is seen as denying Japan recognition of a key component of its self-identity. Statements by Chinese leaders to the same effect constitute an explicit denial of this identity. The article, then, demonstrates the importance of the collective memory of the post-war period for Japanese identity. Whereas a number of scholars have stressed the importance of Japanese war memory for Japan's international relations (Gustafsson 2011; He 2009; Lind 2008), up until now the way in which the post-war period is remembered has been granted scant attention.

Research on identity and Japan's international relations has been concerned with how identity is constructed, how it changes and how it relates to policy outcomes (for an overview of this literature, see Hagström forthcoming). One influential approach has emphasised the role of Japan's pacifist or 'anti-militarist' identity. These studies focus primarily on how domestic identity influences foreign policy. Its proponents regard this identity as relatively stable even though they do not rule out the possibility of a significant change as a result of a major external shock, for example, in the form of a collapse or rupture in the security alliance with the USA (Berger 1998; Katzenstein 1996; Oros 2008). The idea that Japan is now 'normalising' is often ascribed to the emergence of new security threats –

usually in the form of a rising China and/or a North Korea which is developing nuclear weapons and missile technology.

The second major approach focuses on how Japanese identity is constructed through a process of drawing boundaries in relation to specific 'others' (Bukh 2010; Guillaume 2011; Schulze 2013; Tamaki 2010). Boundaries may be drawn in a way that stresses continuity but there may also be change. This article seeks to contribute to the literature on Japan's identity and international relations by applying recognition theory. It thereby offers a conceptualisation of identity change that differs from both approaches discussed above.

The article is structured as follows. First, I outline the article's theoretical approach, which is based on theories of identity and recognition. In short, an identity has to be recognised by others in order for an agent to be able to act confidently. Denial of recognition may therefore result in the abandonment of an identity and the construction of a new one. The second section establishes the importance for Japanese self-identity of the idea that Japan has been peaceful during the post-war period. This might be seen as similar to the approach to the study of Japanese identity discussed above, which emphasises Japan's pacifist or anti-militarist norms. However, while those scholars see a domestically constructed identity as a factor which might influence foreign policy, focusing on recognition means that identity is, to a significant extent, constructed internationally and interactively. This process is significant in itself and not only because the resulting identity is believed to impact foreign policy. In addition, identity is constructed in relation to difference. For example, some identity discourses promoted by Japanese domestic actors who seek to make their preferred vision of Japanese identity dominant construct Japanese identity in relation to contemporary others, for example, China. Significantly, however, in official Japanese discourse, Japan's identity has often been constructed primarily in relation to its past self. External recognition or denial of recognition may strengthen particular identity discourses promoted by domestic actors. The third section shows that many Japanese regard China as denying Japan recognition for its development as a peaceful state during the post-war period. In the fourth part, I examine in greater detail the Japanese government's responses to these denials. The section takes the analysis one step further by demonstrating how the perceived denial of recognition leads to additional effects through actions taken by certain agents. In particular, I argue that the increased ascription of an 'anti-Japanese' identity to China is a way of dealing with what is interpreted as Chinese denial of recognition of Japan's self-identity. Japanese identity entrepreneurs have sought to use this window of opportunity to emphasise Japan's identity as democratic in relation to an authoritarian China. Identity entrepreneurs are political actors who promote an identity that they espouse through the discursive representation of certain issues and actors. What sets them apart from other actors is that they do not merely reproduce but also seek to alter identities. In addition, I suggest that Japanese movements in the direction of an identity shift seeking to make Japan a 'normal' state are strengthened by Chinese denial of Japan's peaceful identity. Finally, I conclude that China and other states can influence Japanese identity by recognising or denying recognition of particular Japanese stories about what Japan is. Whether or not Japan 'normalises' therefore depends in part on which Japanese identity narrative is recognised by other states.

It should be mentioned that the focus of the analysis is on Japanese views. The article does not seek to determine whether or not China *really* recognises Japan's identity. As long as China is seen as denying Japan recognition of its peaceful identity, Japan's identity as well as Sino-Japanese relations will likely be affected. I also do not analyse Chinese views of whether or not Japan recognises China's identity. Nonetheless, the analysis still sheds light on critical issues in Sino-Japanese relations hitherto largely overlooked.

Identity and recognition

Identity construction is the process through which individuals, collectives and states construct narrative accounts of who they are. These stories tell actors who they are as well as how they are supposed to act. States may, for example, tell stories about themselves being super, great or middle powers (Ringmar 2007: 66–77; 2012: 3–7).

The basic understanding of identity in Ringmar's theory of recognition is similar to that found in ontological security theory as it argues that agents need stable and secure self-identities in order to be able to act in a self-confident way. They hence act in a routine-like manner that seeks to maintain their narrated self-identities. The identities of states may be challenged if it occurs to an actor that its self-identity does not correspond with its actions (Steele 2008). In recognition theory, other actors perform a more central role in prompting such challenges because for an agent to be able to act in a self-confident manner its identity needs to be recognised by others. Continuity in recognition makes agents feel secure in their identities. In other words, it enhances ontological security. 'To the extent that we are able to achieve recognition for our performance and to the extent that our audience remains loyal, we are able to increasingly take our identities for granted' (Ringmar 2012: 8).

Recognition is sometimes divided into two types – 'thin' and 'thick'. Thin recognition is about being recognised as a full member of a community. In this sense, it is about *identity with* other actors. Thick recognition, in contrast, acknowledges difference or uniqueness, for example, in the form of specific qualities (Wendt 2003: 511–512). This article is concerned with the latter kind of recognition. 'The political representatives of other communities are to "recognise" that upon which a community founds its self-image – the challenges it has overcome in the past, its power to resist authoritarian tendencies, its cultural achievements, and so on' (Honneth 2012: 29). Mutual recognition, involving two parties recognising each other not merely as equals but as possessing different traits or qualities, can create solidarity and improved relations (Wendt 2003: 511–512). However, such stories will not necessarily be accepted by other states. Others may regard a state's accounts as unreasonable or even hubristic. The audience may, for example, not agree that a state is a great power and instead deny it recognition for the story it tells about itself (Ringmar 2007: 78–83; 2012: 7–8).

Regardless of whether or not it is possible to objectively determine if an actor A denies actor B recognition, it has been argued that it is the subjective feeling of not being recognised or being denied recognition that matters. Identity markers, what we believe makes us what we are, are closely linked to emotions (Lindemann 2010). Denial of recognition may therefore be understood as humiliating and disrespectful (Wolf 2011). What is interpreted as an insult, of course, depends on one's self-identity (Lindemann 2010). For a state, the leaders and people of which see the state as a great power, being called or treated as a middle power will most likely be interpreted as an insult. Needless to say, if this self-identity were that of a middle power the same treatment would not be considered offensive. To this discussion, it might be added that there is a difference between (1) the absence of explicit recognition, (2) explicit recognition, (3) non-explicit acts, behaviour or statements that are interpreted as recognition, (4) non-explicit acts, behaviour or statements that are interpreted as denials of recognition and (5) explicit denials of recognition. An explicit and unequivocal denial arguably matters more and is more likely to provoke a stronger response than, for example, the absence of recognition. Similarly, explicit recognition is likely to be more powerful than non-explicit recognition.

If the stories a state tells about itself are not accepted, Ringmar suggests that three options are available to it. First, it can accept that its stories were inaccurate and that those ascribed to it by others were correct. In that case, it needs to refashion its story about itself and hope that the new narrative is accepted. The second option is for the state to accept that its narrative was incorrect but argue that it can change in order to become what it has claimed that it is. The third option is for it to stick to its stories without altering its behaviour and instead try to convince those who do not believe in the stories that they are actually accurate. Violence, or the threat of violence, may be one way for a state to prove itself. If a state, for example, argues that it is a great power it might attempt to force other states to accept this description through the use of military force (Ringmar 2007: 78–83; 2012: 7–8). This, according to Ringmar, is why Sweden intervened in the Thirty Years War. 'We act, as it were, in "self defence" in the most basic sense of the word – in defence of the applicability of our selves' (Ringmar 2007: 83). The struggle for recognition can thus be a cause of international conflict. I suggest a fourth option; in the face of denial of its identity, a state could increasingly construct its identity as different from that of the denying state, while stressing similarity with third parties to which it appeals for support and recognition without admitting that its story was incorrect.

So whose recognition matters? In his book on Sweden's participation in the Thirty Years War, Ringmar suggests that some actors' recognition matters more than others' and introduces the concept of 'circles of recognition'. For the Swedish king at the time of the Thirty Years War, those countries it identified as friends (mainly fellow Protestant countries) formed a circle of recognition. Sweden hence sought recognition primarily from those countries rather than from its Catholic enemies even though it did want a more limited recognition from its enemies, at least as a 'state worthy of animosity and as an opponent on the battlefield' (Ringmar 2007: 81, 164–170). Other studies suggest that recognition between adversaries matters to an even greater extent. The Soviet Union, Ringmar suggests, desired recognition from the West (Ringmar 2002). Moreover, the Libyan government's politics of recognition toward the USA, argues Lindemann, for a long time helped to keep the latter from attacking the former (Lindemann 2010). Recognition of an antagonist, then, can function as a form of appeasement that makes one's adversary less likely to engage in antagonistic behaviour.

In addition, context matters. The Europe of the 1620s that Ringmar discusses differed significantly from the contemporary world. In a world in which most states are members of the 'international community', this community arguably forms a circle of recognition from which states seek recognition (cf. Murray 2010). This argument notwithstanding, it might be argued that Japan is more concerned with having its self-identity recognised by the USA, a fellow democracy and alliance-partner, than by China, an authoritarian state commonly seen as denying human rights. While this is most probably the case, it does not mean that the Japanese government does not care about Chinese recognition. First, whether China is regarded as a friend or a foe and the extent to and way in which Japan's identity is constructed in relation to China, as well as Japan's relationship with China in general, is likely to be affected by whether China recognises or denies Japan's self-identity. Furthermore, the Japanese government's range of options in bilateral dealings is influenced by its identity as recognised by China. In addition, denial of recognition, especially explicit denials directed toward the international community, might be contagious even when they emanate from actors considered less important.

Japanese self-identity and the post-war

A number of studies have emphasised the significance of Japanese war memory for Japan's international relations (Gustafsson 2011; He 2009;

Lind 2008). In contrast, scholars have granted the Japanese collective memory of the post-war period scant attention. Yet, the collective memory of the post-war era has, I argue, come to occupy an important place in the stories Japanese tell about themselves, especially those told by the Japanese government in the international arena. In this section, I demonstrate the centrality of the post-war period in Japanese self-identity by revealing how it appears in official documents as well as in apologies and speeches delivered by Japanese prime ministers. These representations matter for thick recognition as they contain explicit claims about what is particular about Japan. As the 50th and 60th anniversaries of the end of the war, the years 1995 and 2005 have been especially important occasions for making such representations, and they are still highlighted as significant on the Japanese Ministry of Foreign Affairs' (MOFA) website.

Prime Minister Murayama Tomiichi's 1995 apology in which he expressed 'feelings of deep remorse' and 'heartfelt apology' for Japan's 'colonial rule and aggression' is well known. Less attention has been given to the sections in the statement that refers to the post-war period: 'The peace and prosperity of today were built as Japan overcame great difficulty to arise from a devastated land after defeat in the war. That achievement is something of which we are proud, and let me herein express my heartfelt admiration for the wisdom and untiring effort of each and every one of our citizens' (Murayama 1995).

Prime ministers since Murayama have not only repeated and expressed support for key phrases from his apology but have also further elaborated on and emphasised Japan's positive post-war self-identity as peaceful. Prime Minister Hashimoto Ryūtarō, for example, referred to Murayama's statement during a visit to Beijing in 1997, saying that 'Japan's development was the result of rigorous self-remorse on our past, self-remorse that led us, in the postwar era, to completely abandon the path of becoming a military power and seek to be a pacifist state' (Hashimoto 1997). Similarly, Prime Minister Koizumi Jun'ichirō, after visiting the Chinese People's War of Resistance Memorial Hall in Beijing in 2001, quoted the statement's key passages. Significantly, he emphasised that Japan, by 'squarely facing the past' was able to 'prosper as a peaceful state in the post-war' era, based on 'self-reflection', according to which it can 'never cause another war' (Koizumi 2001).

When he paraphrased Murayama again in 2005 during the Asian–African Conference in Bandung, Indonesia, Koizumi elaborated even further on Japan's post-war achievements: 'with feelings of deep remorse and heartfelt apology always engraved in mind, Japan has resolutely maintained, consistently since the end of World War II, never turning into a military power but an economic power, its principle of resolving all matters by peaceful means, without recourse to use of force. Japan once again states its resolve to contribute to the peace and prosperity of the world in the future as well' (Koizumi 2005).

The most elaborate official story about Japan's identity as peaceful during the post-war era is probably presented in the leaflet *60 Years: The Path of a Nation Striving for Global Peace*, published by MOFA in July 2005. On its first page, it quotes Prime Minister Koizumi's General Policy Speech delivered to the Diet in January 2005: 'In the post-war period, Japan has become the world's second largest economic power. Never turning into a military power and always observing pacifism, Japan has played an active role in achieving world peace and prosperity by contributing financially, such as through Official Development Assistance and contributions to the UN, and by personnel contributions, such as participation in UN peacekeeping operations'. It then paraphrases the Murayama statement and describes how Japan, following the end of the war, started over as a 'nation striving for global peace'. The document states: 'Japan, underpinned by its solid democracy, has resolutely and consistently strived for peace by adhering to a strictly defensive security policy, preventing the escalation of international conflict, and dedicated itself to international peace and stability by mobilizing all its available resources. It has adhered to the Three Non-Nuclear Principles. During these 60 years, Japan has never resorted to the use of force'. Furthermore, the pamphlet described Japan as the 'world's leading donor country' and showed that 12.6% of Japan's total bilateral official development aid (ODA) has gone to China (MOFA 2005). Clearly, this construction of Japanese identity emphasises uniqueness.

When Prime Minister Abe Shinzō visited China in 2006 he stated in talks with Chinese leaders that Japan 'shall look at past history squarely and shall continue to conduct itself as a peaceful nation. Japan has come through the 60 years of the postwar period on the basis of the deep remorse over the fact that Japan in the past has caused tremendous damage and suffering to the people of the Asian countries' (Abe 2006). In 2007, Prime Minister Fukuda Yasuo made a similar statement in Beijing (Fukuda 2007).

In 2009, MOFA published another pamphlet called *Japan and China: Building a Mutually Beneficial Relationship Based on Common Strategic Interests*. Significantly, it featured a section on 'Japan's pursuit of the path of a peaceful country', which stated that Japan's 'progress in the 60 years since the war is grounded on deep regret', which 'is shared by the Japanese people' (MOFA 2009: 2).

Defeat in a war commonly makes an identity change necessary. Since it was unable to defeat the enemy the country was obviously not as great as its citizens may have believed (Ringmar 2012: 8). This was the case for Japan after its defeat in 1945 and this arguably explains the centrality of the post-war period to Japanese identity. Since 1995, Japanese apologies and statements have made increasingly clear references to the post-war period. The need to emphasise that Japan has been peaceful throughout the post-war period would not have been there had it not been for Japan's history as an aggressor. This becomes quite clear in Japanese apologies, which contrast post-war Japan with the wartime 'other' as they depict the past as a foreign country. They present the Japanese story of its peaceful post-war and requests recognition for this self-identity.

Recognition and China's amnesia concerning Japan's peaceful post-war

Chinese patriotic education is frequently described as the root cause of partly violent 'anti-Japanese' demonstrations, which have taken place in China since the mid-2000s. For example, the Democratic Party of Japan's (DPJ) Matsubara Jin responded to the 2005 protests against Japan in China during a speech in the Diet by directly connecting what he labelled 'riots' (*bōdō*), to Chinese patriotic education. He showed a Chinese teacher's manual in which teachers were told to 'stimulate the pupils' minds and encourage them to harbour a strong resentment toward the assaults by Japanese imperialist aggression against China'. Such sentences, according to Matsubara, appeared in abundance in the manual (Diet session 162, Foreign affairs committee meeting 6, 22 April 2005). A *Yomiuri Shimbun* editorial discussing the demonstrations blamed the former Chinese leader Jiang Zemin for launching 'life-long learning' of 'anti-Japanese education' in the mid-1990s and mentioned that his plan for patriotic education laid the foundation for the establishment of more than 200 patriotic education bases. In addition, it claimed that Chinese textbooks feature numerous descriptions that 'deliberately plant anti-Japanese sentiments' in Chinese pupils (*Yomiuri Shimbun* 2005b).

In Diet statements as well as in newspaper editorials, patriotic education is described as problematic partly because it is filled with such detailed depictions of the Japanese military's wartime atrocities. However, the problem with Chinese education is not seen as only related to what it *contains* but also to what it *excludes*. China's patriotic education is regarded as 'anti-Japanese' because its historical narrative largely ends in 1945. Japan's peaceful development during the post-war period is consequently denied, creating a one-sided image of Japan.

In the Japanese Diet, a number of speakers representing various political parties have expressed similar views. For example, in 2006, Takano Hiroshi of the New Kōmeitō argued that Chinese education was 'anti-Japanese' as it devoted considerable space to detailed descriptions of Japanese wartime aggression while not at all mentioning Japan's post-war development as a peaceful nation that has expressed regret concerning the past and provided China with large-scale ODA. He questioned whether it was really possible to build Sino-Japanese friendship on the basis of such education (Diet session 164, Foreign policy and defence committee meeting 22, 13 June 2006).

Around the time of the large-scale protests against Japan in spring 2005, a representative of the Japan Communist Party, Daimon Mikishi, similarly demanded that the Chinese government not only teach young people about Japanese aggression but also about Japanese post-war aid to China (Diet session 162, Investigative committee for international affairs meeting 8, 18 April 2005). Kishimoto Takeshi of the DPJ described Japanese aid to China as something that ought to nurture gratitude. He called for an investigation into what Japanese aid to China had been used for and that the results be disseminated to the Chinese people as this might benefit Sino-Japanese friendship. Foreign Minister Machimura Nobutaka responded that Beijing's international airport had been built with Japanese aid but that the only acknowledgement of this at the airport was a tiny plate in an inconspicuous place (Diet session 162, Fiscal administration review committee meeting 1, 25 April 2005).

In response to the 2005 protests, the *Asahi Shimbun* similarly expressed concern about what it described as misrepresentative and biased Chinese depictions of Japan: 'Through patriotic education, many Chinese repeatedly see the photos and images of the Japanese military's aggression. The other side – the post-war history of the Japan that has a constitution, which forbids the use of force to solve conflicts, does not possess nuclear weapons and has not been engaged in war is practically unknown' (*Asahi Shimbun* 2005).

A related point, which is made repeatedly, is that Japanese expressions of contrition and apologies for its past aggression have not been properly recognised. After Japanese diplomatic missions were attacked in spring 2005, Japan demanded that because it had failed to stop the destruction the Chinese government pay reparation costs and issue an apology. Chinese President Hu Jintao refused to apologise and instead insisted that Japan express regret for its past war of aggression. *Yomiuri Shimbun* criticised Hu, arguing that the claim that Japan has not shown regret is an 'obvious distortion of history'. The editorial stated that official expressions of regret or apology have been made more than 20 times since the normalisation of bilateral relations in 1972. It pointed out that Koizumi apologised just before his meeting with Hu at the Asia-Africa Summit. Hu, however, called for the expression of 'regret to be turned into real actions'. The editorial retorted that in that case, China should also put a stop to its own 'actions' concerning its 'patriotic and anti-Japanese education' (*Yomiuri Shimbun* 2005a). During a visit to China in May 2005, the Liberal Democratic Party's (LDP) Takebe Tsutomu explicitly stated that because 'based on regret, post-war Japan has continued to walk the path of a peace state' it deserved some recognition (*Sankei Shimbun* 2005).

The Chinese Foreign Ministry's agreement in the wake of the 2005 demonstrations to initiate a joint bilateral history research project prompted optimism in Japan. In a Diet debate in October 2006, Higashi Junji of the New Kōmeitō, for example, interpreted it as a sign that the Chinese government would teach Chinese children about Japan's post-war development as a peaceful state. The then prime minister, LDP's Abe Shinzō, lamented that China had previously not evaluated Japan's postwar development positively but said that it was significant that it did now (Diet session 165, The lower house budget committee, meeting 4, 10 October 2006). The next day, the New Kōmeitō's Takano Hiroshi explicitly urged Abe to demand that China teach a 'correct recognition of our country as a peaceful country' during the post-war era (Diet session 165, The upper house budget committee, meeting 1, 11 October 2006).

These expectations of Chinese recognition were actually realised in 2007–2008 when Sino-Japanese relations temporarily improved. First Chinese Prime Minister Wen Jiabao and then President Hu Jintao visited Japan. Significantly, it was not the visits per se that led to improvements in bilateral relations. Instead, it was arguably the fact that during their visits, both leaders recognised Japan's self-identity as a peaceful state during the post-war period that had provided China with ODA. On 13 April 2007, Chinese Prime Minister Wen stated in a speech in the Japanese Diet, which was broadcasted in both Japan and China: 'The Japanese government and its leaders have on several occasions expressed its attitude towards the history issue, officially recognised its aggression, expressed deep regret and apologies to the victimised countries' (Wen 2007). The *Asahi Shimbun* welcomed this clear recognition of Japan's apologies as 'epoch-making' (*Asahi Shimbun* 2007). Wen also mentioned that 'China has received support and assistance from the Japanese Government and people in its reform, opening-up and modernization drive' (Wen 2007). The *Asahi Shimbun* commented that 'this must be the first time many people in China hear the truth' about Japan's aid to China (*Asahi Shimbun* 2007). The *Yomiuri Shimbun* similarly commented that few Chinese knew about the role that Japanese ODA had played in China's development, for example, in developing important infrastructure in coastal regions. At the same time, it expressed appreciation and mentioned that before Wen's visit, state television screened programs about Japanese life and culture for three weeks. It was speculated that the purpose might be to 'correct the anti-Japanese education, which had gone too far and to mitigate anti-Japanese sentiments' (*Yomiuri Shimbun* 2007).

In the Joint Statement issued by the governments of Japan and China in connection with Chinese President Hu Jintao's meeting with Japanese Prime Minister Fukuda Yasuo on 7 May 2008, China again explicitly recognised Japan's self-identity: 'The Chinese side expressed its positive evaluation of Japan's consistent pursuit of the path of a peaceful country and Japan's contribution to the peace and stability of the world through peaceful means over more than sixty years since [the Second] World War' (MOFA 2008). As attempts to improve Sino-Japanese relations, Hu and Wen's visits were especially significant because they involved *explicit recognition* of Japan's post-war self-identity as a peaceful state. The positive reactions to the statements arguably demonstrate that recognition of the achievements central to Japan's identity can contribute greatly to improved bilateral relations.

However, the optimistic reaction to the visits and the expectations raised by the joint history project eventually abated. In a Diet debate in 2010 when protests against Japan were again occurring in China, the LDP's Hirasawa Katsuei stated that in Chinese war museums such as the one located in Jiandao in Jilin province in Northeast China, the Japanese military was shown torturing Chinese while there was no mention of friendly bilateral relations and Japan's abundant aid to China in the post-war period (Diet session 176, The lower house judicial affairs committee, meeting 2, 22 October 2010).

In autumn 2012, when large-scale and partly violent demonstrations against Japan took place in more than 100 Chinese cities, the previous optimism had completely vanished. China's refusal to recognise Japan's post-war identity was again cited as a fundamental bilateral problem. The *Yomiuri Shimbun* mentioned that even though Japan had contributed to China's development by providing Yen-loans with generous terms this spirit of cooperation on behalf of Japan was hardly recognised at all in China. On the contrary, 'anti-Japanese patriotic education' had been strengthened during the 1990s (*Yomiuri Shimbun* 2012). The *Asahi Shimbun* urged the Chinese Communist Party (CCP) to stop using 'anti-Japanism' (*han'nichi*) to deal with its many social problems. In addition, it argued that Japan must work hard to guarantee that Chinese people learn about Japan's 'actual circumstances', as few Chinese knew about Japan's contributions to China's development through more than 3 trillion Japanese Yen (JPY) in Yen-loans (*Asahi Shimbun* 2012).

When the Sino-Japanese joint history research project was conducted, the Japanese researchers similarly stressed the post-war period. When the texts written by the historians were ready to be made public, the Chinese side expressed unwillingness to publish the chapters on the post-war era (Kitaoka 2010: 7–13). The Japanese side had hoped that 'by adding the contemporary period ... Japan's assistance to China and Japan's status as a peaceful state would be included' (Kawashima 2010: 31). Again, this is important as it clearly demonstrates that the problem with Chinese patriotic education is not only regarded as having to do with depictions of Japanese aggression but, more importantly, with Chinese forgetfulness concerning Japan's development and achievements as a peaceful state that provided China with ODA during the post-war era.

The importance of remembering Japan's post-war development is stressed by politicians belonging to various parties, in editorials in the largest newspapers as well as by leading historians. This further demonstrates the centrality of the post-war period to Japanese self-identity. Whereas it has been demonstrated that Japan's war memories are highly disputed (Seaton 2007), consensus concerning the post-war appears to exist among most Japanese. The post-war has provided a positive and relatively uncontroversial memory that serves as a unifying element of a national identity that can be more broadly agreed upon.

While the many examples discussed above concern how China is seen as denying Japan's peaceful post-war identity through education, another incident, which took place following the Japanese nationalisation of three of the Diaoyu/Senkaku Islands, involved a more explicit denial of this identity in the form of a statement by a Chinese senior government official. In September 2012, Chinese Vice Premier Li Keqiang made the following statement when he met with Papua New Guinea Prime Minister Peter O'Neill: 'Both China and Papua New Guinea were victims to the Japanese fascist invasion back in the Second World War'. He continued: 'Japan's position today on the issue of the Diaoyu Islands is an outright denial of the outcomes of victory in the war against fascism and constitutes a grave challenge to the post-war international order. No nation or people who are peace-loving and justice-upholding will tolerate Japan's stance'. O'Neill reportedly replied: 'Papua New Guinea understands China's position and that Japan's move cannot be accepted by the international community. The international community should work together to defend the post-war world order' (MOFAPRC 2012). Arguing that Japan's behaviour denied the post-war order and that such actions would not be tolerated by 'peace-loving' nations in effect denies Japan's identity as a peaceful nation. This was done in an attempt to appeal to the international community. Li drew a line between the peace-loving international community and Japan, excluding the latter from the former (Gustafsson 2014b). If the international community constitutes a circle of recognition, denial of Japan's identity could arguably spread beyond the bilateral context.

Dealing with the denial of recognition

This section goes one step further in analysing the effects of what is regarded as Chinese denial of Japan's post-war identity as a peaceful state by addressing how the Japanese government has dealt with such perceived denial. Because having one's identity recognised by others is necessary in order to act confidently, doing nothing is not an option. What options are available to Japan in its struggle for recognition within the context of Sino-Japanese relations?

One possibility is for Japan to accept what the Chinese denial suggests – that it does not live up to its self-image – and to work harder to be what it considers itself to be. Such an approach would mean accepting that Japan is not sufficiently peaceful and to try harder. Despite much talk about Japanese 'normalisation' and 'remilitarisation', Japan has not waged war since 1945 and consequently has arguably been peaceful. To argue that it has not would require an extraordinarily broad definition of 'peaceful' that it seems unlikely that the Japanese government will accept.

Another option, in the face of denial of recognition is to attempt to convince the other party that one's stories indeed describe the self accurately. In other words, the actor in question would fight for his or her self-identity, possibly through the use of force. In this particular case, however, Japan requests recognition for its identity as peaceful. It would be an obvious contradiction for Japan to force China to recognise its peaceful identity through violent means.

If force is not an option, how can Japan persuade China that its stories are accurate? Since the mid-2000s, MOFA has tried to convince the Chinese foreign ministry to recognise Japan as peaceful. China did make some concessions, including Wen's speech in the Japanese Diet, which, according to Japanese accounts, recognised Japan's identity for the first time. In addition, MOFA managed to make the Chinese side add some material that emphasises post-war peaceful bilateral relations to Chinese war exhibitions (Gustafsson 2014a). However, there are several indications that this approach might be changing.

To begin with, in response to Chinese Vice Premier Li Keqiang's explicit denial of Japan's identity in September 2012, Japanese Foreign Minister Gemba Koichirō wrote an opinion piece that was published in the *International Herald Tribune* to counter the Chinese allegations. In the article, he responded that Japan through its actions in relation to the Diaoyu/Senkaku dispute is 'absolutely not' trying to deny the post-war international order. He also directly addressed Li's denial of Japan's identity as a peaceful state during the post-war period: 'Japan is a peace-loving nation and has greatly and consistently contributed to peace and prosperity throughout Asia in the post-war period. This policy, strongly supported by our citizens, is a hallmark of Japan and will never change'. He further stated: 'In a joint statement between China and Japan issued when President Hu visited Japan in 2008, China itself stated that, "The Chinese side expressed its positive evaluation of Japan's consistent pursuit of the path of a peaceful country and Japan's contribution to the peace and stability of the world through peaceful means over more than 60 years since World War II"'. While it might be seen as an attempt to convince China to recognise Japan's self-identity, there are several factors suggesting that the audience, which Gemba was addressing was not primarily China. To begin with, the article was published in the *International Herald Tribune*, suggesting that the international community was the primary audience. Moreover, Gemba also criticised China:

> As a first step after the war, Japan concluded the San Francisco Peace Treaty, which was signed by 48 other countries, including the United States. The treaty constitutes an important element of the postwar international order, but the Chinese government considers the treaty "illegal and void." In addition, China enacted a Law on the

Territorial Sea and the Contiguous Zone in 1992 that treats the Senkaku Islands as belonging to China, thus trying to unilaterally change the status of the islands defined by the San Francisco Peace Treaty. Which country, Japan or China, negates the postwar international order? (Gemba 2012)

In addition, following Li's statement, the Japanese MOFA began to stress Japan's identity as a peaceful and democratic country in a number of statements and position papers on the Diaoyu/Senkaku dispute published in a number of languages (e.g. MOFA 2013).

Following another speech by Chinese Prime Minister Li Keqiang that similarly denied Japan's identity, delivered in late May 2013 during a visit to the Cecilienhof Palace in Germany where the Potsdam Proclamation was signed in 1945, Japanese Defence Minister Onodera Itsunori made a speech on 1 June 2013 at the Shangri-La Dialogue, an Asian forum on security issues. Onodera responded to what he referred to as criticism that Japan was 'tilting towards the "right"' and that it was 'abandoning its identity as a "pacifist" nation and ... attempting to challenge the existing international order'. He described such views as a 'total misperception' and stated that the Japanese government stands by expressions of 'deep remorse and genuine apologies'. Onodera's speech might be regarded as an attempt to convince China and/or others that Japan's self-identity is actually correct. Much of the speech appears to be directed at the South East Asian nations rather than at China. Onodera emphasised cooperation with ASEAN and that Japan shares universal values, such as democracy, the rule of law and human rights with these nations (Onodera 2013). He did not explicitly describe China as not subscribing to these values but it was arguably implied.

Just before his official visit to the USA in February 2013, Japanese Prime Minister Abe Shinzō stated in an interview with the *Washington Post* that as a country under one-party rule, China bases its legitimacy on patriotic education, which in effect involves teaching 'anti-Japanese' sentiment. He argued that this education has created a 'mood and atmosphere', which undermines China's 'friendly relationship with Japan' (*Washington Post* 2013). Abe, then, depicted the Chinese government's dependence on 'anti-Japanese' patriotic education for its legitimacy as the root cause of the bad state of Sino-Japanese relations. This was the first time a Japanese prime minister has criticised China's 'anti-Japanese' education in a statement directed at the USA and arguably the international community as a whole.

That Abe made such a statement in an effort to appeal to the international community suggests, along with Onodera's speech, that Japan, or at least its current cabinet, might have given up on attempting to convince China to recognise its peaceful identity. Abe and others seem to regard the Chinese response to Japanese attempts as insufficient. In the absence of the possibility of using force, branding China 'anti-Japanese' can be understood as part of an appeal to the international community. It is a way of arguing that China's assertion is incorrect; that the denial of Japan's identity is an inaccurate description that can only be explained by the fact that China is 'anti-Japanese'. Pleading directly to China is portrayed as impossible because of its hostile and undemocratic identity. Significantly, Abe emphasised Japan's identity as democratic, and that the reason that China teaches 'anti-Japanese' education is its authoritarianism. If the rest of the international community accepts Japan's story this might convince China to follow suit. At the same time, such a course of action could be taken to suggest that China should not be accepted as a responsible member of the international community because, unlike democratic states, it irresponsibly relies on negative representations of its neighbour for legitimacy. This might hurt Chinese efforts at being recognised as a responsible power, thereby causing it to strengthen similar appeals to the international community. The result could be a spiral of negative representations of the other before the international audience that might further inhibit mutual recognition. In addition, it is possible to argue that Abe and others are using Chinese denial of Japan's identity as peaceful, which has previously typically been constructed in relation to Japan's past aggressive self, to refashion Japan's identity in a way that constructs it less in relation to its wartime past and to a greater extent in relation to an undemocratic China.

Japan could take the option of refashioning its identity when faced with denial of its peaceful identity even further. The idea that Japan should become a 'normal' state has been a political goal for Japanese conservatives for decades. For those pushing this agenda, denial of recognition of Japan's peaceful identity presents an opportunity for identity change. Some proponents of this change describe Japan's post-war identity as excessively peaceful and argue that it has been mistaken and 'abnormal'. For this reason, they argue that Japan should abandon its 'mistaken' pacifism and 'normalise' through the revision of the pacifist Article Nine of its constitution and the strengthening of its military (Hagström forthcoming; Kō 2005: 346). For example, the commentator Miyazaki Masahiro has argued that China's 'anti-Japanism' (*han'nichi*) has functioned as an 'external pressure' that has given birth to a Japanese 'healthy nationalism' that will replace its 'mistaken pacifism' (Miyazaki 2005: ix–x, 233–236). Those supporting a revision of the constitution, he maintains, have increased significantly thanks to China's 'anti-Japanism' (Miyazaki 2012). Whereas these arguments might partly be characterised as wishful thinking on behalf of advocates of far-reaching identity and foreign policy change, it is clear that significant changes have indeed taken place, including the reinterpretation of Article Nine of the Japanese constitution to allow for collective self-defence (*Japan Times* 2014). Another commentator has stated that in order to become a 'normal country' Japan must stop yielding to China on diplomatic issues such as the Yasukuni Shrine (Komori 2007: 203–207). A Japanese identity shift in the form of such 'normalisation', it is suggested, would entail constitutional revision and less consideration for Chinese views. Of course, China might not recognise such an identity. However, a 'normal' identity offers more options in the struggle for recognition than does a peaceful one as it can be imposed on others through force. Moreover, the more Japan emphasises its identity as different from China, the less important Chinese recognition becomes.

Conclusion

This article has demonstrated that the Chinese government's patriotic education is viewed as the root cause of 'anti-Japanese' incidents in China. The Chinese government has come to be seen as not recognising Japan's identity as a peaceful state during the post-war era. It is regarded as 'anti-Japanese' not merely because demonstrations against Japan and attacks on Japanese material interests have taken place. More fundamentally and importantly, China is seen as 'anti-Japanese' because it is understood as denying a key component of Japan's self-image. The analysis has also shown that when the Chinese leadership explicitly recognised Japan's identity this move was very positively received within Japan. However, when it explicitly denied Japan's identity, Japanese leaders reacted by criticising China for being undemocratic and even 'anti-Japanese'. There are clear signs that Japanese identity entrepreneurs who advocate identity change in the form of 'normalisation' and challenge Japan's peaceful identity as 'mistaken', are attempting to take advantage of Chinese denials of Japan's identity as peaceful.

China (and other countries) can (and do) influence Japanese identity by recognising or denying recognition of specific stories about Japan. The politics of recognition in Sino-Japanese relations can influence the future course of Sino-Japanese relations. The best way for China (and other countries) to make sure that Japan stays peaceful and refrains from 'normalising' is to recognise that it has been peaceful during the post-war period. Recognising this identity might also encourage further contrition on behalf of Japan as this identity is often stressed in relation to Japan's aggressive wartime self. In contrast, if China continues to deny Japan recognition for this identity it may very well lead Japan to refashion its identity in relation to a negatively depicted undemocratic China to a greater extent and in relation to its past aggressive self to a lesser extent.

Acknowledgements

The author would like to thank Hans Agné, Linus Hagström, Ulv Hanssen, John Hennessey, Björn Jerdén, Shogo Suzuki, Taku Tamaki and one anonymous reviewer for insightful comments on earlier drafts of this article. A collective expression of gratitude also goes to the participants in the International Security section of the Swedish Political Science Association's annual meeting in Stockholm 2–4 October 2013.

Funding

This work was supported by the Swedish Research Council [grant number 2012-1150].

Notes

1. In one opinion poll, respondents choose three countries they 'strongly dislike' (*kirai*). In July 1989, following the crackdown on Tiananmen Square in Beijing, 30.2% of Japanese respondents expressed 'strong dislike' of China. After this, it never exceeded 30% until August 2004 when it reached 31.5%. Around the time of the large-scale demonstrations against Japan in China in May 2005, 43.3% of respondents disliked China and in November 2010, the figure reached 68.8% (Jiji Tsūshinsha 1988–2013). A survey on whether Japanese 'feel affinity with China' similarly demonstrated that respondents who 'do not feel any affinity with China' have surged from around 50% in 2003 to 63.4% in 2005, and remained high thereafter, hitting 80.6% in October 2012 (Cabinet Office 2012).
2. This is based on an analysis of the results yielded by a search in the database for Japanese parliamentary debates for sessions in which the word 'anti-Japan/anti-Japanese' is mentioned. The database is available online: http://kokkai.ndl.go.jp.
3. This is based on an analysis of the search results yielded by a search conducted on 18 March 2013 for all books listed in the National Diet Library's catalogue, which mention the word 'anti-Japan/anti-Japanese' in their titles. The catalogue is available online: http://ndl.go.jp.
4. This is based on the analysis of the results of a search for editorials in which the word 'anti-Japan/anti-Japanese' appeared in the *Yomiuri Shimbun's Yomidasu* database.
5. This is based on an analysis of all the results of a search in the *Asahi Shimbun's Kikuzō* database for editorials that mention the word 'anti-Japan/anti-Japanese'.

References

Abe, S. (2006) *Press Conference by Prime Minister Abe Following His Visit to China*, accessed at http://www.kantei.go.jp/foreign/abespeech/2006/10/08chinapress_e.html, 26 June 2013.
Asahi Shimbun. (2005) *Chūgoku no Hōdō: Jijitsu o Tsutaetehoshii* [China's news reports: convey the truth], 13 April.
Asahi Shimbun. (2007) *On Shushō Enzetsu: Nihon e no Hyōka o Kangeisuru*, [Prime Minister Wen's speech: the appraisal of Japan is welcomed], 13 April.
Asahi Shimbun. (2012) *Nittchū Kokkō 40nen: Kōryū Hiroge, Shinrai Tatenaose*, [Sino-Japanese diplomatic relations 40 years: expand exchanges, rebuild trust], 29 September.
Berger, T. U. (1998) *Cultures of Antimilitarism: National Security in Germany and Japan*, Baltimore, MD: Johns Hopkins University Press.
Bukh, A. (2010) *Japan's National Identity and Foreign Policy: Russia as Japan's 'Other'*, Oxon and New York: Routledge.

Cabinet Office (Government of Japan). (2012) *Gaikō ni Kansuru Seron Chōsa* [Opinion Survey on Foreign Policy], accessed at http://www8.cao.go.jp/survey/h24/h24-gaiko/zh/z10.html, 26 June 2013.

Fukuda, Y. (2007) *Forging the Future Together*, accessed at http://www.mofa.go.jp/region/asia-paci/china/speech0712.html, 26 June 2013.

Gemba, K. (2012) 'Japan-China relations at a crossroads', *International Herald Tribune*, 21 November; accessed at http://www.mofa.go.jp/mofaj/annai/honsho/gaisho/gemba/pdfs/iht_121121_en.pdf, 15 August 2013.

Guillaume, X. (2011) *International Relations and Identity: a Dialogical Approach*, Oxon and New York: Routledge.

Gustafsson, K. (2011) *Narratives and Bilateral Relations: Rethinking the 'History Issue' in Sino-Japanese Relations*. PhD Thesis. Stockholm: Department of Political Science, Stockholm University. Accessed at http://su.diva-portal.org/smash/record.jsf?pid=diva2:414566, 15 May 2013.

Gustafsson, K. (2014a) 'Memory politics and ontological security in Sino-Japanese relations', *Asian Studies Review* 38(1): 71–86.

Gustafsson, K. (2014b) 'Is China's discursive power increasing? The case of the 'power of the past' in Sino-Japanese relations', *Asian Perspective* 38(3): 411–33.

Hagström, L. (2008/09) 'Sino-Japanese relations: the ice that won't melt', *International Journal* 64(1): 223–40.

Hagström, L. (forthcoming) 'The "abnormal" state: identity, norm/exception and Japan', *European Journal of International Relations*.

Hashimoto, R. (1997) 'Prime Minister Hashimoto's Speech in Beijing "Japan–China Relations in the New Age: new Developments in Dialogue and Cooperation"', accessed at http://www.mofa.go.jp/region/asia-paci/china/dialogue.html, 25 June 2013.

He, Y. (2009) *The Search for Reconciliation: Sino-Japanese and German-Polish Relations Since World War II*, Cambridge and New York: Cambridge University Press.

Honneth, A. (2012) 'Recognition between states: on the moral substrate of international relations', in T. Lindemann and E. Ringmar (eds) *The International Politics of Recognition*, Boulder, CO: Paradigm, pp. 25–38.

Japan Times. (2014) *Abe guts Article 9*, 2 July.

Jerdén, B. and Hagström, L. (2012) 'Rethinking Japan's China policy: Japan as an accommodator in the rise of China, 1978–2011', *Journal of East Asian Studies* 12: 215–50.

Jiji Tsūshinsha. (1988–2013) *Jiji seron chōsa* [Jiji Public Opinion Survey].

Katzenstein, P. J. (1996) *Cultural Norms & National Security: Police and Military in Postwar Japan*, Ithaca and London: Cornell University Press.

Kawashima, S. (2010) 'The three phases of Japan-China joint-history research: what was the challenge?' *Asian Perspective* 34(4): 19–43.

Kitaoka, S. (2010) 'A look back on the work of the joint Japanese-Chinese history research committee', *Asia-Pacific Review* 17(1): 6–20.

Koizumi, J. (2001) '*Chūgoku Jinmin Kōnichi Sensō Kinenkan Hōmon go no Koizumi Sōri no hatsugen*' [Prime minister Koizumi's statement following his visit to the Chinese People's War of Resistance Memorial Hall], accessed at http://www.mofa.go.jp/mofaj/kaidan/s_koi/china0110/hatsugen.html, 21 May 2013.

Koizumi, J. (2005) 'Speech by H.E. Junichiro Koizumi, prime minister of Japan', accessed at http://www.mofa.go.jp/region/asia-paci/meet0504/speech.html, 21 May 2013.

Kokubun, R. (2006) 'The shifting nature of Japan–China relations after the cold war', in P. E. Lam (ed) *Japan's Relations with China: Facing a Rising Power*, London and New York: Routledge, 21–36.

Komori, Y. (2007) *Chūgoku 'Han' Nichi' no Kyomō* [The lies of China's 'anti-Japanism'], Tokyo: Kairyūsha.

Kō, B. (2005) *Chūgoku, Kankoku han'nichi Rekishi Kyōiku no bōsō* [China and South Korea's reckless anti-Japanese education], Tokyo: Nihon Bungeisha.

Koo, M. (2009) 'The Senkaku/Diaoyu dispute and Sino-Japanese political-economic relations – cold politics and hot economics?' *The Pacific Review* 22 (2): 205–32.

Lind, J. (2008) *Sorry States: Apologies in International Politics*, Ithaca: Cornell University Press.

Lindemann, T. (2010) *Causes of War: the Struggle for Recognition*, Colchester: ECPR Press.

Miyazaki, M. (2005) *Chūgoku yo, 'han'nichi' Arigatō! Kore De Nihon mo Futsū no Kuni ni Nareru* [China, thanks for 'anti-Japanism: now Japan can become a normal country], Tokyo: Seiryū shuppansha.

Miyazaki, M. (2012) 'Senkaku sensō taibōron: sayonara heiwaboke' [On the long-awaited Senkaku war: goodbye complacent pacifism], *Sankei shimbun*, 19 December; accessed at http://sankei.jp.msn.com/life/news/121219/bks12121903010000-n4.htm, 15 September 2013.

MOFA. (2005) *60 Years: The Path of a Nation Striving for Global Peace*, accessed at http://www.mofa.go.jp/policy/postwar/pamph60.pdf, 21 May 2013.

MOFA. (2008) *Joint Statement Between the Government of Japan and the Government of the People's Republic of China on Comprehensive Promotion of a "Mutually Beneficial Relationship Based on Common Strategic Interests*, 7 May; accessed at http://www.mofa.go.jp/region/asia-paci/china/joint0805.html, 21 May 2013.

MOFA. (2009) *Japan and China: Building a Mutually Beneficial Relationship Based on Common Strategic Interests*, accessed at http://www.mofa.go.jp/region/asia-paci/china/relation.pdf, 21 May 2013.

MOFA. (2013) *Position Paper: Japan–China Relations Surrounding the Situation of the Situation of the Senkaku Islands – in Response to China's Weapons-guiding Lock-on*, 7 February; accessed at http://www.mofa.go.jp/region/asia-paci/senkaku/position_paper3_en.html, 13 September 2013.

MOFAPRC. (2012) *Li Keqiang Meets with Papua New Guinea Prime Minister O'Neill*, 11 September; accessed at http://www.fmprc.gov.cn/eng/topics/diaodao/t969873.htm, 15 August 2013.

Murayama, T. (1995) *On the Occasion of the 50th Anniversary of the War's End*, accessed at http://www.mofa.go.jp/announce/press/pm/murayama/9508.html, 23 May 2013.

Murray, M. (2010) 'Identity, insecurity, and great power politics: the tragedy of German naval ambition before the First World War', *Security Studies* 19(4): 656–88.

Onodera, I. (2013) *Defending National Interests, Preventing Conflicts*, accessed at http://www.iiss.org/en/events/shangri%20la%20dialogue/archive/shangri-la-dialogue-2013-c890/second-plenary-session-8bc4/onodera-d174, 29 July 2013.

Oros, A. L. (2008) *Normalizing Japan: Politics, Security, and the Evolution of Security Practice*, Stanford, CA: Stanford University Press.

Ringmar, E. (2002) 'The Recognition Game: Soviet Russia Against the West', *Cooperation and Conflict* 37(2): 115–36.

Ringmar, E. (2007) [1996] *Identity, Interest and Action: a Cultural Explanation of Sweden's Intervention in the Thirty Years War*, Cambridge and New York: Cambridge University Press.

Ringmar, E. (2012) 'Introduction: the international politics of recognition', in T. Lindemann and E. Ringmar (eds) *The International Politics of Recognition*, Boulder, CO: Paradigm, pp. 3–23.

Sankei Shimbun. (2005) *Chūgoku Fukushushō Kikoku: Me ni Shitakunakatta Ugoki* [The Chinese Vice Premier returns to China: a development we did not wish to see], 24 May.

Schulze, K. (2013) *From 'Head of Flying Geese' to 'Thought Leader': the Rise of China and Changes in Japan's Foreign Policy Identity*, unpublished doctoral thesis, Duisburg: Department for Social Sciences/Institute of East Asian Studies, Duisburg–Essen University.

Seaton, P. (2007) *Japan's Contested War Memories: the 'Memory Rifts' in the Historical Consciousness of World War II*, London and New York: Routledge.

Steele, B. J. (2008) *Ontological Security in International Relations: Self-identity and the IR State*, Oxon and New York: Routledge.

Tamaki, T. (2010) *Deconstructing Japan's Image of South Korea: Identity in Foreign Policy*, New York, NY: Palgrave Macmillan.

Washington Post. (2013) *Transcript of Interview with Japanese Prime Minister Shinzo Abe*, 20 February; accessed at http://www.washingtonpost.com/world/transcript-of-interview-with-japanese-prime-minister-shinzo-abe/2013/02/20/e7518d54-7b1c-11e2-82e8-61a46c2cde3d_story_3.html, 15 September 2013.

Wen, J. (2007) *Speech by Premier Wen Jiabao of the State Council of the People's Republic of China at the Japanese Diet*, 13 March, accessed at http://www.fmprc.gov.cn/eng/zxxx/t311544.htm, 23 April 2013.

Wendt, A. (2003) 'Why a World State is Inevitable', *European Journal of International Relations* 9(4): 491–542.

Wolf, R. (2011) 'Respect and disrespect in international relations: the significance of status recognition', *International Theory* 3(1): 105–42.

Yomiuri Shimbun. (2005a) *Nitchū Shunō Kaidan: Kawaranu Chūgoku no "Rekishiteki Jijitsu" Waikyoku* [Japan–China summit: China's distortion of 'historical truth' unchanged], 24 April.

Yomiuri Shimbun. (2005b) *Han'nichi" demo soshi: Risshōsareta chūgoku tōkyoku no "nōryoku"* ["Anti-Japanese" demonstrations interrupted: the Chinese authorities' "ability" demonstrated], 5 May.

Yomiuri Shimbun. (2007) *On Kahō Shushō Enzetsu: Chūgoku no Tainichi Shisei ni Henka ga Mieta* [Wen Jiabao's speech: a change could be seen in China's attitude toward Japan], 13 April.

Yomiuri Shimbun. (2012) *Chūgoku Iatsu Gaikō: Risuku Zōdai de Nihon no Tōshigen mo* [China's coercive diplomacy: the increased risk may curb Japanese investments], 23 September.

International and domestic challenges to Japan's postwar security identity: 'norm constructivism' and Japan's new 'proactive pacifism'

Andrew L. Oros

Abstract Japan today is widely portrayed as on the verge of a significant identity shift that could lead to dramatic new security policies. Yet, Japan's first formal national security strategy, adopted in December 2013, proclaims repeatedly Japan's long-standing 'peace-loving' policies and principles. Why does a conservative government with high levels of popular support not pursue policies more in line with views widely reported to be central to its values and outlook? The answer lies in Japan's long-standing security identity of domestic antimilitarism, an identity under siege to a degree not seen since its creation over 50 years ago, but – as evidenced in Japan's new national strategy document – one that continues to shape both the framing of Japan's national security debates and the institutions of Japan's postwar security policy-making process. Relational approaches to identity construction illuminate challenges to Japan's dominant security identity, but a focus on domestic institutions and electoral politics offers the best course for modeling identity construction and predicting its future resilience.

Japan will continue to adhere to the course that it has taken to date as a peace-loving nation, and as a major player in world politics and economy, continue even more proactively in securing peace, stability, and prosperity of the international community, while achieving its own security as well as peace and stability in the Asia-Pacific region as a 'Proactive Contributor to Peace' based on the principle of international cooperation. This is the fundamental principle of national security that Japan should stand to hold.

National Security Strategy of Japan, 17 December 2013

Introduction

The publication of Japan's first national security strategy (NSS) document culminates the first stage of a controversial and closely followed process of reformulation of Japan's security policies under a reportedly nationalist and conservative government that has sought to respond to 'severe' security challenges (Japan National Security Council [JSNC] 2013: 1). As with much-reported policy announcements under popular conservative Prime Minister Koizumi Junichiro (2001–2006) and before that popular conservative Prime Minister Nakasone Yasuhiro (1982–1987), Japan today is widely portrayed (including in some other contributions to this special issue) as on the verge of a significant identity shift that could lead to dramatic new security policy pronouncements. Yet, the NSS adopted by the allegedly 'hyper-nationalist' cabinet of Abe Shinzō (*New York Times* 2013) proclaims repeatedly Japan's long-standing 'peace-loving' policies and principles. How can one reconcile this apparent contradiction? Why does not a conservative prime minister with high levels of popular support pursue policies more in line with views widely reported to be central to his values and outlook?

Just as with previous popular conservative prime ministers, the answer lies in Japan's long-standing security identity of domestic antimilitarism (SIDA), an identity under siege to a degree not seen since its creation over 50 years ago but – as evidenced in Japan's first NSS – one that thoroughly pervades both the framing of Japan's national security debates and the institutions of Japan's postwar security policy-making process.

> A security identity is a set of collectively held principles that have attracted broad political support regarding the appropriate role of state action in the security arena and are institutionalized into the policy-making process…providing an overarching framework recognized both by top decision makers and by major societal actors under which a state shapes its security practices.
>
> (Oros 2008: 9)

As developed and codified in the early post-World War II period, Japan's postwar security identity is defined by three central tenets: (1) Japan will possess no traditional armed forces; (2) there will be no use of force by Japan except in self-defense; and (3) no Japanese participation in foreign wars.[1] Japan's contemporary security identity continues to be rooted in these core principles, which structures specific policy decisions together with shifting domestic and international circumstances. It is not the policies themselves that define this identity: rather, it is the central tenets of the security identity that structure policy formulation.

Other scholars have articulated principles that have guided postwar Japan in different ways, including by observing continuity of action or by rooting analysis on government policy proclamations. The principles associated with the so-called Yoshida Doctrine are one such example (e.g. Green 2001; Pyle 2007). By contrast, the three central tenets of the SIDA employed in this analysis are drawn from principles articulated by diverse political actors, negotiated through the formal political process (through electoral outcomes, Diet debates, and the crafting of legislation), reified through popular reporting (norm creation), and institutionalized into countless regulations and formalized bureaucratic practices. Once codified, this security identity influences security practice in three ways: '(1) through its influence on policy rhetoric, (2) its structuring of public opinion and the coalition-building opportunities this enables, and (3) its institutionalization into the policy-making process' (Oros 2008: 193).

The Japanese state and Japanese people juggle multiple identities, as apparent from the other articles in this special issue and other recent scholarship related to Japanese identity (e.g., Ashizawa 2013). Moreover, Japanese individuals and groups actively and at times passionately disagree with each other about identity conceptions – such as the contrast between some Japanese pacifists who demonstrate an almost religious devotion to Article Nine of Japan's postwar constitution and some Japanese nationalists who rail against the perceived violation of sovereignty and trust in Japan that Article Nine symbolizes. Alternate identity conceptions of Japan as a victim state, an economic superpower, or as the lead goose in the flying geese model of Japan as leader of Asia, among others, are prevalent and also can be argued to structure policy decisions in certain contexts. In the past several decades, aspiring prime ministers have even taken to writing books that espouse their imagined identity for Japan, such as Prime Minister Abe's conception of Japan as a 'beautiful country' (Abe 2006).

Some states – including postwar Japan – negotiate, construct, and reify a durable 'security identity' that structures policy debate and choices over national security-related issues over time. If successfully constructed and codified, a security identity enjoys broad legitimacy at the level of the general public: it is not merely a creation by political elites. However, as a broad set of principles, it requires interpretation by political elites in order to be translated into specific policy proposals and action. In this way, policy can change over time under guidance of policy elites based on changing domestic and international circumstances, as long as it can be articulated and justified in terms of the security identity – and sometimes, if a powerful political actor wishes to expend political capital, even if the policy cannot be articulated and justified in terms of the security identity. Contestation over the guiding principles, and later the implementation of these principles, has been an enduring facet of postwar Japan, experiencing ebbs and flows in line with substantial changes in Japan's domestic and international environment – despite continuity in the core principles (the three central tenets) upon which the identity is based.

Recent events and government policy decisions illustrate challenges to the dominant security identity that have long taken place, but which have repeatedly failed to change the fundamental nature of the security identity. For example, the distinction between Japan's 'self-defense forces' (JSDF) and the military forces of other states has become less clear as the JSDF develop new – once taboo – capabilities such as mid-air refueling of fighter aircraft and long-distance heavy-lift transport planes, challenging the first tenet of the SIDA (no traditional military forces). Prime Minister Abe's call for Japan to participate in 'collective self-defense' with other states challenges the second tenet of the SIDA: raising the possibility of Japan engaging in the use of force abroad. JSDF participation in limited deployments in the US-led foreign wars in Afghanistan (2001–2010) and Iraq (2004–2006) under the direction of Prime Minister Koizumi challenged the third tenet of the SIDA (no participation in foreign wars), even though the JSDF did not directly participate in combat-related activities. These examples, among many others, illustrate challenges to Japan's dominant security identity and underscore that such challenges are not new to Abe-era Japan. Still, these challenges could have a substantial impact on Japan's long-standing security policies rooted in non-military approaches if successful in modifying the core principles upon which the security identity is based.

To date, however, the underlying principles of the SIDA remain resilient. In part this is because they are vigorously defended by powerful political actors. More broadly, Japan's long-standing security identity endures because it is widely supported by public opinion in Japan's vibrant democracy[2] – and it enjoys this high level of support because it is seen as having contributed greatly to the success of postwar Japan: a country that has not lost a single member of its armed forces to a combat-related casualty in nearly seventy years, and which today is the third-largest economy in the world with living standards among the world's highest. Importantly, however, the identity is resilient because it is adaptable: it is not rooted in unchanging security practices but rather in a set of principles that can be interpreted in line with shifting domestic and international political realities.

By adopting a formal NSS document that will guide Japan's national security policy 'over the next decade', the Abe Cabinet itself provides another important illustration of how the SIDA will continue to structure Japan's security policies for years to come, despite powerful political actors seeking change not just to policy but to the security identity itself. True identity shift – replacing the three central tenets of the SIDA with other guiding principles – is unlikely absent even more dramatic changes to

Japan's international and domestic political environment, and the rise of new 'identity entrepreneurs' who can successfully craft and embed such new guiding principles into a new security identity. Relational approaches to conceptualizing identity can help illuminate the process by which such international changes may be interpreted domestically, and share an interest in the concept of 'identity entrepreneurs.' This article, however, roots Japanese security identity in three principles that only indirectly are relational in nature. As such, the argument could be considered within the broad approach of 'norm constructivism' as defined in the 'Introduction' to this special issue. Unlike some conceptualizations within that broad school that focus on norm creation from an ideational or institutional perspective (e.g., Berger 1998; Hopf 2002), this article argues that attention to the organized domestic politics of identity construction and maintenance in the context of shifts in the international and domestic environment is central to understanding the future of Japanese security identity and resulting security policies.

The remainder of this article will proceed as follows. First, identity as an explanatory variable will be considered vis-à-vis other explanations for both policy continuity and policy change in contemporary Japanese security policy, in particular relational approaches to identity. Next, the role of security identity in contributing to policy continuity across the six prime ministers who served in the era of the 'twisted Diet' (2007–2012) will be examined. Finally, the security policies and ambitions of the second Abe Cabinet will be evaluated in relation to challenges to the SIDA. The conclusion will theorize about possible next steps in the battle over Japan's security identity and the likely impact on policy, and also further consider how different approaches to the study of identity can complement each other to better explain both policy outcomes and the adaptation of the identities themselves.

Security identity and other explanations for policy change and continuity

Public debates about Japan's identity are at the center of all of the central security policy issues Japan faces today. As ably demonstrated in other articles in this collection, conceptions of Japanese identity directly relate to what is outside of or perceived as 'the other' – such as another country or even an entire region. An examination of changing notions of 'the other' offers insight into how Japanese view themselves. How Japanese interact and view each other, however, is also an important area for study. There can be no question that this issue is related to how Japanese view those they perceive or create as 'others,' but a focus on the domestic politics of identity – in particular durable groups of Japanese who support or challenge Japan's postwar hegemonic security identity – reveals insights into

Japanese identity that a focus primarily on 'othering' touches on only indirectly. Postwar democratic Japan is replete with competing groups who advocate for different identities for Japan, including several different schools of conservative thought, different articulations of 'pacifism' (*heiwa shugi*), and even different forms of nationalism on both the political right and political left.

The *politics* of identity politics is often under-appreciated in scholarship on identity. Abdelal, Herrera, Johnston and McDermott (2006) and others have sought to 'bring the politics back in' – as have other contributors to this special issue. More often, however, 'politics' is conflated with the more abstract notion of 'contestation' in ways that obfuscate the organized political aspects of identity politics, particularly within democracies. Domestic power struggles rooted in competing conceptions of Japanese identity have been an important facet of Japanese domestic politics throughout the modern era, both prewar and postwar. Sometimes these debates are explicitly framed in terms of identity – such as Prime Minister Abe's call for Japan to embrace his concept of 'proactive pacifism' (*sekkyokuteki heiwashugi*)[3] – and other times the identity component underlies what to outsiders might seem simply a discussion of a specific policy issue. For example, controversy over the dispatch of the JSDF overseas or whether to relax restrictions on the export of weapons are at least as much debates over identity as they are about the benefits and drawbacks of the policies themselves.

Identity politics over security issues have been especially visible in the tumultuous years since the end of the popular Koizumi administration in 2006 – a period that witnessed seven prime ministers in seven years, the rise and fall of an opposition political party to power, and the return of Abe as prime minister in December 2012. A focus on the domestic politics of identity can offer insights both about Japan's near-term security policy direction as well as on the scholarly issue of how identity can stand resilient in the face of sustained assault by powerful political actors and substantial changes in the international environment. Japan's regional environment has changed for the worse in recent years, including the first real concerns about military confrontation in decades – with China over the disputed Senkaku islands (Diaoyu in Chinese) in the East China Sea. Beyond the territorial dispute, China's rising military spending and more provocative military activities have put great strains on Japan's long-standing non-military security practices, as well as Japan's overall conception of China – as described by Suzuki and Gustafsson in this collection of articles. In addition, North Korea continues to pose serious security challenges to Japan. More broadly, Japan's economic and military might – as well as that of its only formal ally, the US – has declined relative to other states in the region in the past decade. Such shifting material factors outside of Japan – in additional to shifting factors internally (discussed below) – have altered the balance of power among different political actors within Japan.

Some conceptions of identity reject the notion of material factors contributing directly to identity shift, instead focusing on how actors ascribe meaning to such change. As Hagström and Gustafsson write in the 'Introduction' to this special issue, 'we do contest the possibility that these factors can have any precise or clear meaning independent of the discourses in which they are constituted as objects'. This point recalls lengthy discussions within the realist paradigm of threat perception – which, in essence, argues that the idea of threat is not based solely on material factors (e.g. Walt 1985). Substantial changes in material factors combined with observed actor conduct can be reasonably understood to change actor perceptions of 'other' without a lengthy evaluation of discourse and self-other conceptualizations, however. Some changes to the international environment are so dramatic as to not require detailed analysis to understand that the change will be perceived as a threat. Such dramatic change is evident in Japan's regional environment in the past decade.

Scholarship that endeavors to make the connection between material change and threat perception (such as work employing the concept of 'securitization') can be useful to better understand the nature of identity – as seen by numerous contributors to this collection – but can shift focus away from the outcomes effect of identity on policy. Such examinations also can reveal the process whereby new threats are perceived and institutionalized into the policy-making process – such as the notable first mention of China as a 'threat' in Japanese government policy documents and the more recent stark characterization of China as a state that 'attempts to change the status quo by coercion' (JSNC 2013: 5), which also is a useful contribution.

While changes in Japan's international environment may be seen to be pushing Japan to consider a more active military security posture internationally (as multiple schools of realist theory would predict), domestic factors are pulling Japanese policy-makers in multiple directions. On one hand, as argued further below, Prime Minister Abe and his supporters have long sought for Japan to play a more active military role abroad. In this context, recent international developments can be seen more as facilitators than instigators of new policies the Abe administration has advocated for in the area of national security (some of which have passed, many of which have not). The virtual collapse of organized party opposition on the left – exemplified by the rise and fall of the Democratic Party of Japan (DPJ) from political power – further facilitates a shift to more activist security policies abroad.

On the other hand, however, Japanese policy-makers face other domestic political concerns that lead many to question whether Japan should devote more resources to military security. In particular, concerns over Japan's dismal fiscal situation and its rapidly aging demographic profile create great pressure for policy priority to be placed on those areas. The Abe government has reversed a 10-year annual decline in defense spending, but only very modestly – a 0.8% increase in FY13–14 and a proposed 3% increase in FY14–15; even with these increases, Japan will spend less on defense in 2014 than it did in 2000–2004 (http://www.mod.go.jp/e/d_budget/index.html) – despite a greatly increased perception of security threats from abroad among the Japanese public. Japan's debt to gross domestic product (GDP) ratio is the highest of the advanced industrial democracies – even higher than Greece, Ireland, and Italy. The high level of deficit spending greatly constrains substantial future increases in defense spending (De Koning and Lipscy 2013). Moreover, other areas of Japan's budget are expected to rise due to Japan's challenging demographic profile, the most rapidly aging among the advanced industrial democracies. These demographics lead to great pressure for increased spending on healthcare and retirement pensions, potentially crowding out increased defense spending (Glosserman and Tsunoda 2009).

Utilizing the concept of security identity helps to explain the way that domestic and international pressures are reconciled in policy. The SIDA sets boundaries for appropriate action in the foreign policy arena, though it does not rise to the level of a uniformly held causal or principled belief theorized in some conceptions of identity. This facet of a security identity – setting boundaries, not dictating thought – is evident in the examples above, where the head of government himself (Prime Minister Abe) is advocating for pushing beyond boundaries derived from the SIDA. However, because many political actors *do* subscribe to the values and beliefs embedded in the SIDA, the security identity exerts additional influence in some areas of policy-making. In postwar Japan, however, a minority of powerful political actors (including the grandfather of Prime Minister Abe, former Prime Minister Kishi, as well as former Prime Minister Nakasone, among others) has always sought for Japan to play a larger military role in the region – in conflict with the dominant security identity – but their views remained in the minority. Still, these minority views have influenced political debate and some policy outcomes in the past,[4] and have been exerting growing influence on policy outcomes in recent years – a subject addressed in subsequent sections below.

The security identity, therefore, is not always concerned with *what* political actors seek to accomplish but rather with *how* they will attempt to accomplish their goals given the overarching framework (and content) of the SIDA. Thus, at a practical level, this framework can help to explain current Prime Minister Abe's successes and failures to change security policy: Abe is not a subscriber to the core tenets of the SIDA, but he *is* constrained by them. Moreover, by advocating for his preferred policy agenda, and succeeding to some extent, he poses a challenge to the hegemony of the dominant security identity over time.

Newspaper headlines of late attest to the fact that Japan's long-dominant security identity is under siege – from within (by policy elites, such as Abe and others within the Liberal Democratic Party, LDP) and from outside (via Japan's civil society activists as well as international actors), ideationally (those who question the efficacy of the SIDA) and materially (due to a changing international security environment). One can see such challenges to all three 'clusters of order' that Lieberman (2002) conceptualizes as at the core of identity maintenance and hegemony: governing institutions (legislatures, executives, bureaucracies, courts), the 'organizational environment' (parties and interest groups), and the 'ideological repertoire' (newspaper op-eds, intellectuals, popular culture).

The following two sections will elucidate such challenges over two recent periods, during the period of turmoil of the 'twisted Diet' (2007–2012) and under the second Abe government (2012–). In both cases, the findings from earlier work on the effect of security identity on policy-making are confirmed: 'policy initiatives that conform to existing interpretation of the security identity of domestic antimilitarism should proceed quickly and be relatively unhindered, absent other intervening factors such as bureaucratic politics, alliance politics, or personal executive leadership effectiveness', while 'policy initiatives that conflict with the existing interpretation of the security identity should take more time, require extensive use of political capital, and often necessitate substantial political concessions to the initial intent of the policy in order to proceed' (Oros 2008: 17). However, as argued below, the extent of political capital required to enact policy contrary to the three tenets of the SIDA seems to be declining in comparison to earlier periods, and further policy initiatives in this direction appear to be forthcoming.

The 'twisted Diet' and twists in long-standing identity politics, 2007–2012

A great cloud of uncertainty hovered over Japan's security identity and security policies as popular Prime Minister Koizumi handed over the reins of power to his successor, Abe, in September 2006. Then, as now, Japan appeared to face a great challenge to develop cooperative security policies with China and South Korea in particular, and the new prime minister's reportedly nationalist statements and policy initiatives generated substantial concern at home and abroad. The year that followed, however, departed greatly from the expected script: in July 2007 (after Abe had been in office only 10 months) the LDP lost control of the House of Councillors (the less-powerful upper house of Japan's parliament), which created a divided government, or what the Japanese media termed a 'twisted Diet' (*nejiri kokkai*), for the first time under the postwar constitution. In September 2007 Abe resigned as prime minister, reportedly for health reasons.

In the next two years, two more LDP prime ministers (Fukuda Yasuo and Asō Tarō) served for only one year each. Then, in a historic moment in postwar Japanese politics, the LDP lost the House of Representatives election to another party for the first time since the LDP was formed in 1955, to the rival DPJ. As with the first Abe government, however, the DPJ also enjoyed less than one year of control of both houses of the Diet, losing control over the Upper House in July 2010. The period of the 'twisted Diet' and annual turnover of prime ministers continued until December 2012, when Abe led the LDP to an electoral victory in the Lower House, and returned to the prime ministership. The subsequent July 2013 election appears to have locked in LDP control over both houses of the Diet until at least July 2016 (the next required national election, of the House of Councillors), together with its long-term coalition partner, the New Komei Party (NKP).

The frequent party and leadership turnover in the period from September 2006 to December 2012 may partially explain why a dramatic change to Japan's security identity or policies did not take place during this period – i.e., no single leader had enough time to enact substantial change. The period does offer a first opportunity to examine how the SIDA constrained the policy agenda of Prime Minister Abe, in his first term as prime minister, however. Moreover, beginning in September 2009, the period offers the opportunity to examine whether a security identity created and institutionalized under one political party (the LDP) would endure after a new political party took over the reins of political power. Substantial media reporting predicted great breaks from past security practice during this period – from predictions of revision of Article Nine of the constitution under the Abe administration to a wholesale re-crafting of the US–Japan military alliance under the first DPJ Hatoyama administration. However, while the period indeed saw many challenges to the SIDA, it did not see more success in implementing policies contrary to principles embedded in the SIDA than in previous periods.

In contrast, the once-opposition then ruling party DPJ embracing of the vast majority of LDP-advocated and LDP-adopted security policies and approaches marked a historic moment in Japanese security identity and security policy formulation: a moment where the ruling coalition and opposition coalition expressed substantial agreement about the general contours of Japan's security policies. Although some individual politicians of both major parties continue to disagree with some aspects of their party's mainstream positions, the consensus compromise legislation and practices illustrated striking continuity of outcomes – despite many instances of expressed concern that this would not be the case. Multiple factors together explain this striking continuity of policy, but the central tenets of the SIDA provided existing institutions, practices, enabling rhetoric, and public support that greatly contributed to this continuity.

Growing concern over Japan's regional security environment was evident throughout this period, as also discussed in several other contributions to this special issue. In particular, Japan's growing sense of insecurity vis-à-vis China has been noted by the Gustafsson and Suzuki contributions to this special issue. The first concerted policy response to military concerns of a rising China was developed internally within the LDP governments of Abe, Fukuda, and Aso and crafted into a new draft National Defense Program Guidelines (NDPG) in 2009. Before this new NDPG could be formally adopted; however, the LDP lost control of the Diet, and the DPJ rose to power. Over the course of the next year, the security situation vis-à-vis China further worsened, with China's GDP surpassing Japan's to become the second largest economy in the world and the first of what would become a series of escalating disputes over control of the Senkaku/Diaoyu islands in the fall of 2010.

The 2010 NDPG adopted by the DPJ government in December marked a substantial change to Japan's long-standing regional security posture – to the extent that it was widely characterized both within Japan and outside of Japan as a dramatic break from the past. Indeed, although the new NDPG released by the Abe government in December 2013 has received substantial coverage as an example of further 'identity shift' in Japan, it is the 2010 NDPG (that was largely based on a template provided by the previous LDP government) that introduced most of the core concepts that the 2013 NDPG seeks to further advance – such as 'dynamic defense,' increased capabilities for the JSDF, the 'southwestern shift' of the JSDF to respond to the increased China threat, relaxations on arms export restrictions and joint weapons production, and the strategic use of overseas development assistance (ODA).[5]

What is notable about the 2010 NDPG from an identity perspective is that it carefully articulates the rationale for each incremental change in security policy using language and concepts derived from the SIDA. It does not set out a new rationale for Japanese security, but rather argues that new material circumstances require an adjustment of policies largely within the framework of the existing principles of the SIDA of a highly constrained JSDF (tenet one) that would not become involved in foreign wars (tenet three) and would not threaten force to solve international disputes (tenet two). Critics may argue excessive 'concept stretching' – that some principles when pushed too far no longer hold meaning; the vigor with which each component of the new plan was debated and analyzed, and sometimes overturned (such as with an initial plan to further relax arms exports) suggests otherwise. Overall, even new practices were generally described as building on past practice. For example, analysis provided by the research institution affiliated with the Ministry of Defense (MOD) describes new 'strategic ODA' policy as follows:

> Although the strategic use of ODA is not a particularly new approach for Japan, its reconstitution in the context of security policy, together with capacity building support being independently provided by the

MOD, can be expected to give new depth to Japan *[sic]* regional security policy. (NIDSJ 2013: 113)

This explanation thus roots incremental change in past policy practice.

The 2010 Defense 'Guidelines' are just that, however – guidelines for action, not a description of actions taken. Thus, some areas of political sensitivity – such as a relaxation of arms export restrictions or an increase in the defense budget to allow for the planned procurement – require continued political support *after* the NDPG is issued. This, in part, explains why the 2013 NDPG sets out plans for policies that were not yet implemented in the 2010 NDPG. (The changeover of political party also likely contributes to the second Abe administration's decision to release a new NDPG despite much of the 2010 NDPG not yet having been realized.)

A number of important and far-reaching changes to Japan's security practices have been implemented in the years since 2007 – as outlined briefly above – but these changes do not mark a fundamental shift in the principles that guide Japanese security policy. Given the scale of change in Japanese identity in this period as defined in relational terms, such as vis-à-vis China or South Korea as described in other contributions to this special issue, one may expect greater policy change in this period than actually seen. Challenges posed to the SIDA by the first Abe administration in 2006–07 in particular were substantial, but were not realized in actual policy outcomes. Abe's second attempt at challenging existing security policy norms and advocating for a new vision for twenty-first century Japan has been more successful, but also falls far short of an identity shift to date, as argued in the next section below.

Abe 2.0: a second attempt to redefine Japan's security practices

Abe's return to the prime ministership in December 2012 led to the same sort of media firestorm and concerns about rising nationalism in Japan and a dramatic break with Japan's long-standing security practices as it did when Abe took office in September 2006. The similarities between Abe 1.0 and Abe 2.0 did not end there. In December 2012, as in September 2006, Abe would face a scheduled Upper House election in July of the following year. And as in September 2006, Abe made a number of statements in his first six months in office from December 2012 that made headlines around the world for the concerns they raised about Japan's future policy moves rightward – which the *New York Times* and the *China Daily* alike described as 'hyper-nationalism'. Unlike his first experience as prime minister, however, Abe successfully led his party to gains in the Upper House election, and less than one year after assuming office, succeeded in implementing several major pieces of national security legislation that established a new National Security Council for Japan (JNSC), created a system of classification of government secrets (especially related to national security), and led to the issuing of Japan's first NSS and a revision to the 2010 NDPG. These new developments are notable and important. They do not, however, connote a dramatic break from Japan's past practices, rooted in the three central tenets of domestic anti-militarism. Even the more recent and controversial Cabinet decision on 1 July 2014 that sets out a new framework for Japan to engage in military policies related to collective self-defense − military actions with other states not directly involving the defense of the Japanese homeland − was substantially revised from early drafts to conform with the central tenets of the SIDA, in particular the principle that Japan should not participate in foreign wars (Green and Hornung 2014; Oros 2014). (Legislation to implement the July 1 Cabinet decision is expected to be introduced into the Diet in the spring of 2015.)

While Japan's security identity has not been replaced by a new set of guiding principles, a new politics of security has been evident in Japan since the Koizumi period (2001–2006), as discussed in previous sections and further examined by Samuels (2007). Increased public discussion of alternative security policies − including those advocated by powerful political actors − is not the same as a new security identity, or even necessarily new security policies, however. For example, great media and public attention to the idea of constitutional revision of Article Nine in 2007 did not lead to revision of the constitution; similarly, discussion of Japan developing pre-emptive strike capabilities, for example, made headlines but did not result in a decision to pursue the idea.

Looking forward, in the second Abe administration both the policies derived from the SIDA and the hegemony of the identity itself will arguably continue to be challenged, both ideationally and institutionally. Still, substantial institutional and political constraints stand in the way of a realization of Abe's full policy objectives vis-à-vis Japan's future security practices. Ultimately, it will require another victory in elections in both houses of the Diet to achieve one of his primary objectives of security policy: formal revision of Article Nine of the postwar constitution. In the meantime, however, a number of more limited challenges to the principles of the SIDA can be expected, and can be considered from both an ideational and institutional perspective. Ideational challenges to the SIDA confront directly the three core principles upon which the security identity is based. Institutional challenges loom in the form of new processes or structures that contravene the principles of the SIDA, often seeking to replace existing institutions rooted in the security identity. Revision of Article Nine of Japan's postwar constitution would be considered both as an ideational and as an institution challenge, and has been at the center of recent debates about future changes in Japan's overall security posture. Another ideational challenge discussed below is the development of an integrated NSS.

Challenges to the ideational underpinnings of the security identity of domestic antimilitarism

Japan's postwar constitution was officially adopted by a recently defeated Japan on May 3, 1947, under heavy pressure from the occupying American military forces at the time. While especially Article Nine of this constitution – the so-called 'war-renouncing' clause[6] – plays a central role in Japan's postwar security identity, political actors must interpret and enforce constitutional principles. The interpretation of the constitution has been changed numerous times in the postwar period, and was significantly reinterpreted once again in the second year of the second Abe administration. Although conservatives and nationalists in Japan have consistently sought to formally revise Article Nine of the constitution for over sixty years, until the twenty-first century there was no time where it looked as if a vote for revision could pass the necessary two-thirds affirmative requirement in the Diet. The process by which the subsequently required national referendum would be conducted had not even been determined by legislation until 2007 (under the first Abe administration), as no national referendum of any sort has ever been conducted in Japan.

During these over six decades, however, the way that the constitution was interpreted did change. One important constitutional principle that has been reinterpreted in the area of national security policy is the issue of 'collective self-defense' – specifically, whether the JSDF are allowed to participate in military exercises and military combat together with other states for a purpose other than directly protecting the Japanese homeland. At the start of his first term in office, Prime Minister Abe made clear that he would like Japan's military forces to engage in activities related to collective self-defense. The Cabinet Legislative Bureau (CLB) interpretation of this issue, however, stood in conflict with Abe's agenda. It reads (with italics added here for emphasis):

> International law permits a state to have the right of collective self-defense, which is the right to use force to stop an armed attack on a foreign country with which the state has close relations, even if the state itself is not under direct attack. Since Japan is a sovereign state, it naturally has the right of collective self-defense under international law. *Nevertheless, the Japanese government believes that the exercise of the right of collective self-defense exceeds the limit on self-defense authorized under Article 9 of the Constitution and is not permissible.*
>
> (Ministry of Defense [MOD] 2012: 110)

With formal constitutional revision politically unattainable, Abe sought in his second term a re-interpretation of this opinion in 2014. The idea of a reinterpretation of a constitutional provision related to national security is not novel. In conjunction with earlier LDP efforts to expand Japan's international security role, the CLB issued an interpretation that allowed for the JSDF to operate in 'areas surrounding Japan' outside of Japanese territory — with the restriction that the JSDF could *not* operate in the air, land, or sea territory of another state; it also has reconciled the constitutionality of Japan's participation in an integrated missile defense system with the US (which some saw as an exercise of collective self-defense), and a range of other security-related issues over the years.

The July 1, 2014 Cabinet decision that explicitly allows for the JSDF to participate in collective self-defense activities with other states marks a significant change in a long-standing interpretation of appropriate security practices. It calls into question all three tenets of the SIDA: potentially leading Japan's 'self-defense forces' to look and act more like traditional military forces (contra tenet 1), potentially involving Japan in the use of force for something other than Japan's own direct self-defense (contra tenet 2), and potentially involving Japan directly in the fighting of foreign wars in the exercise of collective self-defense (contra tenet 3). In fact, however, Abe has not been able to achieve an overturning of the central tenets of the SIDA via even the second-choice approach of constitutional reinterpretation — at least not to date. The July 1, 2014 Cabinet decision that has been widely reported to have overturned Japan's long-standing policy not to exercise its inherent right to collective self-defense states that such collective self-defense actions would be undertaken is only extremely limited circumstances: only when not acting 'threatens Japan's survival' and 'when there is no other appropriate means available to repel the attack' and, even then, that the JSDF is permitted 'the use of force to the minimum extent necessary...in accordance with the basic logic of the Government's view to date' (Government of Japan [GOJ] 2014: 8). This result is far less than Abe and many of his supporters sought — but their views were overridden by opposition from within the ruling coalition (both within the LDP and especially from the NKP) as well as influenced by strong public opposition. In one sense, it is therefore domestic politics and public opinion that played the direct role in limiting Abe's policy change — but, as with previous attempts to change policy beyond the boundaries of the long-standing security identity, it was the SIDA that provided the framing language, institutional barriers, and garnered public support to re-shape the preferences of a powerful political actor.

Beyond such constitutional issues, the Abe administration adopted three new government documents related to national security policy in December 2013, each of which illuminate Abe's new approaches to security. The new NDPG (and related Medium Term Defense Program document) continue the policies set out in the last published NDPG of December 2010, but also push further Abe's preference for a more activist security policy for Japan and a Japan that possesses greater military capabilities — though the increase is fairly limited and firmly within the boundaries of the existing security identity.

The release of the Japanese government's first published NSS relates to the creation of the new JNSC that was authorized by the Diet in November 2013 (discussed below). It is illuminating of Japan's postwar security identity that Japan has not even had such a formal strategy document in the past seventy years, illustrating how military policy was not seen as a core tool to promote the national interest – though the MOD (and prior to that, the Japan Defense Agency) had developed military defense 'guidelines' by way of the aforementioned NDPG since 1976, which have become increasingly detailed and strategic as they have been updated over the years, especially the 2004, 2010, and 2013 versions. The NSS is crafted (at least in principle, and likely more in practice in future iterations) by a new institution, the JNSC operating within the Cabinet Secretariat, that includes representatives from ministries other than the MOD as well. The prospect of integrating military strategy into broad Japanese national objectives could mark a significant shift in Japan's security identity, but whether this is what actually takes places within this new institution and future iterations of an NSS document remains to be seen; the first attempt does not appear substantially different from earlier NDPGs, though officially now expresses a more whole-of-government approach as the product of an internal Cabinet body. At this point, in mid-2014, however, Japanese policy-makers certainly have many more tools at their disposal to utilize military power to achieve broader national objectives, crossing to some degree previous ideational boundaries.

Challenges to the institutional underpinnings of the security identity of domestic antimilitarism

Beyond challenging the core principles underlying the SIDA, the Abe government has advocated for the transformation of a number of existing institutions derived from these principles, and in some cases the creation of new institutions that depart from the three central tenets of the SIDA. In addition to the aforementioned new JNSC, the Abe government envisions an 'upgrade' to the institutions underpinning the Japan–US security alliance through a crafting of new Japan–US Guidelines for Defense Cooperation by December 2014. In addition, the Abe government has crafted, and seeks to deepen, institutionalized security cooperation with other states in the region, building on recent such developments with Australia in particular. Finally, the Abe government seeks to increase further the capabilities of the JSDF – as evidenced in the new 2013 NDPG and 2013 Medium Term Defense Program documents.[7]

Institutionalized security cooperation with the US has long been a controversial aspect of security policy in Japan, but has grown less so in recent years. Still, the level of cooperation and the sorts of 'roles' that Japan will play within the alliance framework continues to be an issue that challenges

core principles of the SIDA. As noted in a recent report by Japan's National Institute of Defense Studies, 'the scope to the US–Japan alliance has expanded from the "defense of Japan" to "the Asia-Pacific region" and thence to "global cooperation"'(NIDSJ 2013: 118). The last significant expansion of US–Japan cooperation took place under the Koizumi administration with the dispatch of the JSDF abroad to support US combat operations – a decision that was quite controversial and ultimately quite limited in scope. Whether the Abe administration will be able to develop and pass legislation that routinizes or even expands such out-of-area cooperation – or development of 'dynamic defense cooperation' during ordinary times and not just emergencies – remains to be seen. Related legislation is reportedly being considered for the fall 2014 extraordinary Diet session. Other areas of deepened cooperation, by contrast, though new, would be easily incorporated within the SIDA – such as deepened cooperation in regional humanitarian assistance and disaster relief (HADR) and in cooperatively addressing threats in cyberspace: both areas under consideration for deepened cooperation (Hornung and Oros 2014).

The extent to which the JSDF can cooperate with countries other than the US is also an important question raised in Japan's new NSS, and in the 2010 and 2013 NDPGs, that relates to Japan's security identity. Such cooperation need not challenge the SIDA, but it could depending on how it is framed – particularly in areas related to collective self-defense. An expansion of defense cooperation with other states would be a new development – and certainly would present a new image for Japan overseas – but security cooperation with states other than the US in itself would not be an indication of identity shift as conceptualized in the three central tenets of the SIDA; it would depend on the nature of that cooperation.

The development of greater capabilities for the JSDF also can be considered an institutional question in that the JSDF is the primary institution for the implementation of defense policy for Japan. The question of what capabilities the JSDF should have has been controversial since their creation in 1954, and has historically been rooted in the concept of 'minimal force necessary for the defense of Japan'. What was considered minimally necessary is, of course, related to perceptions of threat and also of evolving military technologies. For example, some technologies once considered solely military but which now have widespread civilian uses have become uncontroversial to be employed by the JSDF: such as satellite communications and surveillance satellites. In addition, as international cooperation has become a core mission of the MOD at the time it was established as a ministry (in 2007), new capabilities needed for this mission also have become uncontroversial – such as heavy-lift air transport capabilities, which once were imagined as a threatening means to transport soldiers and weapons abroad but now are seen as a way to deliver humanitarian assistance.

Other aspects of enhanced JSDF capabilities remain controversial and seemingly proscribed by the principles of the SIDA – such as overt strike capability. Such capabilities are reportedly desired by Prime Minister Abe, but notably have not been directly requested in policy documents to date – once again confirming the continued resilience of the SIDA even in changed domestic and international political circumstances. Recent Cabinet Office polling similarly lends support to the idea that the Abe government must be cautious in this area. While longitudinal public opinion surveys conducted by Japan's Cabinet Office show the number of Japanese who believe that JSDF capabilities 'should be increased' has jumped significantly from 14.1% in January 2009 to 24.8% in January 2012 (Ministry of Defense 2012: 474), and most likely have further risen since January 2012 given the tense military stand-off with China, still it is notable that less than one-quarter of Japanese express this view in the latest poll.

Continued ideational, institutional, and other constraints

Abe 2.0 appears more cognizant of the limitations of his political power compared to Abe 1.0. The sorts of security policy change he has initiated in legislation differs from ideas that he and some of his supporters have long advocated for, such as formal constitutional revision, fully exercising the right of collective self-defense, and development of a limited military strike capability. The prioritizing of incremental change to security policies that can be articulated within the existing principles of the SIDA while putting off difficult issues that arguably lie outside the boundaries of the SIDA conforms to the identity-derived predictions of security policy developed in this article.

Still, other – perhaps overlapping – explanations for security policy continuity can be offered outside of the framework of security identity. As discussed in an earlier section above, other domestic political issues also vie for center stage in the new Abe administration – such as the fiscal and demographic issues discussed above, as well as broader issues of economic policy. Surely it was a lesson from the first Abe administration (that lost the Upper House election after only 10 months in power) that voters demand attention to such areas. In addition, the LDP must work together with its coalition partner, the NKP. As in previous LDP-led administrations, the NKP continues to serve as a 'brake' on some more 'proactive' areas of security policy, avowedly for reasons related to the political principles of the NKP. This influence was especially visible in the formulation of the Cabinet decision related to collective self-defense.

Other contributors to this special issue would likely point out, however, that seemingly disconnected 'other constraints' themselves have an identity component. For example, while the difficulty of formally revising the constitution was initially imposed by the US during the Occupation period (1945–1952), it is Japanese themselves who have chosen not to change the process for constitutional revision in the subsequent 60+ years – arguably because of issues related to the postwar SIDA. Similarly, while the die-hard opposition of the NKP to reinterpreting the constitution no doubt is related to principles of the party itself (and to the religious principles of the Soka Gakkai Buddhist sect that forms of the core of NKP supporters), opposition is also rooted in the principles of the SIDA. Thus, it on the broader issue of how relational approaches to identity intersect with the norm constructivism-based approach employed here that this article will conclude.

Conclusion: Towards 'Proactive Pacifism'?

What do recent challenges to Japan's dominant SIDA mean for Japan's future security policies? Is the idea of 'proactive pacifism' a Trojan horse for more wholesale policy shifts in the coming years? Put another way, will Japan's medium-term security future look much like its past? The answer to this latter question is 'yes, to a large degree' — though further changes in the international and domestic political environment will continue to lead to incremental policy adjustments within the general guidelines of the SIDA, as in the past.

Oros (2008) sets out three possible scenarios for Japan's future security practices that remain relevant to the current political situation: '(1) continued policy evolution in line with the existing security identity; (2) new security practices resulting from an unexpected shock that discredits the security identity of domestic antimilitarism; and (3) new security practices resulting from a growing irrelevance and subsequent abandonment of the security identity of domestic antimilitarism' (p. 187). While there still is substantial evidence of Scenario 1 above, as demonstrated in the previous discussion of both the recent DPJ and Abe administrations, there also is growing evidence of Scenario 3. If Japan's regional security environment continues to evolve in the dramatic fashion it has in just the past few years, the SIDA will grow even more disconnected from the previous environment under which it was crafted, which could result in a much more 'proactive' version of the articulated policy of 'proactive pacifism'.

A substantial change in Japan's international strategic environment is one of three 'x factors' set out in Oros (2008) as potential sparks to a broader identity shift in Japan (pp. 189–93). Escalation of the territorial dispute between Japan and China is leading toward such a shift at the moment, while other long-standing potential disruptions (such as a Korean contingency or China-Taiwan conflict) remain possible though unlikely. 'A rupture in the US–Japan alliance' was set out as a second 'x-factor' — though such a disruption seems quite unlikely in the current period of alliance deepening (though a rupture is certainly *possible*, such as in relation to the Senkaku/Diaoyu dispute).

To some extent, the third 'x-factor' set out — 'domestic political realignment driven by rising political populism' — has already occurred and may also partly explain the stress placed on the SIDA. One could consider the rise and fall of the DPJ from power, the rise and fall of the Japan Restoration Party (*Nippon Ishin no Kai*) from popularity, and the fall and rise of the LDP as a sort of political realignment – though it also may be a precursor to a larger realignment in the coming years, or to new extended period of LDP dominance. Thus, as argued in this article, greater attention to domestic political forces on identity maintenance and change is an important continuing factor in analysis of the identity – policy nexus. Abe will need not only to maintain political support over several years to enact the range of security policies on his proclaimed agenda, but also to strengthen political support in the Upper House in order to achieve his long-term proclaimed goal of constitutional revision. Absent such deepened political support, his compromise articulation of 'proactive pacifism' – a formulation in line with the existing security identity – is as far as he will be able to go. What exactly will be the boundaries of this new formulation will the subject of active political contestation in the coming years.

Apart from the connection to future Japanese security practices, an examination of the challenges to Japan's dominant security identity also affords a better understanding of the dynamics of identity resilience and adaptation in conjunction with relational approaches to identity advocated by other contributions to this special issue. In the 'Introduction' to this special issue, Hagström and Gustafsson note the disagreement among those who study identity over the impact of 'material reality' on identity creation and maintenance. Several of the other contributors to this special issue show convincingly how attention to self-other relationships involving actors outside of Japan can explain how changes in objective measures of security – such as levels of defense spending and/or development of new weapons capabilities – may or may not be perceived as threatening and thus affecting Japan's conceptualizations of its own identity. Such insights add greater depth and explanatory power to the analysis offered here that argues that a shifting international environment has been a principal driver of policy change in Japan in the past decade. Thus, domestically derived and relationally derived approaches to identity can be seen as complementary explanations – at least in the case of contemporary Japanese security policy. Future work may productively utilize insights from both approaches to provide a more complete picture of how Japanese identity is both challenged and then evolves in relation to an outside actor such as China or South Korea, presenting a picture that devotes attention both to sources of identity change and to resulting changes in policy practice.

This article argues that greater attention to agents pushing for identity shift can, paradoxically, help illustrate the *resilience* of identity. Future research might consider how relational approaches could better conceptualize how the democratic process of organized politics interacts with self-other conceptions to result in both policy change and identity change. As Hagström and Gustafsson note in the 'Introduction' to this special issue, however, there continues to be a gulf between those who seek to explain how identity is created and maintained (using identity as a 'dependent variable') and those who seek to explain how identity affects policy-making (using identity as an 'independent variable'). Relational approaches to identity conceptualization tend to devote substantial energy to the former; it is a welcome development to see more attention paid to the latter in the contributions to this special issue.

Acknowledgements

I would like to thank Linus Hagström for organizing this special issue and his many suggestions on numerous drafts of this article, the anonymous reviewer for useful suggestions on this article draft, the East-West Center in Washington for providing me a quiet and intellectually supportive base from which to write during my recent sabbatical leave, and Washington College for that sabbatical leave.

Notes

1. Oros (2008) analyzes in depth how this security identity was negotiated, established, and evolved over the course of the early postwar and Cold War periods.
2. Midford (2011) provides an invaluable collection of public opinion polling on Japanese attitudes related to military security which support this claim, although he argues that Japanese attitudes are more in line with what he terms 'defensive realism'.
3. Note that the Japanese government prefers to translate this phrase into English as 'proactive contributions to peace' – which is not a literal translation, but arguably conveys the spirit of the phrase better to a foreign audience.
4. Oros (2008) offers several detailed examples in areas such as Japan's arms export policies, its development of missile defense capabilities, and even deployment of the JSDF abroad in limited areas.
5. The complete text of these Guidelines is available from Japan's Ministry of Defense website at: http://www.mod.go.jp/e/d_act/d_policy/pdf/guidelines FY2011.pdf.
6. The complete text of Article Nine reads:

    i. Aspiring sincerely to an international peace based on justice and order, the Japanese people forever renounce war as a sovereign right of the nation and the threat or use of force as a means of settling international disputes. ii. In order to accomplish the aim of the preceding paragraph, land, sea, and air forces, as well as other war potential, will never be maintained. The right of belligerency of the state will not be recognized. (Cabinet Office, 1947)

7. The complete text of these documents are available from Japan's Ministry of Defense website at: http://www.mod.go.jp/e/d_act/d_policy/national.html.

References

Abdelal, R., Herrera, Y. M., Johnston, A. I. and McDermott, R. (2006) 'Identity as a variable', *Perspectives on Politics* 4(4): 695–711.

Abe, S. (2006) *Utsukushii Kuni e [Towards a Beautiful Country]*, Tokyo: Bungei Shunju.

Ashizawa, K. (2013) *Japan, the US, and Regional Institution-Building in the New Asia: When Identity Matters*, New York, NY: Palgrave Macmillan.

Cabinet Office. (1947) The Constitution of Japan; accessed at http://www.kantei.go.jp/foreign/constitution_and_government/frame_01.html.

Berger, T. (1998) *The Politics of Antimilitarism: National Security in Germany and Japan*, Baltimore, MD: Johns Hopkins University Press.

De Koning, P. and Lipscy, P. Y. (2013) 'The land of the sinking sun: Is Japan's military weakness putting America in danger?' *Foreign Policy On-Line*, 30 July; accessed at http://www.foreignpolicy.com/articles/2013/07/30/the_land_of_the_sinking_sun_japan_military_weakness?page=full.

Glosserman, B. and Tsunoda, T. (2009) 'The guillotine: demographics and Japan's security options', *PacNet* 45, June 17.

Government of Japan (GOJ). (2014), *Cabinet Decision on Development of Seamless Security Legislation to Ensure Japan's Survival and Protect Its People*, 1 July; accessed at http://japan.kantei.go.jp/96_abe/decisions/2014/__icsFiles/afieldfile/2014/07/03/anpohosei_eng.pdf.

Green, M. (2001) *Japan's Reluctant Realism: Foreign Policy Challenges in an Era of Uncertain Power*, New York: Palgrave.

Green, M. and Hornung, J.W. (2014), 'Ten Myths about Japan's Collective Self-Defense Change', 10 July; accessed at http://thediplomat.com/2014/07/ten-myths-about-japans-collective-self-defense-change/.

Hopf, T. (2002) *Social Construction of International Politics: Identities and Foreign Policies, Moscow, 1955 and 1999*, Ithaca, NY: Cornell University Press.

Hornung, J. W. and Oros, A. L. (2014), 'Enhancing U.S.-Japan Defense Cooperation: New Strategies and the Challenges Ahead', in *Challenges Facing Japan: Perspectives from the U.S.-Japan Network for the Future,* Washington, DC: Mansfield Foundation, pp. 63–74.

Japan National Security Council (JSNC). (2013) *National Security Strategy (Provisional English Translation)*, December 17.

Lieberman, R. C. (2002) 'Ideas, institutions, and political order: explaining political change', *American Political Science Review* 96(4): 697–712.

Midford, P. (2011) *Rethinking Japanese Public Opinion and Security: From Pacifism to Realism?* Stanford, CA: Stanford University Press.

Ministry of Defense (MOD). (2012) *Defense of Japan 2012*, Tokyo: Erklaren.

National Institute for Defense Studies Japan. (2013) *East Asian Strategic Review 2013*, Tokyo: Japan Times.

New York Times. (2013) *China's Coercive Play*, 25 November; accessed at www.nytimes.com/2013/11/26/opinion/chinas-coercive-play.html

Oros, A. L. (2014) 'Japan's Cabinet Seeks Changes to Its Peace Constitution – Issues New "Interpretation" of Article Nine. 2014.' *Asia-Pacific Bulletin*, Washington, DC: East-West Center, July 1.

Oros, A. L. (2008) *Normalizing Japan: Politics, Identity, and the Evolution of Security Practice*, Stanford, CA: Stanford University Press.

Pyle, K. B. (2007) *Japan Rising: The Resurgence of Japanese Power and Purpose*, New York, NY: Public Affairs.

Samuels, R. (2007) *Securing Japan: Tokyo's Grand Strategy and the Future of East Asia*, Ithaca, NY: Cornell University Press.

Walt, S. M. (1985) 'Alliance formation and the balance of world power', *International Security* 9(4): 3–43.

Index

Note: Page numbers in *italic* type refer to figures and illustrations
Page numbers in **bold** type refer to tables

Abductions: The Essence of an Abnormal State (book) 84
Abe Shinzō 17, 141; and the Northern Territories dispute 59, 60; and the North Korean Abduction issue 79–80, 81, 83, 84–5, 88; seeks constitutional reinterpretation for new defence policy 152, 153, 158; shift in defense and security policy 142, 144, 145, 150–1, 156; on Sino-Japanese relations 35, 40, 125, 128, 132–3
abnormality of the pacifist identity 82–3, 86
aid to China *see* ODA (official development aid to China)
Alliance for Securing the Territorial Rights to Takeshima 52
anti-Japanese sentiment in China 118–19, 126–8, 129, 132–3
antimilitarist culture as identity 4, 16, 82, 119, 124, 140, 147 *see also* SIDA (security identity of domestic antimilitarism)
Aoki Mikio 59
appeasement and recognition 123
Araki Kazuhiro, General 80, 86
Article 9 of the Constitution 39, 99, 100, 141, 156–7; as constraint on waging war 4, 82, 83; possible revision of 15–16, 133, 148, 151–2

Asahi Shimbun (newspaper) 105, 127, 128; coverage of a 'victimised' Chinese Other 101, **101,** 104–5; and the Senkaku/Diaoyu Islands dispute 106–8, 111
ASEAN+3 37
ASEAN (Association of Southeast Asian Nations) 33, 37–8, 132
Asia as pre-war threat and opportunity 24, 29–32
Asō Tarō 34, 36, 147

banishment of those who sought improved ties with North Korea 78–9
blame on China for dragging Japan into Sino-Japanese War of 1931–1945 106
Bōei taikō (National Defence Programme Guidelines) 38–9

capabilities of the SDF 155–6
Chiang Kai-shek 106
China: association with 'anti-Japanese' sentiment 118–19, 126–8, 129, 132–3; as both security threat and opportunity 28–32, 33–6, 37, 39–40, 149; and recognition of Japan 121, 123, 128–9, 130–1, 133–4; rise of as Japan's 'Other' 14, 96, 98, *101,* 101–13

161

INDEX

China Security Report (2011) 34
Chinese invasion of Vietnam 103–4
Chūkibō (Midterm Defence Programme) 38, 39
CLB (Cabinet Legislative Bureau), the 152, 153
Cold War, the 24, 30, 33, 61, 100, 109; impact of the end of 41, 49, 99, 107, 111–12
collective identity, idea of 10
collective self-defense 152–3, 155
colonial period, the 28, 72, 85
COMJAN (Investigating Committee on Missing Japanese Probably Related to North Korea) 80
conceivability and political possibility 14
conformism through the North Korean abduction issue 79–81

Daimon Mikishi 126–7
defense budgets 16, 145–6
defense cooperation with the United States 99, 101, 110, 154, 155
demographic trends 145–6
Deng Xiaoping 104–5
denial of recognition 122, 130–3
Diplomatic Bluebook of the MOFA 34, 36, 37–8
discourse mapping and decision-making processes 13–14
discrepancy between Northern Territory campaign and Takeshima issue 55
discursive power and identity construction 8, 14
Doi Takako 79
DPJ (Democratic Party of Japan) 36, 79, 113n3, 145, 148, 158; defense policy 38, 149; on the Senkaku/Diaoyu islands dispute 60, 95–6, 110, 111

EAC (East Asian Community) 36
East Asian Strategic Review (2009) 34
economic superpower status 3–4
emotion and rational action 9–11, 16–17

ethnocentricity and Japanese security policy 29
explicit and non-explicit recognition 122

factors contributing to identity change 7–11
fishing industry disputes between Japan and Korea 56, 57–8, 63
foreign and security policy 4–5, 13, 14–15, 16, 29–36, 38–40 *see also* security challenges
Foucault, Michel 13
Fukuda Yasuo 125, 128, 147

Gemba Koichirō 37, 131
Gotō Shimpei 28
Guidelines for Greater East Asia Strategy 30

Hashimoto Ryūtarō 124
Hasuike Tōru 79
Hatoyama Ichirō 33, 99
Higashi Junji 127
Hirasawa Katsuei 78, 83, 88, 129
Hokkaido Alliance, the 52
Hu Jintao 127, 128

Idealist Left, the 103, 104, 105, 107–9, 112, 113n3
Idealist Right, the 99, 102–3, 107–9, 110
identity construction of Japan 6–7, 12, 20, 49, 119–22, 141, 143–4; relational approach to 2, 5, 12–13, 16, 158–9; through 'Others' 97, 99–100, 144–5; through securitization of North Korea 73–4, 87–8 *see also* SIDA (security identity of domestic antimilitarism)
identity entrepreneurs and identity change 7–9, 10, 16, 120–1, 134
identity resilience and change 5–6, 158–9
Ijiri Hidenori 97
Ikeda Hayato 32
Inagaki Takeshi 85
inferior economic status of South Korea 11
international law and collective self-defence 152

162

INDEX

international relations and identity 3
IR (International Relations): and ontological security 11, 49–50
IR (International Relations) during the Cold War 9
IR theory and reification 26–7
Ishihara Shintarō 83, 84, 99, 113
Ishii Kikujirō 29

Japan and China: Building a Mutually Beneficial Relationship Based on Common Strategic Interests (pamphlet) 125
Japanese interest in North Korean issues 75 *see also* North Korean abduction issue, the
Japan Restoration Party 158
Japan-US Security Alliance, the 99, 101, 110, 154
Japan-US trade disputes 103
Jiang Zemin 126
JNSC (National Security Council for Japan) 150, 154
Jōdai Yoshiro 58
Joint Regulation Zone 53, 56
JSP (Japan Socialist Party) 15

Kaifu Toshiki 25–6
Kan Naoto 84, 96, 110
Kazokukai (Association of the Families of Victims Kidnapped by North Korea) 75–6, 80, 84
Kim Jong-Il 72, 74, 77, 79
Kishimoto Takeshi 127
Kishi Nobusuke 27, 31, 51, 99
Kitaoka Shin'ichi 39
Kitazawa Toshimi 38
Koizumi Junichiro 37, 127, 140, 142, 147; on Japan's post-war identity 124, 125; on the North Korea abduction issue 72, 77; visits Yasukuni Shrine 59, 111
Kokaryō Case, the 104
Komura Jutarō 28

Kōmura Masahiko 38
Korea and modern Japan's identity 60–5

Law on the Territorial Sea and the Contiguous Zone 131–2
LDP (Liberal Democratic Party), the 15, 38, 55, 147–8, 158; on China 35, 95–6, 98; on the North Korean abduction issue 72, 76, 78, 79; and shift in security and defense policy 127, 148, 149, 156; and the Takeshima territorial dispute 51, 52, 58–9, 60, 64
Left-wing images of Japanese 'Others' 97, 98, 103, 104, 105, 106–8
Left-wing view of Japanese post-war identity 82, 86, 99
Li Keqiang 130, 131, 132
limits to the diffusion of conformism 81
lobbying to place North Korean abduction issue on the political agenda 75–6, 80

Machimura Kingo 52
Machimura Nobutaka 127
Maehara Seiji 96
Mainichi Shimbun (newspaper) 105, 106
Makita Kunihiko 77
Masumoto Teruaki 84
Matsubara Jin 126
Matsui Ukon 29
media portrayal 101, *101*; of the North Korean abduction issue 76–7, 79, 80–1; of Sino-Japanese disputes 96, 98, 104–6, 118
memorandum by Shimane Prefecture for policy demands to the central government 58–9
METI (Ministry of Economy, Trade, and Industry) 36
MOD (Ministry of Defence) 33–4, 39, 150, 152, 154, 155
Moderate Left, the 107, 108, 112, 113n3
Moderate Right, the 99
MOFA (Ministry of Foreign Affairs) 31–2, 77, 131; and post-war identity 124,

163

125; on regional Asian economy 27, 30, 33, 34, 36, 37; on territorial issues 48, 55, 56, 59, 132
moral righteousness of the Japanese 'Self' 111
Murayama Tomiichi 124

Nakagawa Hidemasa 51, 53
Nakagawa Shōichi 102
Nakajima Mineo 102
Nakanishi Terumasa, Professor 83
Nakasone Yasuhiro 31, 102, 103, 140
National Institute of Defense Studies 155
nationalism and patriotism 10
NDPG (National Defense Program Guidelines) 38, 149–50, 151, 153, 154
NHK 81
NIDS (National Institute for Defence Studies) 34
Nishioka Tsutomu 78, 84
NKP (New Komeito Party) 127, 153, 156, 157
Noda Yoshihiko 79, 110
Nonaka Hiromu 76–7
normalisation as a nation state 15, 20, 119–20, 121, 122, 133–4; and securitisation 73–4, 87–8 *see also* North Korean abduction issue, the
normalization of Japan-South Korea relations 52–3, 61
normalization talks with the Soviet Union over disputed territories 52
norm constructivists and Japanese identity 2, 4–5, 12
Northern Territories campaign, the 55–6, 58, 64
North Korean abduction issue, the 10, 15, 20, 72–3, 75, 75–82, 83–8; and normalisation 72, 73–5, 75, 77, 83, 84, 86–7
NSS (national security strategy) document 139–40, 142, 151, 154, 155
nuclear armament 84

Obuchi Keizō 37

ODA (official development aid) to China 125, 126, 128, 149–50
Ōhira Masayoshi 33
Okada Katsuya 36
Okada Kikujirō 30
Okuno Seisuke 106
O'Neill, Peter 130
Onodera Itsunori 39, 132
ontological security about oneself and identity change 11, 49–50, 61–2, 63, 64
Ōta Masakuni 81, 85
Other-representations 7, 14, 48, 49; the Korean 'other' 60, 61, 63, 64–5; Left-wing images of 97, 98, 103, 104, 105, 106–8
Ōya Bunko (magazine) 48

pacifist identity since the war 17, 25, 82, 103; abnormality of 82–3, 86
Park Chung Hee 61–2
perception of Chinese denial of Japanese identity 10–11, 15, 17, 122, 130–3
political parties in Japan 15 *see also* DJ (Democratic Party of Japan); LDP (Liberal Democratic Party), the
politics of identity politics 144
post-structuralist constructivism in IR 48–9
post-war era and self-identity 123–6, 128–34, 140–1, 152
post-war outlook on Asia 23–4, 25–6, 30–1
pre-war militarism 25
'proactive pacifism' 144, 157, 158

rational action and emotion 9–10
recognition or denial of by Others on the Self's construction of identity 13 *see also* perception of Chinese denial of Japanese identity
recognition theory 120, 121
reification: of Asia as Otherness 24, 26, 27–8, 35–6, 40–1; as social reality 26–7, 33–4, 38–9

164

INDEX

relational approach to Japanese identity 2, 5, 12–13, 16, 158–9
Rhee Line, the 61
Right-wing images of Japanese 'Others' 97–8, 99, 102–3
Right-wing view of Japanese post-war identity 82, 99 *see also* Left-wing view of Japanese post-war identity
Ringmar's theory of recognition 121–3
routinized relationships and ontological security 50

Said, Edward 13
San Francisco Peace Treaty 131
Sankei Shimbun (newspaper) 101, 102, 103, 111
Satō Eisaku 25
SDF (Self Defence Forces) 82, 84, 142, 149, 152–3, 155
SDP (Social Democratic Party) 79
securitisation as argument for normalisation 73–4, 87–8
security challenges 144, 145, 147–9, 151–2, 157–8 *see also* foreign and security policy
security identity 140–3, 146–7
Self and the Other and identity 6–7, 10
Sengoku Yoshito 38, 84
Senkaku/Diaoyu Islands territorial dispute 60, 95, 103, 108, 110, 111; as denial of Japanese identity 130, 131–2; and diplomatic maneouvring 110, 111; as security issue 34, 39, 144, 157
Shangri-La Dialogue, the 132
Shidehara Kijūrō 29
shift in identity and a new security policy 140, 142–3, 144, 145, 148–52, 153–7
Shimane Alliance, the 52
Shimane Prefecture 49, 52, 65; rights to Takeshima 48, 50, 54–5; and the 'Takeshima Day' ordnance 56, 58–9, 64
SIDA (security identity of domestic antimilitarism) 140, 149, 150; challenges to 154–5, 157; setting of

boundaries to foreign policy 146, 148; tenets of 141, 142, 147, 151, 153
Soka Gakkai Buddhist sect, the 157
Southeast Asia as an opportunity 32–3, 36–8
South Korean claim to the Takeshima (Dokdo) islets 47–8, 49, 58, 59, 63
South Korean economy, the 62–3
South Korean territorial sea rule 54–5
Soviet Union, the 109
Sukūkai (National Association for the Rescue of Japanese Kidnapped by North Korea) 75–6, 78, 79
Swedish participation in the Thirty Years War 122–3

Takano Hiroshi 126, 128
Takebe Tsutomu 127
'Takeshima Day' ordinance 56, 57, 58, 59, 64
Takeshima territorial dispute, the 8, 47–9, 50–60, 61, 63, 64
Tamogami Toshio 86, 106
Tanaka Hitoshi 77, 85
Tanaka Kakuei 102
Tanigaki Sadakazu 35
territorial disputes 23, 34, 38, 39, 40, 52 *see also* Northern Territories campaign, the; Senkaku/Diaoyu Islands territorial dispute; Takeshima territorial dispute, the
thick recognition 121, 124
'twisted Diet,' the 147–8

Ugaki Kazushige 29
UNCLOS (United Nations Convention on the Law of the Seas) 56
United States, the: as depicted by Right and Left in Japan 96–7, 108–9; as dominating 'Other' 99–101, *101,* 103, 105, 111–12
use of North Korean abduction issue to promote a right-wing agenda 72–3, 76, 77, 87

165

victim and aggressor discourse in the North Korean abduction issue 85–6
visit of Chinese president and prime minister to Japan 128–9, 131

Watanabe Wataru, Colonel 30
Wen Jiabao 128, 131

Yamagata Aritomo, Field Marshall 28
Yasukuni Shrine, the 59, 111, 133

60 Years: The Path of a Nation Striving for Global Peace (leaflet) 125
Yokota Megumi 83, 85
Yokota Sakie 83
Yomiuri Shimbun (newspaper) 48, 96, 101, *101,* 126, 127; on anti-Japanese sentiment in China 128, 129
Yoshida Doctrine, the 82, 99, 141
Yoshida Shigeru 30–1, 99